Welfare, Choice, and Solidarity in Transition

Reform of the welfare sector is an important yet difficult challenge for all countries in transition from socialist central planning to market-oriented democracies. Here a scholar of the economics of socialism and post-socialist transition and a health economist take on this challenge. This book offers health-sector reform recommendations for ten countries of Eastern Europe, drawn consistently from a set of explicit guiding principles. After discussing sector-specific characteristics, lessons of international experience, and the main set of initial conditions, the authors advocate reforms based on organized public financing for basic care, private financing for supplementary care, pluralistic delivery of services, and managed competition. Policy-makers need to achieve a balance, both assuring social solidarity through universal access to basic health services and expanding individual choice and responsibility through voluntary supplemental insurance. The authors also consider the problems that undermine effectiveness of market-based competition in the health sector.

JÁNOS KORNAI is Allie S. Freed Professor of Economics at Harvard University and Permanent Fellow at the Institute for Advanced Study at the Collegium Budapest. He has a long list of publications, including more recently *Highway and Byways: Studies on Socialist Reform and Postsocialist Transition* (1995), *Struggle and Hope: Essays on Stabilization and Reform in a Post-Socialist Economy* (1997) and *On Health Care Reform* (1998).

KAREN EGGLESTON teaches health economics in the Department of Economics at Tufts University and is a Research Associate at the Kennedy School of Government at Harvard University. Her research interests include comparative health policy, payment system incentives, health-sector reforms in China, and the economics of contracts.

Federico Caffè Lectures

This series of annual lectures was initiated to honour the memory of Federico Caffè. They are jointly sponsored by the Department of Public Economics at the University of Rome, where Caffè held a chair from 1959 to 1987, and the Bank of Italy, where he served for many years as an adviser. The publication of the lectures will provide a vehicle for leading scholars in the economics profession, and for the interested general reader, to reflect on the pressing economic and social issues of the times.

Welfare, Choice, and Solidarity in Transition

Reforming the Health Sector in Eastern Europe

János Kornai and Karen Eggleston

CAMBRIDGE
UNIVERSITY PRESS

CAMBRIDGE UNIVERSITY PRESS
Cambridge, New York, Melbourne, Madrid, Cape Town, Singapore,
São Paulo, Delhi, Dubai, Tokyo, Mexico City

Cambridge University Press
The Edinburgh Building, Cambridge CB2 8RU, UK

Published in the United States of America by Cambridge University Press, New York

www.cambridge.org
Information on this title: www.cambridge.org/9780521159371

© János Kornai and Karen Eggleston 2001

First published 2001
First paperback edition 2010

A catalogue record for this publication is available from the British Library

Library of Congress Cataloguing in Publication Data

Kornai, János.
Welfare, choice, and solidarity in transition : reforming the health sector in
Eastern Europe / János Kornai and Karen Eggleston.
    p. cm. – (Frederico Caffè lectures)
Includes bibliographical references and index.
ISBN 0-521-79036-0
1. Health care reforms–Europe, Eastern. 2. Medical policy–Europe, Eastern.
3. Health planning–Europe, Eastern. 4. Medical care–Europe, Eastern.
I. Eggleston, Karen. II.
Title. III. Series.
RA395.E852 .K67 2001
362.10947–dc21   00-045500

ISBN 978-0-521-79036-9 Hardback
ISBN 978-0-521-15937-1 Paperback

Contents

Figures

Tables

Acknowledgments

The publisher gratefully acknowledges the following for permission to reproduce copyright material:

The European Bank for Reconstruction and Development for permission to reproduce tables 2.1, 5.18 and 8.4 and figures 5.3 and 5.4, which first appeared in *The Economics of Transition*, 2000 (8), Blackwell Publishers; The Organization for Economic Cooperation and Development for permission to reproduce tables 3.1 and 4.1, which first appeared in *OECD Health Systems: Facts and Trends, 1960–1991*, OECD, 1992 and *The Reform of Health Care Systems: A Review of Seventeen OECD Countries*, OECD, 1994; the American Public Health Association for permission to reproduce Table 9.5, which first appeared in the *American Journal of Public Health*, 1998 88 (8); Elsevier Science for permission to reproduce figure 9.1, which first appeared in *Health Policy*, 1999 42 (1).

1

Introduction

The health sector in post-socialist Eastern Europe suffers from a great many serious problems and concerns. The need for radical reforms is generally agreed, but opinions differ on what actually needs to be done, and how and when. Sharp debates take place, sometimes behind closed doors and sometimes in public, within the countries concerned and within the international agencies and academic institutions that are giving advice regarding economic and social transformation.

The authors of this book take positions on the issues being debated. We explain what direction we think the reforms should take and argue our point of view. We do not make detailed recommendations. The emphasis in our remarks is on the desirable features of reform that are common to all the countries examined.

While the book does not avoid taking up a position, it seeks to point to the difficulties that loom in the path of implementing reform. It sets out to identify the trade-offs. It points out what a country will win and lose, and what risks and dangers it will face in taking the approach recommended.

The purpose behind the book is to make recommendations that will facilitate reform. The economic-policy recommendations appear in part II. The preceding part I discusses the points of departure upon which the recommendations are based.

The subject-matter is vast. It is worth establishing first of all

what criteria the authors used to narrow the scope of inquiry.
Although our recommendations may be of broader interest,
they are specifically addressed to ten post-socialist countries
of Central and Eastern Europe (CEE), namely Albania,
Bulgaria, Croatia, the Czech Republic, Hungary, Macedonia,
Poland, Romania, Slovakia, and Slovenia. The Yugoslav successor states that have suffered gravely from war, and will
continue to suffer for some time, have been omitted. There is
no discussion in this book of the Soviet successor states. The
ten countries are referred to for brevity's sake as "Eastern
Europe," although this is not geographically accurate.

Wherever possible, the tables and examples incorporate
the data and experiences of all ten countries. Unfortunately,
this could not be done consistently, because abundant data
and descriptive materials could be obtained only from some
countries and relatively little from others. The largest body of
information was available from Hungary, as one of the
authors is Hungarian. He was able to gain access to nonpublic, internal information and the findings of in-depth
examinations, and to initiate research into the situation.
Nonetheless, the book is not about Hungary or about two or
three specific countries, but about Eastern Europe.[1]

Health-sector reform has been defined in many different
ways. This book takes a relatively narrow interpretation, confined to structural and institutional changes. It does not
directly address the otherwise important question of whether
the resources available for the health sector are sufficient or
lacking. Nor does it discuss how these resources should be
allocated among the activities and organizations that
promote the improvement of health. The question addressed
here is a different one: what economic and political institutions should govern allocation of health-sector resources in
Eastern Europe?

[1] The predecessor of this work was Kornai (1998b), which appeared in
Hungarian and dealt expressly with the Hungarian health-care reform.
Although there is much overlap between the two books, one of the reasons
for going beyond the first book was to extend the inquiry beyond Hungary
and discuss the reform problems of Eastern Europe comprehensively.

There is hardly an aspect of human life that poses so dramatically as health care the issue of scarcity, a fundamental question of economics. Science and technology are constantly making enormous strides. Even the richest of countries, with the most lavish spending on health care, could effectively use extra dollars or euros to relieve human suffering and save or extend lives. Every spending decision both allocates and excludes. Directly or indirectly, it decides who shall be deprived of certain health-care services. Phrasing the dilemma in this way suffices to show what a weighty question it is. Who is authorized to decide who utilizes resources for health-care purposes, in what quantities, and on what occasions? Should it be patients, doctors,[2] or the health-sector apparatus? Should it be employers, insurers, or the government and the majority in Parliament? This book considers how that power should be distributed. Its subject is not the allocation of health care, but choosing the political and economic mechanism that will decide that allocation.[3]

It should be pointed out here that the book employs the expression "welfare sector" as a generic term. It embraces (to name only the more important components) health care, education, pensions, care of children and old people, and social assistance for the needy. One of the central issues in the reform debate is to decide which welfare-sector activities should remain under and which should be removed from state control – in other words, which spheres should be included in the "welfare state."[4] Although one division of the welfare sector, health care, is placed to the fore throughout the discussion, some of what is said can be applied to the

---

[2] Throughout the book we use "doctor" and "physician" interchangeably and use the broader terms "medical professional" and "provider" to include nurses, physicians' aides, etc.

[3] The expression "political and economic mechanism" is used in the sense in which it was applied in the debates on socialism. It covers a specific configuration of property rights, decision-making spheres, incentives, and forms of coordination.

[4] As the description shows, the expression "welfare state" appears in this book in its European sense. This differs from American parlance, where the definition of "welfare" is narrowed down to social assistance.

welfare sector as a whole, or to other branches of it besides health care.

It emerges from what has been said already that the book is not confined to the economics of health care. Indeed, it is not simply concerned with some important economic aspects of the welfare sector, because it goes beyond the borders of economics. This is an interdisciplinary study centered on the ethical and political–philosophical aspects of reform. It sets out to analyze not only the economic context of the issue, but its social and political environment as well.

For whom is the book intended? It mainly addresses two groups. One consists of those with an interest in the post-socialist transition in Eastern Europe. This interest may not be confined to the health sector; it may extend to the reform of other sectors. This group may find it instructive to consider the changes in the health sector, since these raise several problems common to changes in other areas. The other target group of readers consists of those concerned with health-care reform, whether in Eastern Europe or elsewhere. Although the changes in Eastern Europe have several specific features and the book's recommendations do not aspire to universal validity, the line of argument may yield more general lessons, valid beyond the bounds of Eastern Europe.

The authors would like the book to be comprehensible not just to health economists, but to a broader readership that includes politicians, legislators, party officials, civil servants, doctors, academic economists, political scientists, and press and media journalists. We must apologize to specialists in the field for having to stop and explain some concepts and connections with which they may be already familiar.

We want to measure the book's success not simply by approval from our academic colleagues (welcome though that would be), but by whether it manages, even indirectly, to exercise some influence on the course of events. This aspiration explains why the book is a hybrid. It is not a pamphlet written by politicians and PR people; it is much longer than that in any case. It is apparent that it is written by academics, but it is not an academic monograph, because the emphasis is on recommendations for reform.

The book is the work of two authors. János Kornai has specialized in conducting research on the problems of Eastern Europe. He has spent decades studying the socialist system and reforms of it – and, in the last decade, the transformation that followed the collapse of socialism. It seemed that the experience of his earlier research could be applied to this new field. Where the reform of the socialist health-care sector had yet to take place, a fragment of socialism had survived in the midst of a capitalist market economy.[5] The main features and concomitants of socialism appear clearly: bureaucratic overcentralization, the absence of price signals or distortion of prices, chronic shortage, queuing and forced substitution, and the "black" economy. Where reform gets under way, the questions that immediately arise are familiar to all who took part in and analyzed the earlier debates about market socialism. Can market coordination be introduced while state ownership remains? How far should centralization or decentralization be allowed to go? What function do prices have, and what cost elements should be covered by revenue from sales? Is it possible to harden the budget constraint and impose financial discipline if that inevitably brings losses and hardship for the public? Regrettably, participants in the world-wide debate on health care have not drawn on the intellectual resources of the debates about socialism. They feel that every question and every answer has to be discovered anew. Perhaps this book can help to alleviate this shortcoming, by trying to import into the lively and varied polemic on health care such experiences and ideas, which are sinking into oblivion. Here in the introduction it is

---

[5] When public ownership and administrative allocation still characterized the welfare sector in Israel, one economist asked the ironic question (paraphrasing the debate between Trotsky and Stalin): "Can socialism be built in half a country?"

enough simply to mention this connection, to which the discussion will return on several occasions.

The other author, Karen Eggleston, is a health economist. She completed her studies recently, in which she gained an insight into the modern literature on health care and had an opportunity to acquaint herself with various conflicting views. Her own research has mainly been concerned with the incentives influencing health care. In writing this book, she was also able to make use of experience she gained while studying the health sector in China.

We hope that our two bodies of knowledge and experience will produce a special blend that helps to enrich the literature on health-care reform.

The use of the first person plural in many places in this book is designed to express the personal, individual character of the proposal, not the originality of the idea behind it. Our assertions rest on our own assessment of the situation and reflect our own system of values. Reform proposals often result from committee work, so that the final text reflects a compromise between the views of committee members. This applies still more at a later stage, when the reform is being enacted by Parliament. By then, it embodies numerous compromises struck during the political process of legislation, and various concessions made by the experts who drafted the bill and the politicians who voted for it. We do not belong to the health-sector bureaucracy, nor are we invited experts of a political party or members of Parliament. That means we can express our opinions without making compromises for the sake of agreement. We realize that if there turn out to be people in the government or the administrative system in any of the Eastern European countries who agree with our proposals, they will probably have to make concessions on some issues, against their better judgment, to ensure practical implementation. We think the established division of labor means it is their job, not ours, to make those concessions. Let them decide, according to their feelings of political responsibility and their ethical notions, how far those concessions should go. We have a different job, because we, members of the academic community, have different opportunities open to us. We want to utilize the advantages we gain from that division of labor, in being able to express our views consistently, as our convictions dictate.

Finally, let us say something about the tone of the book.[6] We sense deeply what health and illness mean to everyone, which we have learned from our own experiences in life. There were two occasions when the first author lay in a ten-bed ward of a Budapest hospital after a serious operation, and was able to study the socialist health sector closely. On one occasion he was taken to a private clinic in Geneva after a road accident. Although he was in great pain, they did not set about treating him until it became clear who was going to pay. There he learned to his cost what a "pure market" entailed. Personal experience, of course, is not even the most important aspect. We have sensed several times the anxiety, fear and pain of our relatives in times of illness and defenselessness. During such illnesses, and sad to say, after a good many deaths, we have often asked ourselves: was everything possible done to cure the patients and save their lives? To what extent could the state of the health sector be blamed for their suffering, or, in the worst case, death? We feel this empathy not only for family and friends, but also for all our fellow human beings. Even so, our aim when writing this book has not been to seize every chance to write a heartrending description of present conditions, or pin blame on society, governments, or politicians. Precisely because the situation is dramatic in many respects, the best way to help

---

[6] The problem of terminology in this book should be mentioned here. Each country in Eastern Europe has its own terms for the various health-sector institutions and the various components of the economic and political mechanism. Simply to translate these literally into English would lead to terminological confusion. Moreover, the terminology in the English-speaking countries is not uniform either. To avoid ambiguity, this book consistently uses the expressions current in the United States.

is not to dramatize and work up people's passions, but to think the tasks out, calmly and dispassionately. Figuratively speaking, our ideal is not a doctor who bursts into tears on seeing how ill the patient is, but one who reassures the patient and family and soberly considers what remedy or treatment will be of most avail.

The book is the end product of a long process of research. The work of János Kornai, the first author, took place under the auspices of Collegium Budapest, Institute for Advanced Study. He received financial support from the Hungarian National Scientific Research Foundation (OTKA T 018280 and T 30080), from the Hungarian Ministry of Finance, and from the European Commission DG Research INCO Programme, which supports the "Institution-Building" Project of Collegium Budapest. He wishes to express his gratitude to them all.

János Kornai has given several lectures on the subject-matter of the book, including at the Washington conference of the National Academy of Science, Harvard University, the World Bank, the Berlin Wissenschaftskolleg, and the Hungarian Medical Association. The debates following these lectures provided much inspiration for his work. Part of the book constituted the Federico Caffè Lecture he gave in Rome; this gave us the honor of having this book published in the Caffè Lecture series.

Karen Eggleston, the second author, would like to thank Harvard University's Kennedy School of Government and the National Bureau of Economic Research program of pre-doctoral fellowships in aging and health economics, which provided generous financial support during the period when she first began to work with János Kornai on the issues of transitional economy health-sector reform. She is also grateful to Tufts University Department of Economics for reducing her departmental responsibilities during the Fall of 1999, when this book was taking final form.

The two authors would like to express their joint gratitude

to all of their colleagues who read the studies that were the antecedents of this book, for their thought-provoking comments and suggestions. Of those who contributed in this way, they would like to single out the following: Géza Bálint, Nicholas Barr, David Cutler, Zsuzsa Dániel, Guy Ellena, Béla Fekete, William Hsiao, Csaba László, Mária Kovács, Péter Mihályi, Thomas McGuire, John McHale, Joseph Newhouse, Winnie Yip, and Richard Zeckhauser.

Many people assisted us in the research for and compilation of this book. Mention must be made, with great appreciation, of the help we received from Ágnes Benedict, who contributed to our work with inspiring ideas and suggestions, ingenious collection of data and dedicated assistance in the editorial process. We also received valuable support from Mária Barát, Cecília Hornok, Béla Janky, and Virág Molnár. Brian McLean made excellent translations of the parts of the book that were originally written in Hungarian. Julianna Parti gave very circumspect and thorough assistance with the editing of the manuscript. We greatly appreciate the willingness of Cambridge University Press to publish the book. We would like to express our thanks to Ashwin Rattan and Barbara Docherty for their editorial assistance.

Part I

Points of departure

Introduction to part I

There are several starting points for the line of argument whose destination is a sketch of the guidelines for the reform. First of all, the basic principles of the reform have to be weighed (chapter 2). Then there needs to be an examination of the characteristics of health care that differ from those of other sectors (chapter 3). The next step is to study international experience. It has to be clarified whether there is a country whose structure and institutions can be taken as a model, and what positive and negative lessons can be drawn from studying international developments (chapter 4). Finally, knowledge is required of the inherited attributes of the health sector in post-socialist Eastern Europe. The initial state and the historical path that led to the point of departure constrain later action (chapter 5).

The order follows the logic of comprehension and elucidation. However, when reformers set about devising a plan of action, they have to consider all elements at once – principles, sector-specific characteristics, the lessons of international experience, and the main set of initial conditions – and keep them in mind simultaneously.

2

The general principles of reform

Although the book confines itself to discussing health-care reform, the principles expounded in this chapter have a validity that extends beyond the health sector. Those who accept these principles may apply them to reforming other sectors of the welfare state inherited from the socialist system, such as the pension system, the public assistance and unemployment benefits system, or the financing of education. The comments have been phrased to apply to the welfare sector as a whole.

Some of the principles expounded in this chapter are universal in character, in our view, and therefore not restricted to any country, region, or set of initial conditions.[1] Others have been suggested by the present state of the welfare sector in the post-socialist countries. We have tried to formulate principles that are valid for every post-socialist country and to that extent the chapter points beyond conditions specific to Eastern Europe (as defined in the introduction).

Altogether nine principles are advanced.[2] The first section

---

[1] Principles similar to those recommended in this book have been expounded by some reformers in developed countries as well. See, for instance, Jakobs (1991), Cassel (1992), and Oberender (1992) on the Austrian debate, and Ham (1997: 58–9) on the Swedish position.

[2] Why precisely nine? We do not claim that this set of principles embodies some kind of whole. Perhaps some principle or other could be omitted, or others added to the set. The text could be expressed otherwise, even if the discussion were confined to those who approximately endorse the position taken in the book, at least in their overall view of the world. The authors are certainly relieved to have stopped at nine, avoiding any hint of "ten commandments."

presents those ones related to fundamental values. The next section concerns the desirable attributes of the reformed welfare sector's institutions. The final section considers the allocation proportions appropriate to the welfare sector.

It would have been better to have conducted a far more rigorous, axiomatic discussion that started from postulates and auxiliary postulates and the conclusions to be drawn from them. It would then have appeared that the principles are not just listed one after another, but bear logical relations to each other, forming a closed theoretical structure. For simplicity and congruence with the tenor of the rest of our book, we apply a lower level of abstraction, and the discussion is less rigorous. However, we hope it may, at least, help to raise the debate from the details of some proposal or other to matters of principle. The medium level of generalization applied here seems to suffice for one of the book's objects – to provide common underlying principles for otherwise separately treated parts of the reform: pension reform, health reform, allowances reform, and so on.

We have expressed the principles in the imperative, addressing the "reformer." This might be a politician, an official, an expert adviser, a union official, or an academic. However, it also reveals a *credo*, since it espouses the authors' own set of values, which underlie the proposals.

Many readers may be surprised to find abstract, normative principles launching a discussion of the economic mechanism behind the welfare sector. It is certainly unusual. Most proposals go straight to practical matters. At best it becomes possible after studying the proposal to deduce something about the principles the author may espouse. Sometimes it emerges that the author was guided merely by practical considerations that turn out, if examined according to a stricter, normative line of argument, to be inconsistent – or, more bluntly, devoid of principle. We will risk putting our cards on the table. We will state beforehand what principles guide us in framing the proposals, and try to infer our practical recommendations consistently from them.

Ethical postulates

Although we are economists, our point of departure is not economic principle. Attention is given to economic principles later, but we do not consider them the fundament of the reform.

It is mistaken to advance as the main argument for reforming health care – or more generally, the welfare sector – that "there is not enough money," "the state coffers are empty," or "there is a serious budget deficit." If economic development succeeds in ending the budget deficit, will that mean there is no need to reform the welfare sector after all? In that case, will it be desirable or even possible to reverse the measures taken because money was tight?[3]

We advance here two ethical principles that form the starting point for our line of argument, and which reformers should abide by, in our view.[4] The institutions and allocation proportions that develop during the reform should accord with these moral imperatives.

Principle 1 (sovereignty of the individual): *The transformation promoted must increase the scope for the individual and reduce the scope for the state to decide in the sphere of welfare services.*
The main trouble we see with the welfare sector inherited from the socialist system is that it leaves too wide a sphere of

---

[3] A careful examination of China's health-sector policies and performance in the 1990s well illustrates that the need for reform is not obviated by robust economic growth. See for example, World Bank (1997a) and Yip and Hsiao (1999).

[4] We have tried to produce a "minimalist" solution. In other words, we want to present the minimum number of requirements, i.e. only as much as seems necessary and sufficient as an ethical starting point for the reform.

resources in the hands of government, the political process, and the bureaucracy, rather than the individual. This trespasses on fundamental human rights such as individual sovereignty, self-realization and self-determination.[5] When public spending on welfare decreases, along with the taxes to finance it, citizens are not just having entitlements withdrawn from them. More pertinently, they are regaining rights of individual disposal.

Principle 1 includes not only the individual's decision-making rights, but the requirement that individuals take *responsibility* for their lives. They have to quit the habit of allowing a paternalist state to do their thinking for them (and be helped in their detoxification cure by the reformers). After that, they will have a far greater right to choose, but they will also be responsible for their choices and have to take the consequences if they decide unwisely. In most of the Western world this is seen as a trivial, obvious requirement, imbibed by citizens with their mother's milk. Generations growing up under the socialist system have had the opposite instilled in them. They learned that the ruling party and the state were responsible for everything, and individuals had to accept their decisions, feeling they were in good hands. So many people in post-socialist countries, when they have a problem, think at first not to solve it for themselves, but to call on the state to help. The state will be at hand, so that they need have no thought for the morrow.[6] The reform of the welfare sector

---

[5] Numerous authors have dealt with the interpretation of individual freedom. Isaiah Berlin's study (1969) is especially important for applying the distinction between positive and negative liberty. The negative freedom of individuals is threatened by a hyperactive, disproportionate, paternalist welfare state. It would be desirable for society to develop in a direction that protects and reinforces individuals' negative freedom while enhancing their positive freedom. In this sense Amartya Sen (1990) considers the assertion of individual freedom to be an obligation upon society. See also Sen (1996).

[6] A representative survey taken in Hungary in 1996 at the first author's initiative under the auspices of the research institute TÁRKI sought to gauge the public's attitude to reforming the welfare sector (Csontos, Kornai and Tóth 1998). One question was, "How are you preparing for

relies on developing a new ethos that places the sovereignty and responsibility of the individual to the fore. It seems desirable to establish institutions that induce everyone to bear the main responsibility for what happens to them in the future, in line with principle 1.

It also follows from principle 1 that although no society can function without some governmental coercion, it is desirable to minimize this, and place in the forefront the principle of *voluntary action*. Paternalism tries to force happiness on people. Instead, people should be allowed to succeed for themselves.

Principle 2 (solidarity): *Help the suffering, the troubled and the disadvantaged.*

Many religions, including Judeo-Christian and Buddhist ethics, urge compassionate solidarity. So do labor-movement traditions and left-wing political beliefs. The same sentiments may arise out of plain human goodwill, a sense of fraternity and community, and an innate sense of altruism, without necessarily being based on any specific world view or intellectual tradition.

Much of the literature on the welfare state, including health reform, places the dilemma of "equity versus efficiency" at the center of the analysis. The procedure here does not follow that tradition, which opposes an extremely important ethical postulate with an instrument – the requirement of efficiency in serving human welfare. The requirement of encouraging efficiency also features in the nine principles presented here, as principle 4, but with the lower "rank" of

your old age?" The answer chosen by 51 percent of respondents was that they had not thought about it yet.

According to the findings of a later, follow-up survey, the situation has changed somewhat since then. In 1999, only 33 percent of respondents who were economically active said they had not thought about preparing for their old age (communication from TÁRKI). It should be added that a successful pension reform introducing a private segment was implemented in Hungary between the times of the two surveys, which may have alerted the public to the pension problem.

an instrument, not as a basic ethical postulate. On the other hand, equal rank as a basic ethical postulate has been given to the principle of sovereignty, which is absent from the vocabulary of many Eastern European reformers, or mentioned only in passing.

Unlike the system of axioms in mathematics, which is expected to be contradiction-free, conflicts may occur among the basic postulates of ethics. Fortunately, there is not a conflict in every case; principles 1 and 2 are compatible in some decisions. For instance, individual sovereignty is quite compatible with voluntary charity. To take another example, the type of support for needy people that helps them to adapt to difficult circumstances reinforces their sovereignty rather than reduces it.

Advocates of libertarian ethics are not prepared to go further than that (Epstein 1997), and oppose all legal and bureaucratic compulsion on principle. They reject all forms of redistribution by the state, including the idea of compulsory insurance, because that infringes individual sovereignty and restricts people's right to use their own property as they see fit.

We do not subscribe to such libertarian philosophy. We are aware that there may be a strong conflict between principles 1 and 2, which have been accorded equal rank. We are prepared to accept state coercion to fulfill certain tasks, where it has been endorsed by the democratic political process, deeming that it is preferable to aim at sober compromises in cases where principles 1 and 2 conflict.

The implementation of principle 2 cannot be left solely to individual charity. In that case, some of those in real need might well be omitted from the circle of those receiving support. It has to be prescribed by law that the state must help the suffering, the troubled and the disadvantaged.[7]

---

[7] On the issue of social assistance and other redistributive measures see Atkinson and Micklewright (1992), Andorka, Kondratas and Tóth (1994), Sipos (1994) and Milanovic (1996).

We approve of the fact that the law obliges citizens to take out certain types of insurance. This restricts the application of principle 1, because voluntary action gives way to a legal requirement, but it does not have a paternalist intent. It is guided by collective self-interest. We know any humane society will feel compelled to care for the sick, the homeless, and the elderly if they are left without means. They will be supported in the last resort at taxpayers' expense. It is to avoid this undesirable external effect that the law should oblige all citizens to obtain at least minimum insurance coverage (see Lindbeck and Weibull 1987).

Principle 2 – solidarity, society's collective altruism – steps in to help those not capable of paying for compulsory insurance. So the difference between this proposal and the schemes prevalent under socialism is conspicuous. The proposal is minimum compulsory insurance, with voluntary insurance above the minimum and help for the needy by redistributive means. The initial position, inherited from the socialist system, has been universal entitlement, with the whole task of insurance channeled through paternalist state redistribution. The first seems to us the healthier, more efficient compromise between principles 1 and 2.

Neither principle 1 nor principle 2 *excludes* the possibility of legislating universal state commitments, but they do not require them either. Other considerations may render it necessary or desirable for all citizens, or all employees, to receive guaranteed entitlements. But still other factors, such as scarce economic means, may argue against universal entitlements.

Principle 2 conflicts with the political rhetoric that seeks to turn the middle class into the main beneficiary of tax policy and redistribution.[8] The middle class, by definition, is not the one in greatest need of assistance. Yet much of the

---

[8] This demand often appears in American political debates on taxation and redistribution. Recently, the same demand came up in the Eastern European discussion and actual political praxis as well.

redistributive process took place within the middle class under the socialist system, and the same applies to some extent in all countries where universal entitlements have been used extensively. The truly needy are those who have never risen into the middle class, or have sunk below it.[9] These are the people whose assistance principle 2 brings into the foreground.

Behind principle 2 lies the fundamental demand that every member of a community should be capable at least of satisfying his or her basic needs.[10] This does not imply that the state itself has to provide services to meet the basic needs of *everyone*, free or as a preferential benefit. Most members of society are capable of obtaining these by their own efforts. The principle of solidarity need apply only to those incapable of fulfilling even their basic needs.

Principle 2 cannot be called an egalitarian requirement. It does not override principle 1. Neither does it call for equal incomes and equal consumption, including equal health care, for all. It is motivated by compassion, and all it seeks to guarantee is that no one in need of assistance will be left to their fate; everyone will have equal access to a minimum level of services. Principle 2 includes giving every citizen a chance for successful self-fulfillment. There must be compassion shown for those who will not receive the initial opportunity without state assistance. The criterion of solidarity also justifies active assistance to the disadvantaged, to provide them with their initial opportunity. On the other hand, solidarity should not be used to justify crude, artificial attempts to level the wide differences between people.

[9] Warnings are heard, during the debates in Eastern Europe, about a sharp deterioration in the financial situation of the earlier middle class, especially some of those in intellectual occupations. Action to correct this can be justified by the principle of solidarity (principle 2). The main form it should take is not benefits, but support for adaptation: occupational retraining and changing jobs and homes, to meet the needs of the new employment structure.

[10] Let us leave open here the question of how to define "basic needs" – what foodstuffs, what kind of housing, and what health care it should include. The concept of basic health care is examined in detail in chapter 6.

We want to dissociate ourselves strongly from those who appeal to the solidarity principle or advance egalitarian arguments for denigrating the importance of the individual sovereignty of citizens. We have encountered in the debates on health reform the idea that this requirement meets the demands of wealthier people, able to afford to choose among doctors, hospitals, or therapies. We are convinced that individual sovereignty is not a luxury good. Rich and poor alike have the right to choose. Although the choice is a money matter in part, there are many cases when the chance to choose does not depend simply on ability to pay, but on whether people are offered and advised about alternatives at all.

In light of principle 2, it is worth considering the question of uncertainty about the future. A person not dependent on anyone at present may become dependent in the future. But according to principle 1, it is primarily individuals themselves who must prepare for such contingencies, by saving and building up reserves, and by voluntarily buying private, commercial insurance coverage. Although certain exceptions might be considered, in principle they should be entitled to state assistance on a solidarity basis only if they encounter problems for which they could not have prepared by such individual means.[11]

Principle 2 includes solidarity and a fair distribution of life's cares and joys between generations. The present generation should display care and consideration for future generations. There is no moral justification for making life easier today by leaving future generations with grave debts, with economic time bombs that will explode in the more distant future.

Certainly the poor and disadvantaged deserve compassion from society. But most people on the recipient side find

---

[11] Much confusion has been caused by confounding risk-sharing insurance, placed on a commercial basis, with assistance based on altruistic solidarity. It is especially confusing when the two become mingled in the definition of "social insurance." On the connection between the two institutions, see Csaba (1997). We will return to this later.

"charity" demeaning. The needy must be helped mainly by giving them opportunities to work and skills to better their own circumstances in life. The degree to which claimants can help themselves and adapt to the prevailing conditions must be weighed when determining the degree and type of help they receive (see n. 10 above).

One more comment seems apposite, to conclude the discussion of the ethical starting points. The line of argument in this book does not start from *ultimate* values of freedom, equality, well-being and material welfare, or social justice. The relationships between ultimate values and social organization[12] are the concern of studies in political theory dealing with the ethical foundations of a "good" society. This book does not set out to contribute to the analysis of these deeper problems. We hope that principles 1 and 2, which identify intermediate ethical requirements, not ultimate values, can provide a broad platform acceptable to people who take differing views on freedom, equality, and social justice.

However, principle 1 will be alien (and principle 2 may be superfluous) to those whose axiomatic point of departure is collectivist: *subordination* of the individual to the interests of a specific community, whether a nation, a race or a class, or the tenets of a religion. We own that the reform this book advances differs in essential ways from the kind of changes any collectivist notion would suggest.

It is instructive, in the light of what has been said, to consider the findings of a public opinion poll conducted by Professor Richard Rose, under the "New Democracies" project in 1992 (Rose and Haerpfer 1993). The researchers analyzed the responses to four questions, to decide whether respondents' ideas were closer to an individualist view of the world or to a collectivist one. The results appear in figure 2.1.

---

[12] To single out a few, especially influential works from the vast literature on the subject: Berlin (1969), Rawls (1971), Sen (1973 and 1992), Nozick (1974), and Buchanan (1986). For a broad survey on the debate on the philosophical ramifications of the modern welfare state, see Culpitt (1992).

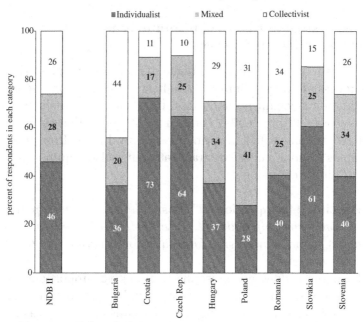

Figure 2.1 Value choices

Notes: Those in the experiment were asked to choose from among an individualist and a collectivist alternative by answering four questions. The categories were compiled as follows: Individualists: three or four individualist preferences. Mixed: two individualist and two collectivist preferences. Collectivists: three or four collectivist preferences.
NDB II: the average in countries in the New "Democracy Barometer II" survey, i.e. all the countries included in the figure plus Ukraine and Belorussia.
Source: Rose and Haerpfer (1993: 71).

In every country except Bulgaria and Poland, more people were inclined to take an individualist rather than a collectivist approach. In three countries about two-thirds of the population favored individualism. Out of the eight countries, in six the proportion of those with consistently collectivist views is less than a third. The poll's definitions cannot be said to coincide exactly with those of this book. Nonetheless, it is remarkable that the idea of individual sovereignty and responsibility should lie close to the value system of much of the post-socialist region's population.

The desired attributes of institutions and coordination mechanisms

Let us now turn to another plane of reform principles. The process of reform eliminates or alters old institutions, coordination mechanisms and rules of the game, and establishes new ones. Principles 3–7 concern the attributes these should have. To some extent the principles follow directly from principles 1 and 2, but the desirable attributes also require some additional components.

Principle 3 (competition): *There should not be a monopoly of state ownership and control. Let there be competition among various ownership forms and coordination mechanisms.*

Principle 3 does not prescribe quantitative proportions. It does not say what shares the state and nonstate segments should have. Whatever the case, the nonstate sector has to attain a critical mass that ends the state sector's enervating monopoly and the chance for the producer (the welfare state) to dictate to the consumer. Although there are considerations of efficiency that argue in favor of competition (see principle 4), the main source of principle 3 is principle 1: there must be competition so that citizens can choose. If they do not like what they receive from state institutions, they can avail themselves of nonstate goods and services as well.

The survival of the socialist system in the welfare sector has the serious consequence of leaving citizens defenseless in several important fields, although the decisions now come from a more diffuse "state authority," instead of the Politburo. What resources go to health care and what income elderly people receive depend on squabbling parties, subordinating their policies to rivalry for popularity, and on the relative strength of lobbies and groups of bureaucrats reaching compromises behind the scenes. Principle 3 seeks to place a much larger proportion of such decisions in the hands of the individuals concerned. At least for a sizable part of this expenditure, let them decide individually what they want to spend on their health or other welfare services and that of their families, how they want to prepare for their old age, and so on. This becomes possible if some welfare resources cease to go through the bureaucratic mechanism, funded by taxes collected by the state and allocated by the state, and households and individuals become able to decide about them through the other great coordination mechanism, the market.

Principle 3 seeks to open the welfare sector to private, non-state institutions, both profit-seeking and not-forprofit. Let there emerge private hospitals, clinics, medical test laboratories, kindergartens, schools, old people's homes, and commercial insurance companies through the foundation of new organizations or the privatization of existing ones owned by the state. Alongside the purely state-owned and the purely forprofit, private providers, there is ample scope for founding nonstate, nonprofit organizations as well. The owners or controllers of these could be societies, foundations, churches, professional associations, large employers, associations of smaller employers, and so on.

The function of applying principle 2 (solidarity) can be shared among the state, the nonprofit segment of the welfare sector, and private charitable activities.

What the public wants is security and this the state has to provide, argue those who believe in fully nationalizing the welfare sector. In our view, this is a flawed argument. Sophisticated writings on uncertainty propose (and common sense also suggests) a simple rule: hedge your bets. To put the matter in investment-portfolio terms: diversify. It would be a mistake, for instance, to entrust all one's retirement savings to a single private pension fund, for if it managed the money dishonestly or unwisely, the insured would be in deep trouble. Similar problems may occur if total reliance is placed on the state. By the time a person retires, the political authorities of the day may have decided to ignore the question of how much contribution has been paid over the years.[13] Alternatively, the pension may be eroded by surges of policy-induced inflation, and by indexation rules that whittle away its real value. So the most expedient proposals for pension reform are those that rest on several pillars, allowing different pension schemes to be used concurrently.[14] Similar "multi-pillar" solutions should be considered to fund the other subsectors of the welfare sector.

Public opinion is dispersed widely about which pillars, or combination of pillars, to prefer. The spread of opinion is exemplified in the findings of the Hungarian public-opinion poll mentioned earlier, shown in table 2.1.[15]

There is a danger that parliamentary procedures, based on the majority principle, will yield reforms that may cause one form of ownership and/or one form of control to predominate. (For instance, the status quo, the domination of state forms, or high level of centralization may remain or, on the contrary, a rapid and radical, total privatization and decentralization may be forced through.) In our view, principle 1 suggests that citizens should not be forced into any particular scheme. So far as possible, let individuals choose for themselves. There should emerge a "menu" of various forms of ownership and mechanisms of control and coordination from which citizens can select. They should be able to learn,

[13] This applies in most post-socialist countries today. The "pay-as-you-go" system and repeated changes in pension rules, coupled with tendencies to level out pensions, have loosened the correlation between the actual pension and the pension premium contributed during the active phase of the pensioner's lifetime.

[14] The Hungarian Pension Reform Act of 1997, and also the proposals elaborated by the Polish government, are based on such a multi-pillar solution. For an excellent survey and careful proposals see World Bank (1994). For a critical assessment of the World Bank report see Beattie and McGillivray (1995), and the rejoinder by the principal author, James (1996). The World Bank proposals are also analyzed and criticized in Diamond (1996).

[15] A follow-up survey to this research asked whether respondents would support the idea of having several, competing health-insurance schemes, so breaking the quasi-monopoly of social insurance up to now. (see chapter 9, p. 332 below and tables 9.2–9.4).

Table 2.1 *Institutional choices: support for state, market, and mixed solutions in Hungary, percentage distribution of answers*

Alternatives	Financing of		
	Higher education	Hospital care	Pensions
Centralized state solutions	42.1	35.5	21.4
Mixed structures	43.5	44.1	56.6
Market solutions	12.1	17.9	18.5
Unable to decide	2.2	2.5	3.5
Total	100.0	100.0	100.0

Note:
The research institute TÁRKI conducted a survey in 1996 to find out how informed the Hungarian population was about the relationship between welfare services and taxation, and about the preferences concerning various institutional alternatives. The sample size was about 1,000 individuals. As for the three alternatives referred to in the table, the first represented the status quo – i.e. services financed and run by the state or by semi-governmental agencies. The third alternative represented a decentralized and to a large extent privatized welfare sector. The second alternative incorporated multi-pillar institutional arrangements. It would have been worth offering more than one mixed structure, but the time limits of the survey did not allow for that.
Source: Csontos, Kornai and Tóth (1998: 307).

from their own and others' experience, to experiment and to modify their positions. That is one more reason why competition is needed in the welfare sector. In the presence of competition, selection can be made not only through the friction-ridden transmission of the political process, but directly, through the market choices that households make.

There is much opposition to applying principle 3 apparent in Eastern Europe. It is understandable that those who currently enjoy a monopoly of ownership or regulation should fear for their power or their incomes, but many people's aversion to the appearance of private ownership and the market is generated by ideological prejudices. The discussion on reforming the welfare sector brings out anti-capitalist, anti-market arguments in the rhetoric not only of radical socialists, but even of avowedly conservative politicians. This ideological opposition is an important terrain for a phenomenon already mentioned in the introduction: the survival of the socialist system, in this case in the indoctrinated prejudices of a high proportion of the public.

Principle 4 (incentives for efficiency): *Forms of ownership and control that encourage efficiency need to emerge.*
This principle is reasonably self-evident and will be discussed in more detail in chapter 3. The only reason for including it among the declared principles is that politicians and academics who defend the status quo in the welfare sector tend to forget it.

The incentives for efficiency (and here there is a substantial difference from present practice) must be given on the demand side as well, to citizens as *recipients* of welfare services. This means that with only the rarest exceptions, services should not be free. Instead of having state subsidies to force the price down below the market level, there should be state assistance, targeted to those for whom it is justified, in voucher form, for instance.[16] (This would normally apply to those in need, in line with the principle of solidarity.) Even if the state or the insurer covers most of the cost of a good or service, recipients should make a co-payment,[17] so that they appreciate that the good or service is not free.

Proper incentives on the demand side include inducing efficiency in the insurers that largely finance the welfare ser-

---

[16] A debate is going on on the advantages and disadvantages of vouchers in welfare services. For a survey see Culpitt (1992).

[17] Throughout the book we use "co-payment" to refer to a recipient's (e.g. patient's) out-of-pocket spending for a good or service, such as a doctor's visit or a prescription drug.

vices. This is one of several arguments against the monopoly of the monstrous "great wens": the central, state health insurance and pension authorities. Where there is no competition, there almost never is sufficient incentive for efficiency and thrift.

The same argument applies on the supply side, to the organizations that provide the health, education, and other services, and care for children and the elderly. When commenting on principle 3, we cited the sovereignty of the individual as an argument for competition. Let no one be left at the mercy of a single monopoly organization. We realize that both forprofit and nonstate, nonprofit insurers and providers may try to cut costs at the expense of recipients (the patient, or the child or old person requiring the service). However, the same may occur under state ownership and control if state institutions are urged to cut costs and no longer have the chance to scatter money left and right. Unlimited expansion of costs versus savings at the expense of those receiving the services form the horns of one of the welfare sector's gravest dilemmas. We will return to this question in the more detailed discussion of the health sector in chapter 3.

Another aspect of incentives and efficiency to consider is the most expedient mechanism for allocating investments and generating and utilizing savings and reserves. Two pure cases can be distinguished. The first applies most consistently under the socialist system, when the pension system and all the other welfare services operate on a nationalized, "pay-as-you-go" principle. Households are not expected to save for security purposes. Instead they are forced to pay taxes that finance all investment and all welfare services. Total centralization leads to low efficiency, and not just with welfare services, but in the selection and execution of investment projects.

The other, diametrically opposite pure case, would be one in which the accumulation of reserves was left entirely to households and firms. Each household would place these in a portfolio, dividing them among banks, mutual funds, insurance companies, pension funds, and so on. The financial sector, i.e. the credit and capital markets, would in turn use this huge stock of savings in a decentralized fashion, to finance investment. That would be complemented by firms' decentralized savings and investment.

One thing has conclusively emerged from the great historical contest between the socialist and capitalist systems. A system in which decentralized investment based on private ownership and competition predominates is more efficient than one in which centralization and state ownership prevail. The implications for welfare-sector reform are straightforward. The savings set aside for illness, unemployment, accident, or old age constitute so much of the total savings that it cannot be right simply to hand them to the bureaucracy. The bulk of this vast quantity of savings should be employed in a decentralized way. Following this line of argument to its conclusion, principle 4 (incentives to efficiency) provides a further, weighty argument in favor of principle 3 (the spread of competition and nonstate institutions). However, it does not follow from this that an utterly decentralized investment mechanism is to be recommended. It is justifiable to assume that there will be a permanent need for some state investment financed out of taxes.[18]

Principle 5 (a new role for the state): *The main functions of the state in the welfare sector must be to supply legal frameworks, supervise nonstate institutions, and provide ultimate, last-resort insurance and aid. The state is responsible for ensuring that every citizen has access to basic education and health care.*
Our commentary on principle 5 needs to be prefaced by a general observation. It has been implied in the arguments so

---

[18] There has been detailed discussion in economic writings about what cases justify state selection, financing, and/or implementation of investment.

far, and now has to be stated plainly, that the state referred to is one with normally operating democratic institutions. The legislature is elected under legally defined conditions through a contest between political parties. The government is confirmed in office by Parliament. There is an independent judiciary. There is freedom of speech, assembly, and the press. The requirements of a constitutional state pertain. Democracy has not advanced or consolidated to an equal extent in the ten Eastern European states examined here, but each has developed the minimum configuration of institutions required for democracy to operate. We ignore here the question of how many of the principles and practical proposals put forward in this book could be implemented under a dictatorial regime, because our message is addressed in any case to states that operate in a democratic framework.

To return to principle 5, the essential requirement is a radical transformation of the state's role, along the lines suggested by principle 1, increasing the sovereignty of the individual. Let us briefly review the functions of the state in a reformed welfare sector:

- By passing and enforcing the new legislation required, the state acts as guardian over the legality of the welfare sector's operation. It is important that citizens be able to seek legal redress in the courts against the government and its apparatus, insurers, hospitals, doctors, old-people's homes, or other bodies, if their civil rights are infringed.
- The state needs to establish suitable bodies to exercise supervision over the welfare sector and its various subsectors (health care, medical insurance, pension-fund management, and so on). These should be complemented by a watchdog role for claimants' and users' associations, the press, and civil society as a whole.

- The state should underwrite the savings that citizens place with insurance institutions and pension funds.[19]
- As mentioned earlier, it is desirable to assign a role to nonstate organizations in applying the principle of solidarity. Nonetheless, there is no way the state can avoid making a substantial contribution as well. We do not agree with those who would rather hide this away among other public expenditure, lest the voters notice.[20] It needs to be stated openly that state assistance is being paid to those in need, out of revenue from the taxpayers.
- Declaring that the state bears responsibility for basic health care (and similarly, for basic education) leaves open the question of how and through what kind of institutions this responsibility is to be met. It neither includes the requirement nor precludes the possibility that institutions owned or controlled by the state take part in providing the service, or that the state budget contributes to financing it. Which approach is preferable depends on what form of ownership will be most effectual under the conditions in the country concerned. Retaining or eliminating state ownership is a means, not an end.

It is clear from what has been said that this book does not advocate a laissez-faire program. It does not seek to relieve the state of its responsibility for the welfare sector, even if

---

[19] Presumably some kind of nonstate or quasi-state reinsurance institutions can be established to safeguard citizens' insurance investments against failure by a particular insurer. It will suffice if the state provides a guarantee of last resort, should the reinsurer be unable to cover the loss. The function of an "ultimate insurer" is still a fiscal burden, but a far smaller one than entire state financing of all welfare services.

[20] Most people have a sense of solidarity with the community. For example, in Hungary, the poll mentioned earlier (Csontos, Kornai and Tóth (1998) showed that many childless respondents would also be willing to pay the tax to support higher education. It would probably be possible to find similar examples from other countries and for other welfare expenditures as well.

many tasks will be performed by enterprises based on private ownership and by nonprofit institutions organized by various communities, coordinated mainly by the market and spurred on by competition. This must occur under rules set by the state, under the supervision of the state and civil society. The state must also contribute its economic resources where there is an inescapable need to do so.

The various instances of market failure have been sufficiently clarified by economists.[21] There is justification for state intervention in cases where the market has failed, provided there is no reason to fear that state activity will cause still greater failure. Public-choice theory and research into bureaucracies[22] explain the conditions and consequences of various forms of government failure. However, there is often a problem with gauging the relative probability of market and government failure, and the scale of the damage they would cause. This book therefore leaves open the question of how big the segment of the welfare sector under state ownership or direct state control should be. If the public, through the political process, expresses a wish that some of the financing for health care or other welfare services should still come from the state budget, that certain hospitals remain in state ownership, and so on, and if they are willing to pay tax to support these, that wish should be respected. The second proviso (willingness to pay the associated tax burden) leads on to the next principle, which concerns transparency.

---

[21] Here and later on in this book we use the expression "market failure." It has been clarified theoretically in economics that market failure ensues from a specific configuration of market participants and their environment. The theory is not that the market becomes inoperable in such cases – that it is unable to perform its coordination tasks at all. It says simply that it cannot perform them so well as it can under conditions more favorable to the operation of the market (primarily in a situation of so-called "perfect competition"). Different situations can produce different market failures. The best account of market failure is still found in the classic paper by Francis Bator (1958). See also Stiglitz (1986).

[22] See Buchanan and Tullock (1962), Tullock (1965), and Niskanen (1971).

Principle 6 (transparency): *The link between welfare services provided by the state and the tax burden that finances them must become apparent to citizens. The practical measures of reform must be preceded by open, informed public debate. Politicians and political parties must declare what their welfare sector policies are, and how they will be financed.*

The principle falls into several parts. The first sentence was inspired by a serious problem: citizens do not discern clearly that they, as taxpayers, bear the costs of the services of the welfare state in general, and of the state-financed health sector in particular. Understanding of the relationship between taxes and state spending is vague or distorted everywhere in the world, but the fiscal illusions are nowhere so pronounced as in the post-socialist societies, where people have been indoctrinated for decades with the idea that health care is "free."[23] It can be hoped that resistance to a decentralizing reform will fall sharply once citizens recognize that it is the taxpayer who pays for every state service, and correctly assesses the size of that payment.

Ultimately, the citizens collectively have to pay for welfare services. However, under conditions of political democracy citizens can choose, through the political process, between two primary channels of payment. One is "tax paid by household $\rightarrow$ state budget $\rightarrow$ state welfare service." The other is more direct: "insurance premium paid by household $\rightarrow$ insurer $\rightarrow$ welfare service covered by the insurer."

This leads to the second and third part of principle 6: the need for debate and for transparency of political choice. Political parties in real life seldom put their ideas on the welfare sector – and, specifically, on the health sector – clearly before the electorate, either because they have not

---

[23] The survey taken in Hungary (Csontos, Kornai and Tóth 1998) revealed, for instance, that only a fifth of respondents could estimate within a ±25 percent margin of error what tax burden was imposed by ostensibly free state health care. The rest of the sample either gave guesses even further from the truth, or could not answer the question at all.

thought out their proposals thoroughly enough, or because they want to conceal their intentions.[24] Since this chapter does not fall within the province of positive political economy, it does not address the question of why this is so, or whether it can be changed. In line with its normative character, it puts forward requirements. Principle 6 is addressed to the better side of all politicians. If they wish to be honest with voters, they should tell the voters frankly what they would like to do about pensions, health care, and other welfare services. Other addressees are academics like ourselves, who research the subject. We have no stake in gaining popularity. We are not running for elected office. We have a duty to discover and demonstrate the gains and the social costs of alternative ideas for the welfare sector. Finally, the principle is addressed to citizens. They should try to discern from the policy statements of politicians and parties what they really intend to do about the welfare sector, and remember this when they vote.

It is hard for voters to clarify parties' intentions and to reach a voting decision. After all, when voting for a party or a candidate, they are choosing between packages of policies. Voters voting for *A* rather than *B* may have to overlook the fact that *B*'s welfare policies are more attractive and decide in *A*'s favor because they prefer *A*'s broader economic, judicial, foreign, and other policies to those of *B*.[25]

These very difficulties provide additional arguments for principles 1, 3, and 5: there must be a reduction in the set of welfare services whose control takes place by way of the political process.

---

[24] Utter disregard for principle 6 was of the essence of the socialist system. *By comparison*, the democratic system has made great progress in applying it. However, there can be few illusions about how consistently the principle applies in actual practice in a parliamentary democracy.

[25] It would exceed the scope of this book to discuss how far this problem might be resolved by a system of referenda on important legislation. Except in a few countries, democratic constitutions allow political decisions to be put to a referendum only in exceptional cases.

Principle 7 (the time requirement of the program): *Time must be left for the new institutions of the welfare sector to evolve and for citizens to adapt.*

The reformed welfare sector will contain several institutions that were unknown under the socialist system. Some will be new foundations, such as private clinics and hospitals, kindergartens, or nonstate pension funds. Others will arise by a change in the ownership form of state-owned organizations – for instance, if a team of doctors operates a group practice in a public hospital under a leasing contract. Advocates of reform cannot, in our view, leave these developments entirely to spontaneous processes, for several reasons. The creation of new institutions and transformation of old ones require carefully designed rules enacted by the legislature or local government. Some new organizations will emerge at the initiative of governmental agencies. In some cases political pressure will be needed to set the process of change in motion. It might be added that, by definition, a change in the role of the welfare *state* can occur only with the state's involvement. In sum, while many parts of the evolutionary process of institutional transformation will happen spontaneously, this book does not advocate a reform pattern based solely on spontaneous change.[26]

Equally, we would oppose forcing through the fastest possible reform of the welfare sector at any price. There are crises in which a government has to enforce a painful and unpopular economic adjustment program, which may have to include some items that cause a rapid fall in welfare spending by the state budget. That is one thing, and comprehensive reform of the welfare sector is another. The second is not fiscal fire-fighting, but a radical social transformation, which cannot be conducted at breakneck speed. Sufficient time must be allowed for drafting the program carefully and obtaining political support for it.

[26] These remarks are compatible with the theory of institutional innovation and the evolutionary perception of the history of changing economic institutions. See Davis and North (1971) and North (1990).

The question of political support was mentioned under principle 6. The better the public understands the social costs and likely benefits of the reform, the readier it will be to provide informed support. Whenever possible, time must be given for citizens to adapt to the new situation. The problem of differing *degrees of adaptability* was mentioned under principle 2. Reformers must display calm insight and humane understanding of the fact that people have different powers of adjustment.

As far as the state of the economy allows, suffering can be mitigated and the process of adaptation encouraged by assisting those who suffer heavy losses from the reform. However, assistance for an unlimited period should be given only to those who are truly unable to adapt. For everyone else, assistance should be for a *temporary* period. (For instance, there could be temporary compensation for the needy when a price subsidy is withdrawn.) Individuals should receive a period of grace, but they have to recognize that they will need to adapt to the new situation once the period of grace is over.

The desired proportions of allocation

Principle 8 (harmonious growth): *Let there be harmonious proportions between the resources devoted to investments that directly promote rapid growth and those spent on operating and developing the welfare sector.*

Two extreme views appear in the debates about welfare-sector reform. One places a biased emphasis on the losses entailed in the transition, and fails to acknowledge that the best way to overcome the present problems is through lasting growth in the economy. However trivial a truism this may be to an economist, it is constantly ignored by those who favor maintaining the welfare sector's status quo. Sometimes they scornfully dismiss the elementary economic argument that the living standard of the majority in post-socialist countries can never be raised even to the present average level in the

West until there is sufficient investment to produce lasting and sufficiently rapid growth.

At the other extreme is a view that tips the balance between welfare spending and fast growth inducing investment projects in favor of the latter. Statistical examinations covering several countries show that in the long term, the fastest growth has taken place in the East Asian countries, which spend relatively little on welfare services. Authors either leave Eastern European readers to draw their own conclusions from this, or state plainly: if you want to catch up with the West, follow the East Asian model.

To the first author, as a member of the older generation, this growth fetish sounds familiar. One of the watchwords of the Stalinist–Khrushchevite economic policy was, "Let us catch up with the West as soon as possible." The growth fetish led to a strategy of forced growth and consequent distortion of the economic structure, one result of which was that people's immediate welfare needs were ignored.[27] This kind of bias caused grave problems under the socialist system, whose consequences have not been overcome to this day. It would be a shame to start all that again.

A different conclusion is reached if the international comparison is based not on the relationship between welfare spending and the *rate* of growth, but on the one between welfare spending and *level* of economic development. As a country progresses in its economic development, state spending on health, education, culture, and care of children and the aged increases. The connection is not deterministic, as it is affected by several other factors as well, such as the political complexions of governments and the country's cultural traditions. Still, there is a strong relation between overall economic development and government spending on human welfare. This is exemplified by spending on pensions in the 92 countries in figure 2.2. (The relation between health

---

[27] The study published almost thirty years ago, *Rush versus Harmonic Growth* (Kornai 1972) already argued against this growth fetish.

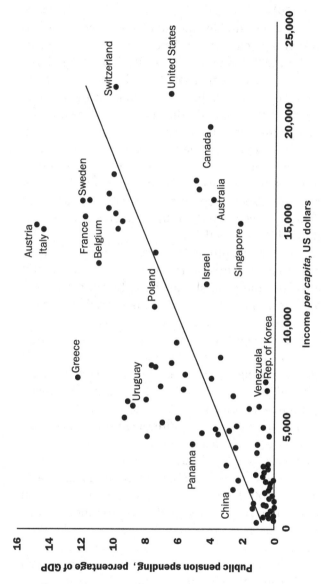

Figure 2.2 Relation between income *per capita* and public pension spending

Note: Because of space limitations, not all data points are identified. The sample comprises 92 countries for various years between 1986 and 1992.

Source: World Bank (1994: 42).

spending and economic development is discussed in chapter 5, p. 176)

Departure from a desirable amount of government welfare expenditure for a given level of development may occur in either direction, with too much or too little spending. Some socialist countries overcompensated for the excesses of the Stalinist period by letting their welfare spending run away at a later stage in their economic development. Prompted by their paternalist ideology and a desire to placate the public, the state undertook greater obligations than its resources warranted at that economic level. This can certainly be said of the pension system in Eastern European countries such as Bulgaria, the Czech Republic, Hungary, Poland, and Slovakia. This applies not only to the written state commitments, but to fulfillment of them.

It is vital to restore the proper balance here by approaching the problem from two directions. State commitments, and entitlements from the state should be reduced, while economic growth is promoted. This will make possible a steady rise in the absolute level of welfare spending, coupled with a fall in its relative weight. We would not venture a quantitative golden rule for ensuring harmonious proportions. It would be a stimulating research task to reconsider this field in the context of the post-socialist transformation. However, although principle 8 does not incorporate a method of quantification, it embodies a strong warning against blatant distortions and misleading political slogans.

Here let us refer back to principle 1. One reason individuals need to be entrusted with more economic choice is because it is doubtful whether central planners are even capable of reaching an appropriate decision on these fundamental proportions. Is the reason why the state should intervene in the main allocation proportions that it needs to "defend" health care and education from the decisions of households, because they spend too much on investment or on the financing of the bureaucracy? We hardly think there is a danger of that. On the contrary, the likely outcome of the individual decisions, aggregated at a national level, would be that society's voluntary, decentralized decision-making, added to total public welfare expenditure, caused more to be spent on health, education, and other activities in the welfare sector than central planners would devote to them.[28]

Another comment has to be made on health-care spending specifically, rather than welfare spending in general. Whatever the proportion of spending determined by state or household decisions, and let us add, whatever the ratio of public to private ownership in the sector, there is a risk that the proportion of health spending to GDP as a whole will run away. This depends largely on what incentives influence the providers and the patients. We will return to this later in more detail. All we wish to do here is to register that principle 8 requires fulfillment of the task of cost containment.

Principle 9 (sustainable financing): *The state budget must be continually capable of financing fulfillment of the state's obligations.*

While principle 8 concerns the desirable allocation of real resources, this principle points to the financial aspects. Self-evident though this requirement may seem, infringement of it was what ended the "taboo" treatment of the welfare state in many countries.

Several economies show a substantial budget deficit, including almost every post-socialist country. The financial deficit of some subsectors of the welfare sector can be

---

[28] This seems to be confirmed by experience under the socialist system. The iron hand of Stalinist economic policy ensured that the state did not "overspend" on hospitals, housing, etc., concentrating resources on developing heavy industry and increasing military might instead.

The argument can also be illustrated in the OECD context. The United States, with its highly decentralized system for deciding the matter, is the OECD country that devotes the highest proportion of GDP to health care. The United Kingdom, with its tax-financed, government-controlled, highly centralized National Health Service, devotes a much lower proportion.

discerned, at least in part, in cases where the budget system earmarks the revenues designed to cover specific types of welfare spending. The deficit has already appeared, or is likely to burst forth eventually, according to projections. In some other subsectors even of these countries, and in the overall state welfare sector of some other countries, the funds required to defray welfare services are not distinct from those for covering other expenditure. State welfare expenditure is paid out of general tax revenues, which makes it hard to determine the relative part played by welfare spending in the overall fiscal deficit.

This book does not set out to analyze the various specific causes of fiscal deficit at different times or in different countries. Nonetheless, it is worth paying attention to calculations that show how the welfare commitments legally enshrined in a particular country will become unsustainable eventually – other circumstances being equal and taking into account the likely economic growth rate and demographic trends. It looks as if state health care services, with great pressure upon them from the demand side, will eventually become impossible to finance. The date when the experts predict that the system will reach the financing limits varies from country to country. In some cases, the gap can be bridged by raising taxes, and in some cases not. This is partly an economic question – higher taxes dampen incentives and impede investment – and partly a political one – the unpopularity of tax increases must be weighed against the unfavorable effects on public opinion of cutting welfare spending. Ultimately it seems that in most post-socialist countries, the need to improve the fiscal balance will eventually necessitate cuts in state welfare spending.

Although we have left principles 8 and 9 to the end of the discussion, they are no less cogent than principles 3–7 concerning the desired attributes of institutions and coordination mechanisms. We think the established cast list for the debates on reforming the welfare sector has become untenable. Here we refer only to the discussion in academic circles. Defenders of the welfare state rightly describe in dramatic terms the sufferings of the destitute and disadvantaged, but they dismiss scornfully any mention of the need for harmonious economic proportions. That they see as no concern of theirs, because it rests on narrow fiscal arguments that no compassionate person would consider. On the other side there can be read economic arguments that devote a paragraph to the need for a social safety net, but the authors have failed to think through all the social consequences of the rules they propose. Both sides usually refrain from backing their positions with ethical criteria. We think it is high time to insist on a synthesis of outlook, in ourselves and in others. Neither side has a right exclusively to espouse either social criteria or economic arguments.

Concluding remarks

An examination of principles 1–9 leaves open a number of important questions whose discussion would extend beyond the scope of this book. Further theoretical analysis is required to decide how far the various pairs and subsets of principles can be reconciled and how far they conflict – in other words, how far there are trade-off relations between them. For instance, principle 1 (individual sovereignty and responsibility) and principle 5 (the responsibility of the state) are not irreconcilable, although clearly the further one goes, the less scope there remains for the other.

Given such trade-offs, no prior theoretical consideration can preclude the need to make a specific, responsible choice in each case. It was remarked in relation to ethical principles 1 and 2 that they conflict with each other. Let us repeat the warning here for the whole set of nine principles. As Victor R. Fuchs, one of the leading theorists in American health economics, put it concisely, "The hardest choices in life are not those that must be made between good and evil. The most difficult choices are those that force a decision between good and good" (Fuchs 1998: 216). Fuchs goes on to quote Isaiah Berlin, "The need to choose, to sacrifice some ultimate values to others, turns out to be a permanent characteristic of the human predicament" (Berlin 1969).

Even so, we would like to hope it has not been fruitless to present a systematic review of these principles. The system in which they appear and the way they are summarized, as mentioned earlier in the chapter, should serve as a set of memoranda, a *checklist* to prevent any principle from being forgotten when actual programs, legislation, and regulations are drafted, evaluated, and enacted. Even where decision-makers are obliged to make a concession on some principle, let them do so consciously, wrestling with their conscience and common sense before accepting the compromise. Those who truly espouse the principles proposed in the book will refrain from the extreme enforcement of any that would thereby conflict with others.

An objection can be made to the subject for the chapter. It can be argued that the scope for reform is already determined in all the post-socialist countries. It is constrained by the economic and political conditions, which ultimately ordain what kind of reform can take place. If reformers really want to fight for their ideas, they will have to make concessions. They may even have to manipulate public opinion. It does not always serve their purpose to state clearly and plainly what principles they follow, what they intend to do, or what results their actions may have.

The fate of reforms is obviously decided in the political arena. One task of academic research that we consider important is to examine the chances for welfare reform in terms of political economy.[29] The rest of the book contains several ref-

---

[29] On the political economy of reforming the welfare sector and/or cutting back government social transfers, see Lindbeck *et al.* (1994) and Lindbeck 1996, 1997), which deal with Swedish experience, and Nelson (1992), which analyzes the problems in some Latin American, Asian, and African

erences to the political conditions for reforms in the health sector. However, we hope it proves useful, as a complement to such positive research, to approach the issue from the opposite end as well. The question to ask is not simply how we can and must take the next steps, starting from our present initial position. It is also vital to ask where we truly want to go. Especially with the welfare sector, it is worth considering the *desired terminal state*.

The nine principles expounded here are not tied to a particular party in the post-socialist Eastern European region. They cannot be pigeon-holed politically in the usual way. They are neither "left-wing" nor "right-wing," or to use American terminology, they do not fit in with traditional "liberal" or "conservative" ideas. They are dissociated from the earlier strand of social democracy, which saw as its main task the fullest possible construction of a welfare *state*. That approach can be blamed historically for the exorbitant lengths to which this was taken. The book also dissociates itself from cold-hearted radicalism, from the idea of dismantling all the achievements of the welfare state, and from the ideologues uncritically biased against the state and in favor of the market. The set of nine principles represents a specific "centrist" position, and although dissociated from the traditional left and right wings, it draws notable ideas and proposals from both. Our motive in doing so is not to make both sides like what we say. That might well rebound, satisfying neither side. We have drawn up the set of nine principles in the belief that they form an integral whole.

The attitude of mind behind this book is akin to that of many other authors, in political and academic life alike. Perhaps it is not too soon to call this an international trend, which has yet to find an apposite name for its view of the world. It does not seek a third way between communism and

countries. Hausner (2001) and Nelson (2001) deal with the welfare-state reforms taking place in the post-socialist countries, with Poland and Hungary as the main examples.

capitalism. It has both feet planted firmly in capitalism. However, it does seek, not just by wishful thinking but by building up suitable institutions, to ensure that capitalism has something more than a human face – a human heart and mind as well. It seeks to build more firmly on individual responsibility, the market, competition, private ownership, and the profit motive than old-style social democracy used to do, while rejecting more strongly the proliferation of bureaucracy and centralization. On the other hand, it does not endorse any Eastern European variants of ultra-conservatism. It seeks to apply the principle of solidarity not simply through individual charitable action, and, within bounds, it is prepared to countenance state redistribution for this purpose. It has no illusions about the market, and does not reject all state intervention out of hand.

The course of history over the next decades will decide what effect this emerging intellectual and political trend has on transformation of the welfare sector.

3

The characteristics of the health sector

Having discussed the principles that apply to the whole welfare sector, the rest of the book is solely concerned with the health sector. Each branch of the welfare sector has specific features. This means they cannot all be reformed along the same lines. Indeed it is widely agreed that health care differs strongly from other social services, and that its specific characteristics require close attention when reforms are being planned and implemented. This chapter examines these special features.

A general overview

We focus on the universal characteristics of the health sector, which apply in all countries and under all socio-economic systems.[1] Later chapters discuss features specific to historical conditions in Eastern Europe.

Few if any of the characteristics examined here, when considered separately, are unique to health care. Several may be found in other areas as well. The specificity of the health sector stems from possession of all these characteristics at once. Furthermore, some characteristics assert themselves with great intensity.

---

[1] In compiling this survey we have drawn upon many sources, including Arrow (1963), Besley and Gouveia (1994), and several chapters in the *Handbook of Health Economics*, edited by Culyer and Newhouse, all of which provide more detailed references to the literature. We cite herein only a few sources of outstanding importance.

The value attached to health

Health is a state that most people attach great value to gaining and keeping. Although this may seem obvious and trivial, it deserves to be mentioned first. Health is not the prime consideration for everyone – some people put other goals before it – but the preference expressed as "health comes first" is the predominant one. The value attached to health is especially high when trouble appears, when the person concerned or a loved one falls ill, when acute pain is suffered, when illness impedes work, or when it brings the fear of death.

Any comparative assessment of the pleasure or utility offered by various goods and services is fraught with difficulties. In the case of health it is especially difficult to apply the traditional and widely accepted economic measure of value: a good or service is worth as much as a consumer is willing to pay for it. Even when there are legitimate reasons for avoiding a market assessment of value, the absence of such a straightforward criterion is problematic. How much money will compensate for the physical and mental suffering caused by illness? How much is it worth to prolong life by a couple of years? What is the money value of improving the quality of a patient's life? Though courts or insurers may manage to put a figure on the economic value of a person's life, no one can really say how much a human life is worth.[2]

In most societies, the exceptional value attached to health elevates the importance of medical care and health insurance. It is important to remember, however, that health is affected by many factors outside of medical care, such as nutrition and genetic endowment. Especially powerful are a person's individual lifestyle choices, such as whether to exercise, smoke, or drink alcohol in large quantities. Many sectors of the economy affect health, for instance through environmental pollution or industrial accidents. Medical

---

[2] For a discussion of the value of risks to life and health, see Viscusi (1992).

care providers are not the only professionals whose judgment may be a matter of life and death: think, for instance, of a pilot's or a driver's job. What is specific to the medical-care sector is that its effect on health, suffering, and life and death is direct, constant, and very potent.

In light of these considerations, those shy of the market may justifiably warn that this is an area where the market may fail. Health, some argue, "has no market value," or to use Marxist phraseology, "is not a commodity."

However, the difficulty of measuring the value of health does not free society from making choices. Resources are scarce; trade-offs are inevitable. The central distributor of resources, whether under a dictatorship controlling a socialist economy or under a parliamentary democracy, likewise faces insurmountable difficulties – precisely the same difficulties, on a national scale, that the individual faces. How many new factories is it worth sacrificing to build a new hospital? How much imported oil should be forgone in favor of an imported medical instrument?

Here (and in other contexts, as will be seen later) the "market failure" and "government failure" have a common origin. The cause is primarily that health, reduction of physical suffering, and survival have an exceptional value incomparable with anything else.[3]

The norm of equal access

Most people accept as a moral precept that everyone has a right to basic health care; society must ensure that people can exercise this right in practice. Even those (like the authors)

---

[3] Some literature on health care treats as a primary characteristic the asymmetric nature of information possessed by doctor and patient. Although such asymmetry is important (and discussed further below), we do not choose to list it first. Even patients who are themselves doctors, possessing the same information as those treating them, have the same experience as other patients: there is nothing with which they can compare the value of their own health or survival.

who normally reject radically egalitarian ideas recognize the need to allow all to satisfy their basic health-care needs (and basic educational needs, for that matter).

Defining "basic needs" raises some ethical, economic, and political problems, however. Analysis of the question features primarily in literature on income distribution and public finance. Here suffice it to quote the classic words of Adam Smith: "By necessaries I understand not only the commodities which are indispensably necessary for the support of life but whatever the custom of the country renders it indecent for creditable people, even of the lowest order, to be without" (Smith [1776] 1937: 821). Adam Smith derives the concept from the valid norms of society, not from physical or biological factors. Basic needs are fulfilled by those goods and services which according to social norms are indispensable to a decent human existence.[4]

Because of the first characteristic mentioned – the special value attached to health, avoiding suffering, and saving life – most people are prepared to accept *specific egalitarian principles* for the allocation of health-care services.[5] These principles are deeply rooted in the system of social norms of modern society. No one could declare with a clear conscience that in a situation where someone rich and someone poor were suffering from the same grave illness, the rich patient should be saved and the poor patient be allowed to die. Moreover, people may consider it ethically disturbing if some who are disadvantaged by poor health have to pay many times the amount others have to pay to obtain basic health insurance.

---

[4] Drawing upon Rawls' (1971) *A Theory of Justice*, Daniels (1985) develops a theory of just health care that is compatible with the distinction between basic and supplementary needs and services, with a definition of basic services that is inevitably *society-relative.*

[5] Tobin (1970) termed "specific egalitarianism" the situation in which society attaches special importance to limiting inequality in access to a specific good or service. Many of those who generally oppose redistribution in favor of poorer people find this more acceptable if it promotes health among such people.

This norm of equal access could be taken as applying to health care principle 2 (the ethical postulate of solidarity) described in chapter 2. The healthy identify with the sick and want to see their compassion apply in practice, through a suitable socio-economic mechanism. The question of how the specific egalitarianism applicable to health care translates into practice is discussed in detail later.

What follows concerns those characteristics of the health sector that are connected with uncertainty and information. Although this book is about the Eastern European reforms, whose initial state is the early 1990s, when the health sector was centralized and uniformly financed out of central tax revenues or compulsory contributions, it is easier to convey the message markedly if this is ignored for a moment. The assumption made in the following paragraphs is that citizens may buy an insurance policy to suit their needs on a decentralized insurance market. As the arguments later in the book will show, the characteristics discussed here exert their effect even if the initial status quo remains, although in a different form, of course.

Uncertainty and the demand for insurance

One very important characteristic of the health sector is that the need for medical care is largely unpredictable. Unlike food, education, or many other goods considered necessities of life, an individual's demand for health-care services is uncertain. Of course some medical care, such as pre-natal and childbirth services, may be foreseeable, but most illnesses and injuries requiring immediate and intense medical attention are unpredictable. The distribution of medical expenditures is highly skewed. Researchers have found that generally in a large population in any given year, if the population is ranked according to health-care spending, the most costly 1 percent of patients accounts for approximately 30 percent of total health-care spending, and the most costly 10 percent of patients accounts for as much as 75 percent of total spending. Individuals are faced with tremendous uncertainty about whether they might be among the large medical care users in any given period.[6]

Most people, recognizing this uncertainty about their future state of health, would be ready to take out voluntary medical insurance. Insurance is a mechanism for transferring money from when it is needed less to when it is needed more. Insurance is more practical and effective than individual "saving for a rainy day" or attempting to borrow enough money to cover expenses after illness strikes. By pooling one's own risk with that of others who also purchase insurance from a given insurer, an individual can secure some protection against the financial risk of ill health by paying a reasonable amount at regular intervals.

Of course the health sector is not the only area in which uncertainty and insurance play an important role. Yet there are important aspects of insurance in this sector that, in combination with other characteristics, give rise to distinctive institutional features.

For example, when taking out homeowners' insurance against the risks of uncertain natural disasters, a consumer can usually buy insurance to cover the full value of the home and its contents, except perhaps for some "priceless" heirlooms. As already noted regarding the value of health, however, the problem of compensating for loss of "priceless" commodities is even more intense for health. In truth, what is called "health insurance" is actually "medical-care insurance": it offers insurance against the risk of payments for medical services that reduce suffering or prolong life, but usually fall far short of restoring full health. There simply does not exist an "ideal" health-insurance policy that insures that health will be restored, and pays the health-care provid-

---

[6] Moreover, once ill or injured, a patient is often highly uncertain about what form of treatment will be most effective in restoring health. See Arrow (1963).

ers only according to how much the patient benefits from medical care.[7]

Uncertainty and the resulting demand for insurance gives rise to another central institutional feature of health-care markets (Ellis and McGuire 1993): insurance imposes a third-party payer between the consumer and the provider. Thus the health sector features a triad of consumer, insurer/payer, and provider. The presence of the third-party insurer means that the demand price – the price that the consumer faces when buying the good – can be set somewhat independently of the supply price – the price that the supplier receives when selling the good. (In fact, in most cases there is an important fourth party as well, a *sponsor* such as a government agency or employer, which mediates the flow of funds between consumers and insurers or health plans, and also may or may not contribute to the costs of insurance. We discuss the implications of this in more detail later.)

Finally, it is important to realize that insurance differs from other goods and services in that the cost of supplying insurance depends on who buys it (Cutler and Zeckhauser 2000). Let us consider a decentralized insurance market in which consumers are free to decide which insurance policy to buy and insurers are free to decide what premium to charge. If high-cost consumers (for instance, those suffering from chronic illness or older age-groups whose members fall ill more frequently and severely) buy an insurance policy, that policy will be expensive to supply. In contrast, if infrequent users of medical care (for instance, healthy young people) enroll in a given insurance plan, that plan will be relatively inexpensive to supply.

Since the cost of supplying insurance depends on the characteristics of the purchasers, it is important to consider to what extent information about those characteristics is known

---

[7] In this sense a "perfect market" for health insurance is unattainable, and many other social institutions may evolve or need to be developed to fill in the gap (Arrow 1963).

to purchaser and supplier. This brings us to the question of asymmetry of information.

Asymmetric information

This is one of the most comprehensively studied phenomena in modern economics. Asymmetry of information appears in any market where one party to the transaction, such as the seller, knows more about the transaction than the other party (e.g. the buyer). Such asymmetries are widespread and important in the health sector.

For example, in the market for health insurance, it is often the demand side (the consumer wishing to buy insurance) who possesses more information about the transaction – his or her current and future state of health and propensity to use medical care – than the insurer supplying insurance. Consider the economic mechanism of commercial insurance. The greater the risk and/or size of a possible loss, and the fuller the cover for the insured, the higher the premium charged by the insurer. If the insurer and the insured have exactly the same information about the risk of loss, the premium can be set to charge the insured the actuarially fair amount (i.e. the expected cost of loss), no more and no less. When information is asymmetric, however, the premium may exceed or fall short of the actual cost of covering the loss, depending on who enrolls. Asymmetry of information about an individual's health-care needs can cause severe problems in any mechanism for health insurance, as will be discussed in more detail under adverse selection below.

Asymmetry of information is also important in the allocation of medical care. The supply side (the doctor, the institution providing the health care) generally knows more about the subject of the transaction – the appropriate treatment of the disease, its full costs and benefits, including risks and side-effects – than the demand side (the patient and the insurance institution paying on his or her behalf). Such asymmetry of information strongly affects behavior on both sides. A medical care provider, for instance the doctor, may rely upon this better knowledge to encourage overspending, or, on the contrary, to refuse to incur some costs, according to the system of incentives that apply (see p. 84). The patient lacks the professional skill and experience to question the provider's recommendations.

Principle 1, the first ethical postulate listed in chapter 2, sovereignty of the individual, requires that this kind of informational asymmetry be reduced as far as possible. This is partly contingent on the patient's legal rights. It also depends on the conventions and codes of behavior in the medical community. The economic mechanism plays a part as well. With most patients, the greater their freedom of choice, and the more they are affected financially by the cost of treatment, the stronger their inclination to require information from those treating them.

Selection

The previous characteristics lead to the problem of selection. Here (and under moral hazard below) we describe the phenomenon and highlight connections with the principles expounded in chapter 2, and defer discussion of empirical evidence, practical experience, and potential remedies to the section on incentives (p. 79). All economic coordination mechanisms select among the potential consumers. The mechanisms typical of a centrally managed, planned economy – administrative rationing, a coupon system, queuing – provide some people with a desired good or service while depriving others of it, according to various criteria (for instance, what position people hold in the political hierarchy, what connections they have with the powerful or with the health-care bureaucracy, whether they are willing and able to bribe those who decide on hospital admissions, etc.). Market coordination clearly selects according to different criteria from these, depriving those who cannot or will not pay the market price.

In health economics, the aggregative term "selection" is used to refer to a specific problem that arises when insurers and providers are trying to provide health insurance and medical care to a group of people, who are facing unequal chances of sickness (risk heterogeneity) and who have some choice regarding insurance and health-care delivery (Newhouse 1996). Although this problem is most severe under market coordination, no supplier of insurance, and no hospital, clinic, or other provider, even in some other structural–institutional context, escapes it completely. We will briefly describe the two important aspects of selection: adverse selection and risk selection.

Adverse selection[8]

People differ in their health status and their desire to use medical services. Those who are or expect to be in worse health will obviously need more nursing, more treatment, more medicines, and more care. Although the relation between severity and length of illness on the one hand and cost of treatment on the other is complex, it is certainly positive on average. Those who expect to need more medical care will therefore be eager to buy more generous insurance to cover their expenses. Conversely, those who are young and healthy may begrudge the money to buy even a meager insurance policy.

This self-selection into different insurance plans is termed *adverse* because of the following problem. If insurers are not privy to the same information about need for medical care as their potential customers (i.e. there is asymmetry of informa-

---

[8] Adverse selection (reverse selection or counterselection) occurs in many kinds of transaction. One pioneering study (Akerlof 1970) dealt with the used-car market, another important article with the insurance market (Rothschild and Stiglitz 1976), and so on. The discussion here is confined to the sphere of medical insurance – to a very special case within "adverse selection" as a whole.

tion as discussed previously), then they must set the price for insurance – the insurance premium – at some average level. Insurers may be required to do so by regulations designed to protect social solidarity as well. If an insurer attracts a large number of enrollees who cost more than this predicted average, then the insurer loses money and will probably be forced to raise the premium. A higher premium will further discourage healthier consumers from choosing that plan, leaving the insurer with an adverse selection of consumers to insure. If the insurer faces a hard budget constraint – that is, cannot count on subsidies to cover financial losses – then an insurer who consistently attracts enrollees of higher-than-expected cost will eventually go bankrupt, leaving its customers without cover.[9] Adverse selection may cause generous health plans to disappear because they fall prey to a premium death spiral: sicker-than-average people enroll, costs increase, and premiums are raised, until eventually not even relatively well-to-do but extremely unhealthy consumers can afford to pay the high premiums that the plan would require to break even.

Adverse selection prevents some consumers from buying the insurance that they would desire, and forces some consumers to pay very high insurance premiums. If broad sections of the population are prevented, therefore, from obtaining access to basic health care, we consider this an affront to the ethical principles of both individual sovereignty and solidarity.

The problem of adverse selection does not arise simply because commercial insurers are "greedy and wish to make a profit." Any organization offering health-insurance coverage,

[9] The organization deciding on the expenditures (a company, for instance, or a hospital) faces a soft-budget constraint if its revenues remain consistently below its expenditures, but it can still operate, because some institution (such as the state, for instance) is prepared to bail it out. The organization faces a hard-budget constraint if it cannot survive a chronic deficit. For a detailed explanation of the concept of soft- and hard-budget constraints and an account of the theory behind the problem, see Kornai (1980, 1986, 1998a) and Maskin (1996).

including not-forprofit insurers and the government, faces the same dilemma: those most willing to join are those who cost the most.

Risk selection

(This is also known as "cream skimming," "cherry picking," or "plan manipulation.") The tendency of high-cost consumers to prefer generous insurance plans gives insurers an incentive to structure their insurance policies to discourage enrollment of the sick and encourage enrollment of the healthy. Insurers financially benefit when they can effectively combat adverse selection and instead are able to "cream skim" the low-risk, relatively healthy consumers. In a free market, health plans can risk select in many different ways: they can exclude coverage of services valued by high-risk individuals (such as short waiting times for cancer specialists); offer services that attract low risks (such as fitness club memberships); locate facilities in healthier neighborhoods; target advertising to healthier communities; design supplementary insurance benefits to attract lower-cost enrollees, etc.

"Cream skimming" may appear not only in the conduct of insurers, but in the behavior of doctors, hospitals, and other health-care providers as well. If the incentives that influence their decisions induce them to do this (for instance, if a hospital has to keep expenditures within a budget and the budget constraint is hard), they may have a vested interest in turning away costly cases. They can always claim that some other provider will have a better understanding of the particular patient's problems. "Skimming" and other selection problems are explained here and on p. 88 in the context of a decentralized insurance system, but similar abuses may appear in other mechanisms (for instance, in a state-controlled, centralized system financed out of taxation).

To return to the subject of insurance, the result of these many phenomena is that under a free market for health insurance, many consumers – especially the high-risk individuals most in need of coverage – may find coverage prohibitively expensive or simply unavailable. All consumers, even low-risk individuals, will be deprived of the ability to insure against becoming a high risk in the future and having to pay high premiums or becoming uninsured. Ultimately, many people are left without insurance if a decentralized insurance market is left to itself, free of intervention. Both phenomena, adverse selection and risk selection (skimming), conflict sharply with principle 2, the principle of solidarity. Selection also infringes upon principle 1, the principle of consumer sovereignty, since selection deprives some consumers of effective choice regarding health-care coverage. Nor does it satisfy the requirement of principle 4, for incentives for efficiency. So any reform designed to uphold the principles espoused in chapter 2 must not favor the development of any mechanism that tends innately to produce adverse and risk selection. The inescapable conclusion is that medical insurance cannot be left solely to voluntary contracts with commercial insurers. A certain amount of insurance cover has to be made compulsory, thus restricting the principle of individual sovereignty in at least one dimension to achieve social solidarity and individual choice along a different dimension. In light of the characteristics so far listed, it is apparent that any society that guarantees access to basic health care for everyone must subsidize premiums for those unable to pay and use compulsion to extract premiums from those unwilling to pay. In addition, there is a need for many other measures to avoid, or at least substantially reduce, among all participants in the health sector, the harmful effects of adverse selection and risk selection.

Moral hazard

This is one of the known consequences of all kinds of insurance. The none-too-apposite term refers to the fact that the greater the cover provided by the insurer, the weaker becomes the incentive for the insured to avoid trouble, or, if it has occurred, to minimize the loss. For instance, if an agricultural insurance policy gives full cover against damage by insect pests, there is no point in spending money on insecticides, or if the insects attack, of preventing their spread.

This phenomenon can also be found in the health sector, on the patients' and the doctors' (providers') side, and in a heightened form.[10] Let us take the pure case where the insurer (whether in public or private ownership) pays the whole bill for medical treatment. On the one hand, there is good reason for preventing disease, because even full financial cover will not compensate the patient for the associated suffering or mental stress. Furthermore, there is no guarantee of a complete recovery, regardless of what treatment is obtained. On the other hand, the problem of moral hazard appears once the problem has occurred. There is nothing to encourage patients to make sparing use of medical resources.

Generally uninformed and helpless patients try to defend their interests almost blindly. Most of them assume that more expensive treatment will be better as well. They have heard at least that dearer treatment involves costlier diagnostic procedures, better paid, more experienced doctors, more cutting-edge procedures, and more expensive – therefore probably more modern and effective – drugs. So patients as a group press providers and insurers to spend more.

Providers are often allies in this. Their professional conscience prompts them to heal their patients as quickly and effectively as possible. Depending on how they are paid for their services (see p. 84), doctors will have little if any interest in limiting the costs of care. Here the asymmetry of information appears in relation to a coalition of the doctor and the patient allied against the insurer. The insurer has little

---

[10] On this, see above all the classic, pioneering work by Arrow (1963), and the writings of Feldstein (1973) and Pauly (1986, 1992).

recourse for investigating the details of treatment and judging the appropriateness of care in each individual case. Instead, the insurer is normally obliged to finance the demand created by the patient and provider (i.e. pay the full bill for treatment), irrespective of whether the spending was economical or extravagant.

When patients as a group overuse medical services because they appear close to "free," eventually the cost of supplying insurance will rise. Patients will rarely recognize, however, the connection between their own specific spending and a general increase in health insurance premiums, even if they are taking out individual policies under a decentralized insurance system. *A fortiori*, the relationship between the expenditure on a particular patient and the compulsory social-insurance contribution or health tax will become looser still if the costs are paid by a vast insurance fund covering millions of patients.

The problems associated with moral hazard reveal that principle 4, incentive for participants in the process to pursue efficiency, often does not apply sufficiently in the health sector, particularly in pre-reform transitional economies. Deterring moral hazard will usually require imposing on the patient and/or provider some of the costs of care at time of use. For example, patients may be required to pay a fixed amount, or *deductible*, before the insurer will reimburse expenses. Patients may also be required to pay a fixed amount for each good or service (a co-payment) or a percentage of total medical-care costs; this is known as *co-insurance*.

Imposing deductibles and co-insurance on patients will therefore to some extent limit inefficient overuse of medical care. This amelioration of moral hazard comes at a price, however. Deductibles and co-insurance re-impose financial risk on consumers and may decrease their access to medical care. As a result, health insurance involves a conflict between principles 2 and 4: spreading risk and assuring access to basic health care to everyone on the one hand and giving appropriate incentives for efficient use of medical care on the other. We return to the problem in detail on p. 80 below.

Supply-side power and monopoly

Systems of organization that create a monopoly, or lead to a situation close to a monopoly, are quite common on the supply side of the health sector. This is partly a natural result of the scale of production that high-technology services may entail. In a small community, for example, it may not be practical to have more than one hospital. In thinly populated rural areas there may not be enough consumers to support many different competing health plans.

Supply-side power in the health sector is also frequently the result of less desirable forces. Providers benefit financially and in terms of prestige and autonomy when they have market power. In many countries physicians try to combine into organizations that resemble guilds, excluding market competition.[11] In a decentralized insurance system private medical insurance companies may try to organize into a cartel. Without regulation, the health sector can be a hotbed for such efforts to limit competition artificially. All these tendencies conflict with principle 3: the requirement that competition should develop.

The dilemmas faced by the reform in the Eastern European countries are especially difficult. The state or quasi-state social-insurance institution that finances health care under the socialist system has a *de facto* monopoly: it does not compete directly with other insurers. This is what the post-socialist transition receives as an initial state. Is it worth retaining the monopoly, or should it be broken? We return to this question in detail.

[11] Organization in the form of a guild may have favorable effects as well. The members of the association or chamber gain a feeling of responsibility for the whole profession and may apply peer pressure on their colleagues if they do careless work. In many ways, people in the same profession are better placed to monitor one another's performances than administrative supervisors or patients are.

The defenselessness of the patient

If there is perfect competition, the buyer and the seller have equal rank and neither is superior to the other. In the health sector, as the characteristics already listed make plain, there is no trace of perfect competition or equality of rank between the provider and the patient. Doctors have power over their patients, irrespective of the social system or economic incentives at work.[12] This supply-side power is partly the result of asymmetry of information as already discussed, but not exclusively so. Even if patients are adequately informed, those treating them have greater scope and responsibility for decision-making than have their patients, the persons most concerned. Even if doctors wanted to, they could not involve patients in every decision. Think of an extreme example: the defenselessness of a patient during surgery or unconsciousness for some reason. Nor is it certain that all doctors in all situations would want to share information with their patients and involve them in decision-making, since this would imply restricting the doctor's own power. Therefore, even under the best of circumstances, patients are in a situation that to some extent infringes upon principle 1, the sovereignty of the individual.

Despite the necessity of delegating some decision-making power to medical-care providers, it is not immaterial how frequent or extensive the infringement on individual sovereignty is. One important characteristic of various health-care systems is the extent to which the sovereignty of individual choice is restricted. The pre-reform, classical socialist health-care mechanism placed tight limits on choice, so that the defenselessness of patients was great. Under such a system, individuals become helpless, passive beneficiaries of – or sufferers from – the paternalist treatment that is thrust upon them. It is dictated for them administratively who shall be their primary-care doctor. It depends on

---

[12] There is an excellent account of this in Losonczi (1986).

that doctor whether they are sent to a specialist, what tests are conducted, which hospital they are sent to, and so on.

This utter helplessness can be eased, but not eliminated, if the reforms give more scope for choice. The degree of defenselessness in the reformed health sector depends on the laws governing the doctor–patient relationship and the written and unwritten code of professional medical practice. It also depends on specific attributes of the economic mechanism (including the assertion of principle 3, the creation of competition), and the financial incentives influencing the doctor and other medical providers.

Mounting costs

The costs of health care in most countries are steadily rising. This increase can be broken into two components. On the one hand there is an increase in health-care spending measured in real terms. On the other there is a relative increase in costs, compared with the general rise in prices. The combined effect of the two in the OECD countries appears in table 3.1.

Experts disagree on how to explain the rise in costs. There are various factors at work.

- An important tendency, which is conspicuous in the health sector but appears in other fields as well, is that technological development is increasingly cost-intensive. A fundamental cause of cost growth is the increasing capabilities of medicine (Newhouse 1992). Technological change – in the form of new drugs, procedures, and equipment – has revolutionized treatment for many health conditions, increasing both utilization and the cost of a given level of utilization.[13]
- While the cost-increasing effects of rising income and

---

[13] A survey of 50 leading health economists in the United States found that 81 percent agreed with the statement that "the primary reason for the increase in the health-sector's share of GDP over the past 30 years is technological change in medicine" (Fuchs 1998: 227). Kornai and McHale (1999) find strong statistical evidence of a technology effect, which has

technological development apply in other sectors as well, there are three other factors that apply more specifically to health care. The first concerns technological development, just mentioned. The great technological development taking place in health care is usually not accompanied by labor savings. It tends to increase the effectiveness of the medical procedure while involving the same or an increasing quantity of work. Prevention and treatment leading to a substantial improvement in the patient's condition or a complete cure become more frequent and successful, without lessening the work of the doctor and auxiliary staff. The health sector is not alone in this respect. However, in most "regular" sectors technical development brings direct labor savings as well. So the output of the health sector (and the other sectors that resemble it in this respect) will grow relatively more expensive by comparison with the products of the other, "regular" sectors. This relative increase in price is inevitable even if there are economic incentives that otherwise work against an extravagant allocation of expenditure.[14] In other words, the health sector, like many service industries, is labor-intensive and experiences less increase in productivity than many capital-intensive industries.

- Health-care spending rises as people live longer (thanks partly to technological development and the effectiveness of the health sector's work). The average health-care spending on the elderly is known to be far greater than average spending on the young.[15]
- Finally another factor, discussed already, is the problem

added 1.4 percentage points to the health-spending growth rate of OECD countries since 1980.

[14] See the classic, pioneering studies by Baumol (1963, 1988).

[15] The average health-care spending on a pensioner is almost two-and-a-half times higher than the average spending on a person in employment in Hungary, and more than twice in Slovenia (see tables 6.1 and 6.2, pp. 205 and 206). Kornai and McHale (1999) estimate that for industrialized countries a 1 percentage point increase in the share of the population between 65 and 74 raises national health-spending growth by 0.7 percent.

Table 3.1 Prices and volume in health expenditure growth, OECD countries, 1980–1990 (average annual rates of increase, percent)

Country	Share of total expenditure on health in TDE 1980[a]	Nominal health-expenditure growth	Health-price deflator	Total domestic-expenditure price deflator	Medical-specific price increases[b]	Health-care benefits volume growth	Population growth	Per capita health-benefits growth	Share of total expenditure on health in TDE 1990
Australia	7.1	11.8	7.6	7.3	0.3	3.9	1.5	2.3	8.3
Austria	7.7	6.6	5.1	3.7	1.4	1.5	0.2	1.2	8.4
Belgium	6.5	7.9	4.9	4.2	0.6	2.9	0.1	2.7	7.9
Canada	7.5	10.7	6.9	5.1	1.8	3.5	1.0	2.5	9.5
Denmark	6.7	7.2	6.1	5.9	0.2	1.0	0.0	1.0	6.7
Finland	6.4	12.7	8.8	7.1	1.7	3.5	0.4	3.1	7.8
France	7.5	10.4	5.2	6.2	-0.9	5.0	0.5	4.5	8.8
Germany	8.4	5.0	3.4	2.6	0.7	1.5	0.3	1.2	8.8
Greece	4.0	22.6	16.9	18.3	-1.2	4.9	0.5	4.4	4.9
Iceland	6.5	40.1	32.9	32.3	-0.2	5.4	1.2	4.2	8.5
Ireland	8.1	7.7	9.1	6.8	2.2	-1.3	0.3	-1.6	7.6
Italy	6.6	14.8	10.7	10.0	0.6	3.8	0.2	3.5	8.1
Japan	6.5	6.0	2.4	1.5	0.9	3.6	0.6	3.0	6.7
Luxembourg	6.8	8.7	5.4	5.0	0.4	3.2	0.4	2.8	7.0
Netherlands	8.0	4.4	2.5	2.0	0.5	1.8	0.5	1.3	8.4

New Zealand	7.2	12.3	11.5	9.8	1.6	0.6	0.7	−0.1	7.3
Norway	7.1	10.0	7.1	7.2	−0.1	2.8	0.4	2.4	8.0
Portugal	5.1	22.6	17.5	17.1	0.4	4.3	0.0	4.3	6.1
Spain	5.4	14.4	9.3	8.9	0.4	4.6	0.4	4.2	6.4
Sweden	9.2	8.9	7.1	7.6	−0.6	1.7	0.3	1.4	8.6
Switzerland	7.0	7.1	4.4	3.5	0.9	2.6	0.6	1.9	7.9
Turkey	3.7	51.7	47.9	45.0	2.0	2.6	2.4	0.2	3.8
United Kingdom	5.9	9.8	7.6	6.1	1.3	2.1	0.2	1.9	6.0
United States	9.2	10.4	6.9	4.1	2.7	3.3	1.0	2.3	12.2
Europe	*6.8*	*12.3*	*9.1*	*8.6*	*0.5*	*2.8*	*0.4*	*2.5*	*7.5*
OECD total	*7.0*	*11.8*	*8.7*	*8.0*	*0.7*	*2.9*	*0.5*	*2.4*	*7.8*

Notes:

[a] TDE = Total Domestic Expenditure.

[b] "Medical-specific inflation" is defined as the excess of health-care price increases over those on all goods and services. A few 1990 ratios and 1980–90 rates are projections of a likely outcome. The underlying statistical series are consistent for the full decade but unobserved discontinuities cannot be precluded. The European and OECD averages are arithmetic; both exclude Turkey.

Source: OECD (1993: 23).

of moral hazard. The fuller the coverage provided by the medical insurance, the more patients and doctors find that costs can be shifted onto the other insured and therefore cease to control them.[16] Part of the general cost increase could stem from the spread of insurance, and the dynamic moral hazard effect of opting for more expensive treatment when someone else bears the cost. At this point, there is often an infringement of principle 4, incentives for efficiency.

The factors that tend to bring an increase in health-care costs in the developed countries have a similar effect in Eastern Europe.

This completes our list of the characteristics of the health sector. The combination of these characteristics makes the health sector distinctive. It is worth repeating the warning to those preparing reforms in transitional economies not to apply mechanically the patterns applicable in the more "regular," business sphere that lies nearer to the theoretical model of perfect competition. Careful account must be taken of the health sector's specific characteristics.

Nevertheless, having emphasized the specific features of the health sector, it is worth adding that in many respects it behaves in the same way as other sectors of the economy. It would be a mistake to obfuscate these characteristics and ignore the well known, fundamental regularities of economics that apply to this sector as well. Let us mention here just one connection, the well known three-way relationship between price, demand, and supply. For instance, if the buyers on the demand side are paying an expense out of their own pockets, a higher price will reduce demand. The same applies to institutional buyers, so long as there is a hard budget constraint. On the supply side, if the provider is inter-

---

[16] The cost-increasing overuse from moral hazard is especially severe if the insurer pays without a murmur any bill the provider sees fit to charge. This is very commonly the case under the "fee-for-service" settlement system, which is described in more detail on p. 84.

ested in increasing the difference between revenue and expenditure, a higher price will increase supply, other factors being equal. This applies to privately owned, directly profit-oriented organizations, to doctors and other medical personnel in private practice, and to publicly owned hospitals and clinics operating under a hard budget constraint.

Ultimately, reformers have to pay attention concurrently to the attributes health care shares with other sectors and those specific to it.

Provision and financing: classification

This section sets out to classify the alternative forms of organization and financing of the health sector on an abstract plane. We focus on methods of organization, ownership forms, and financing, de-emphasizing the question of which configurations are characteristic of various socio-economic formations, countries, or periods of history. Later we draw upon this taxonomy in discussing incentives, country experiences, and recommendations for health-sector reform.

Four key entities

Just as in other areas of the economy, for the health sector a fundamental distinction can be drawn between the supply and demand sides. In health care, the "supply side" refers to the provision (or delivery) of health-care services to patients. The "demand side" refers to the method of financing health care and organizations representing consumers in purchasing health coverage.[17]

In the simplest of health systems, patients buy services directly from health-care providers. There are only two

[17] We were obliged in the earlier part of the book to use certain concepts that have remained unclarified until this section. This is because we felt that to have stopped and defined them earlier would have interrupted the line of argument.

agents: the patient as the buyer and the individually practicing doctor or other provider as the seller. As emphasized on p. 51, however, uncertainty regarding the need for expensive medical services leads consumers to want to purchase health insurance, introducing intermediaries between consumers and providers.[18] One such intermediary is the health insurer or health plan. In this case the health sector features not just a dichotomy between buyer and seller, but a "health care triad" of consumer, insurer, and provider.

As discussed earlier, many people would become uninsured if an insurance market is left to itself, free of intervention. The norm of equal access therefore gives rise to another intermediary between patient and provider. We call this fourth key agent the *sponsor*. Examples include government agencies and employer groups, or large employers that purchase health coverage on behalf of specific beneficiaries, such as their own employees. The primary function of the sponsor is to mediate between its beneficiaries and insurers. It acts on behalf of its consumers to gather information, select a few reputable insurers from which its consumers may choose, and monitor quality. A sponsor requires authority to set the "rules of the game" (such as nondiscrimination against high-cost patients) and to redistribute funds among competing insurers (to combat selection); this regulatory-like authority is usually derived from being a government agency or an employer with market power over insurers. The other possible role of the sponsor is to contribute to financing health expenditure. This the sponsor can do in several ways, for instance by paying some or all of the patient's insurance costs, by paying the provider directly, or by paying part of the provider's bill. The sponsor may also have a third, more

---

[18] Individuals who consult a doctor can rightly be called "patients." However, most of those who take out health insurance are healthy people, so that we have preferred in general to use the broader, more neutral term "consumers" for them.

general regulatory function (such as licensing providers), which is not considered in this section.[19]

We return later to the role of sponsors and the degree of integration among sponsors, insurers, and providers. First, however, we consider the basic "menu of choice" for organizing and financing health-care services. Table 3.2 is designed to make this easier to review.

The supply (provision or delivery) side

Ultimately, of course, patients receive health-care services from individual providers – doctors, nurses, and other health-care personnel – but the subject of inquiry here is the institutional, organizational framework and the forms of ownership in which the individuals work. The following pure forms appear (see the columns of table 3.2):

(1) *Organizations* Doctors, nurses, and other medical personnel are employed by some kind of organization (such as a firm, a public hospital, or a university). Those financing health services often pay the organization directly, instead of reimbursing individual patients for their expenses.

Such organizations can be classified according to who exercises property rights over them. Three pure cases can be distinguished:

(1.1) *State-owned organizations.* Public or state-owned provider organizations can be subdivided further. There may be a monopoly provider – i.e. a single national, bureaucratic, hierarchical state organization – or some kind of decentralized set of

---

[19] The regulatory function is ignored here because regulation can also be performed by an institution (for instance, a state supervisory body) that has no part in financing. An already complex, compound system of classification would be complicated further if the alternative forms of regulation were incorporated into it as well.

Table 3.2 *Provision and financing: classification of alternative mechanisms*

Demand (Financing)	Supply (Provision)			
	(1) Organizations			(2) Private entrepreneurs
	(1.1) State-owned	(1.2) Private nonprofit	(1.3) Private forprofit	
(A) State financing	National Health Service (United Kingdom) Public provision (Soviet Union)	National health insurance (Canada)		
(B) Compulsory insurance			Social insurance (Germany)	
(C) Voluntary insurance			Mainly private insurance (United States)	
(D) Direct patient payment				

Note:

On the difference between the British and the Soviet models see chapter 5, especially n. 2 (p. 138).

organizations, owned by local government, for instance.

(1.2) Organizations with a *nonprofit, nonstate owner* (for instance, a charitable foundation or a church).

(1.3) Organizations with *private, profit-seeking owners.* In real life there are several mixed cases, composed of elements of the pure forms, which may be combined in several ways. Here are some examples:

- A hospital or outpatient clinic in state or nonprofit, nonstate ownership may not confine itself to providing health care through its own employees. It may contract certain tasks out to privately owned, forprofit organizations that act as subcontractors. (For instance, a hospital may have a private firm perform certain laboratory tests.)

- The opposite may occur. A private medical practice owned by its doctors may offer certain services within a state or a nonstate, nonprofit hospital or clinic. The private practice may collect fees for these services, while paying rent for the premises or a charge for using the hospital infrastructure.

- A distinction can be drawn between a case where a company operates a private hospital, for instance, for profit, and one where a profit-making enterprise provides a medical service for its employees, such as a doctor's office. In the second case the firm is not doing this particular activity for profit, but as a benefit in kind for its employees.

- Physicians, nurses, or other trained health workers may divide their time, spending some of it working under one form of ownership and some of it under another, including form (2).

(2) *Self-employed professionals* Health-care providers often deliver services as independent, self-employed professionals or private entrepreneurs. The criterion here is not whether the doctor or nurse is officially

registered as self-employed, pays tax as such, and so on. The essential feature is that the health care is provided independently, not by a member of an organization. In this case it is the self-employed individual who is paid by the patient, the insurer or the sponsor.[20]

Although we have focused here on the organization and ownership of providers, the same system for classifying organizations can apply to sponsors and insurers. For example, the sponsor can be (1.1) a state organization (such as a state agency or local government); (1.2) private nonprofit (such as a regional or national health-insurance fund); or (1.3) private forprofit (such as a large employer). Insurers or health plans can also fall into any of these categories.

The demand (financing) side

The ultimate recipient of health care is the patient, of course. However, when examining the economic mechanism, the question hinges not on the recipient, but on the entity that pays for the service. Here we focus on the source of the funds that are eventually used to pay health-care providers. The following pure cases are distinguishable (see the rows of table 3.2):

(A)   *State financing* The state finances health care through the budget, out of tax revenues. In other words, the purchase is not made out of a special extra-budgetary fund with special sources of revenue.

(B)   *Compulsory insurance* Individuals have a legal obligation to insure themselves. This alternative can be broken down into subcases. There may be one national,

---

[20] In many cases, a self-employed physician employs a nurse or secretary paid out of his or her own pocket. Since this arrangement consists of an employer and one or more employees, it should be classed, strictly speaking, as an organization. Nonetheless, this book leaves such minimal "organizations" in the "self-employed" category, reserving the concept of an "organization" for larger units such as a hospital or a polyclinic.

monopoly institution acting as the social-insurance organization, or a set of regional monopoly insurers, or a decentralized system of insurance institutions that compete for enrollees, so that consumers can choose among insurers for their compulsory policies.

Note that it is common to distinguish "public" from "private" financing, but these terms blur the distinction between (A) and (B) as alternative forms of public financing and between (C) and (D) below as variations of private financing.

(C) *Voluntary insurance* Individuals (or individuals and, as sponsor, their employers) may take out voluntary commercial insurance with an insurance institution.

In cases (A), (B), and (C), usually the sponsor or the insurance institution pays the provider instead of the patient. Some insurance systems require the insured to contribute a co-payment.

The distinction between cases (B) and (C) is fundamentally important to the operation of the health-care mechanism. The compulsory medical insurance can be taken out with a private insurer in some countries, but in most it has to be done in the form of "social insurance" with a special semi-state, nonprofit insurance institution established for the purpose. We discuss this arrangement in more detail later.

(D) *Direct payment by individuals* Patients pay the provider for their treatment out of their own pocket. This form of financing is often called "self-pay."

As on the supply side, there are various combined forms of financing. The most important of these is a combination of (D), direct payment, with (A), (B), or (C), payment by the sponsor (e.g. the state) or the insurer. The connection may be a legal part of the written insurance policy, whereby the patient pays part of the cost (such as a flat-rate deductible payment or a proportional co-payment). On the other hand it may take a semi-legal or illegal form, whereby the insurer pays, but patients still add something from their own pockets. Such gratuities are discussed later in more detail.

In general, these various forms of financing do not preclude each other. The same patient may take part in several at once. For example, a consumer may have voluntary as well as compulsory insurance, while receiving some state-financed services and paying directly for some other services.

The degree of integration between purchasers, insurers, and providers

Finally, it is useful to clarify alternative linkages between supply and demand, delivery, and financing. One important characteristic of a health-care system is the degree of integration between sponsors, insurers, and providers (see figure 3.1). Two pure forms can be distinguished:

(I)   *Integration* The two functions, financing and delivery, are performed by the same legal entity. Instead of having distinct roles for purchaser and provider, an integrated health service fulfills both roles (or all three roles of purchaser, insurer, and provider). Here are two examples:

- The pre-reform, classical socialist health-care system, consisting of a single large organization, combines form (1.1) on the supply side (a state monopoly of delivery) with form (A) on the demand side (direct financing of health care out of the state budget).
- The National Health Service model originated in the United Kingdom and has been adopted in many countries colonized by Britain and other developing countries, such as India, Bangladesh, Nigeria, Kenya, and Sri Lanka (Hsiao 1999). This system also combines state-owned health-care facilities on the supply side (1.1) with state general revenue financing on the demand side (A). Public hospitals and outpatient facilities are funded through salaries and

I. Integration   II. Separation

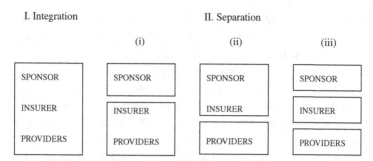

Figure 3.1 Types of integration

Note: The diagram refers to the sponsor and the insurer in the singular. With some mechanisms, there may be more than one sponsor and more than one insurer concurrently. There will be several providers in all cases.

budgets. The state functions both as sponsor, i.e. the purchaser of services on behalf of patients, and the owner–operator of provider organizations.

(II) *Separation* In some systems, the two functions of purchaser and provider are kept strictly separate. One natural person or legal entity provides the health-care service and another person or entity pays for it. The latter purchaser role may be fulfilled, for example, by a government agency or a national insurance fund (that combines the sponsor and insurer roles). The sponsor may also redistribute funds among insurers to assure that although consumers pay the same rate, insurers are paid rates reflecting the risk of their insureds.

There are three variations of systems that split the roles of purchaser and provider.

In the first (II.i), the sponsor role is separate, but the insurer and provider roles are integrated. This form is commonly (but somewhat confusingly) referred to as integration of provision and financing. For example, a private insurance institution may have its own doctors who supply most basic health-care services and decide about referrals to outside organizations (for instance, a specialist clinic or a hospital).

This arrangement combines form (1) on the supply side (an organization as provider) with forms (C) and (D) on the demand side (the insurer paying and the patient contributing). The insurer–provider organization may contract directly with a sponsor. Often many such insurer–provider organizations compete for enrollees. This is a modern form increasingly prevalent in the United States, where these institutions are known as managed care organizations such as health-maintenance organizations (HMOs). (More will be said about HMOs later.) However, it should not be thought that these are an American invention. HMOs existed earlier, not only in the United States, but also in Europe. This was the situation, for instance, in Hungary before the socialist period. This was the form in which the health-care associations of some professions (such as journalists) operated, as did the insurance schemes of some large state-owned and private enterprises (such as the Hungarian State Railways). Similarly, there were three large insurance institutions in pre-war Croatia: one for miners, one for other private employees, and one for state employees. Each had its own network of providers (WHO 1999b: 4). In the old, pre-war institutions and in the present HMOs, the in-house doctors may not provide a full range of medical services. The insurer retains the right to refer the insured to other organizations for specialized services, upon the recommendation of its own doctors. The key distinction here is that the insurance function is integrated with the provider organization, at least for a broad range of medical services.

Alternatively, the sponsor and the insurer may be integrated, but separate from providers (II.ii). For example, under the National Health Insurance system in Canada, each province operates a compulsory insurance program for its residents under federal guidelines, paying independent providers. In the United States, some large employers are self-insured, contracting directly with provider groups to deliver health-care services for employees. Under this form, the integration of sponsor and insurer generally precludes competition among alternative insurers, although patients may have a broad choice of providers.

Finally, all three roles of sponsor, insurer, and provider may be performed by separate legal entities (II.iii). The sponsor usually manages competition among several alternative insurers. Consumers can then choose from among competing insurers. For example, an industry association or large employer may act as a sponsor for its employees. It contracts with several health plans from which employees choose, and also covers part of the insurance premia. The health plans, in turn, contract with independent providers and provider organizations to deliver health-care services to patients.

It has been necessary to give a dry list of these categories to make the later analysis plainer and clearer, and to ensure that the recommendations can be formulated unambiguously. The review is already useful in one respect: it shows how varied a menu of possibilities there is. The choice is not just between a pair of alternatives: a state health sector *or* privatization. There are several forms on the supply and the demand side, which may be linked or integrated in numerous ways, and many mixed and parallel possibilities. It would be a grave mistake to oversimplify the problem of choice.

Payment system incentives

Incentives are critical in determining to what extent a health sector embodies the goals a society wishes the system to fulfill. We have suggested in chapter 2 several such goals or principles for reform in transitional economies. Although the primary focus in this section is principle 4 – the need for forms of ownership, payment, and control that encourage efficiency to emerge – policy-makers should be aware that incentive mechanisms are also critical in upholding or undermining choice, solidarity, competition, financial sustainability, and other principles surveyed earlier. For example, incentives are key in determining to what extent patients, especially those disadvantaged by more severe and expensive medical problems, have access to effective choice of insurers and providers (principle 1). In addition, international comparisons of health-care spending underscore the importance of incentives in explaining the level and growth of expenditures, directly impacting the financial sustainability of a health-care system (principle 9).

Whatever the other characteristics of the chosen economic mechanism of the health sector are – ownership structure, degree of decentralization, predominant form of financing – there will be incentive problems. Trade-offs are inevitable to balance competing principles. In this section, we focus on demand-side and then supply-side incentive trade-offs. Specific policy recommendations are deferred to later chapters.

The term *payment system* is used here broadly to refer to both consumer insurance and provider reimbursement. That is, a payment system entails two major components: how consumers are insured against the risks of medical expenditures, and how health-care providers are paid for their services. The payment system determines what incentives apply to consumers, insurers, and providers. It is desirable to structure the system so that health services are produced and used efficiently (neither "too little" nor "too much"), and that patients have access to risk spreading and quality care. Adverse and risk selection, which compromise choice and solidarity, are to be avoided.

Demand-side incentive problems center on *moral hazard*, the problem (introduced on p. 59) that fully insured consumers tend to overuse services that appear "free" at point of service. This problem will be most severe when the provider has an incentive to indulge or encourage overuse (as discussed under supply-side incentives below). Deductibles, co-payments, and co-insurance – some positive amount of *demand-side cost sharing* – will prevent wasteful overuse without overly discouraging use of needed services.

Although demand-side cost sharing can help to achieve efficient utilization, there is another problem: as noted earlier, demand-side cost sharing tends to defeat the purpose of insurance by making the consumer pay unpredictable, nontrivial co-payments. In other words, it imposes risk on consumers who would like to avoid (or insure against) risk. Therefore, health insurance involves a fundamental trade-off between giving appropriate incentives for efficient use of medical care and spreading risk (Zeckhauser 1970). Increasing the generosity of insurance spreads risk more broadly but also leads to increased losses because individuals choose more care (moral hazard) and providers *ceteris paribus* supply more care (Cutler and Zeckhauser 2000). Well designed health insurance policies include a sliding scale, with the co-insurance rate declining as total health spending of the insured person increases. Such an insurance policy would also limit the patient's total financial liability with an expenditure ceiling.

A heuristic diagram may be useful for visualizing this incentive trade-off. Figure 3.2 represents the incentives associated with setting the patient co-insurance rate (level of demand-side cost sharing). As the co-insurance rate increases, patients use fewer services. This price responsiveness is effective in curbing moral hazard, but may lead to inefficiently low use of health care at very high co-insurance rates.[21] Simultaneously, as the co-insurance rate increases, the inefficiency associated with loss of risk spreading also increases, adding to the ranks of the underinsured and uninsured.

These trade-offs have been couched primarily in efficiency terms; but there are also solidarity concerns (principle 2).

---

[21] In the limit, 100 percent co-insurance means the patient is paying the full cost of care out of his/her pocket and is therefore uninsured. In this situation a large number of patients may forgo necessary care.

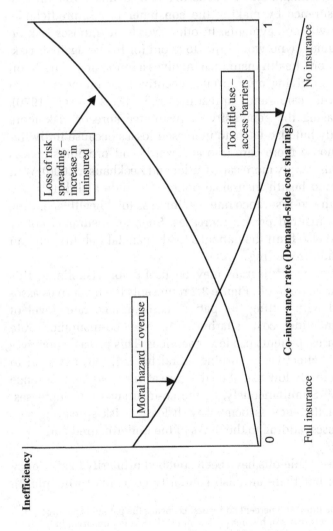

Figure 3.2. Trade-offs in setting the consumer co-insurance rate

Rejecting totally free service and introducing co-payments conflicts with the solidarity principle and its application to health care. A fixed fee for each doctor's visit or prescription drug will be more of a burden on the poor than on those with higher income.[22] Demand-side cost sharing therefore represents a barrier to accessing health-care services that may be disproportionately burdensome for the poor.

Empirical evidence

How significant is the problem of moral hazard? Many researchers have examined the responsiveness of patients to demand-side incentives.[23] The focus has been on the price responsiveness of consumers' demand for medical care. Economists measure this price responsiveness in terms of the percentage change in use relative to the percentage change in price, called the *price elasticity*. The elasticity is expected to be negative: an increase in price leads to a decrease in use.

Early studies yielded widely varying estimates of the price elasticity of health care (ranging from about −0.1 to −1.5). The RAND Health Insurance Experiment − a large social experiment in the United States in the 1970s that randomly assigned nearly 6,000 people into different insurance plans and studied their health care use over a 3- to 5-year period − yielded an overall medical-care price elasticity of about −0.2 (Newhouse and the Insurance Experiment Group 1993:121). In other words, a 10 percent increase in the price of medical services results in a 2 percent decrease in demand for those services. This figure is now widely accepted.

Of course, certain specific services may entail different levels of responsiveness. For example, demand for treatment for urgent health conditions requiring hospitalization is not

---

[22] In economics terminology, demand-side cost sharing is a regressive form of financing because it entails poorer people paying a higher percentage of their income for health care than richer people do.

[23] For a summary of this research, see Zweifel and Manning (2000); Cutler and Zeckhauser (2000).

very sensitive to price at all. In contrast, use of dental care and outpatient mental health care has been found to be more responsive to price than other kinds of medical care. This suggests that although it would be foolhardy to expect co-payments for inpatient care to reduce expenditures significantly, it may be appropriate to impose higher co-payments for more discretionary services.

In sum, considerable empirical evidence confirms that demand for health care is price-responsive. A key question in designing a payment system is choosing the appropriate level(s) of demand-side cost sharing for different health-care services. A very high level discourages drastically wasteful overuse but also imposes risk and represents a tax on the sick, a barrier to access.

Supply-side incentives

Payment systems also create certain supply-side incentives. Considerable evidence suggests that the structure of provider reimbursement affects the quantity and quality of health-care services. The supply-side analog to patient co-insurance is the share of cost borne by the provider at point of service: *supply-side cost sharing* (or *risk sharing*). This denotes a sharing of risk for costs of care between the payer and the provider. The payer could be an insurer, or a sponsor paying an integrated insurer–provider organization. As we will illustrate, a higher degree of supply-side cost sharing in effect imposes a harder budget constraint on the provider when deciding on appropriate treatment for a given patient.

One way to pay health-care providers is cost reimbursement. If the provider is compensated for all the costs of care – complete cost reimbursement – the provider bears no risk. In reality, the payer does not know the exact costs of care, but only what the provider charges for a given set of services. Therefore reimbursement is usually based on a price schedule. One very common contract is *fee-for-service* (FFS) payment, wherein the provider is paid a pre-determined fee for each service rendered. The fees may correspond to competitive market prices, or, more commonly, are administered prices negotiated or unilaterally set by a government or social insurance agency. Usually fees are meant to equal or exceed the cost of providing the service.

Since under full-cost reimbursement or FFS payment the provider bears none of the costs of care, these payment alternatives involve no supply-side cost sharing. The provider in effect faces a soft budget constraint. There is no financial incentive to control costs or to limit the number of services provided, because all costs will be reimbursed. In fact, if the fee for a service exceeds the cost of provision, the provider will be financially rewarded for providing large amounts of that service, whether or not patients' benefit justifies the cost. Since providers almost always are better informed than and wield great influence over their patients regarding treatment choices, patients usually adhere closely to provider recommendations, and those recommendations may be influenced by financial reward. FFS payment is therefore frequently associated with high levels of use and may encourage overuse, especially of the most profitable services. The term *supplier-induced demand* refers to the controversial phenomenon of a health-care supplier (physician or other provider) manipulating patients into receiving more services than they would want, so that suppliers can increase their income (Cutler and Zeckhauser 2000). FFS payment with a positive profit margin per service financially rewards supplier-induced demand.

To address the tendency of FFS to lead to high and open-ended costs through an increase in the quantity of services provided, several countries have combined FFS with other measures. In Japan, for example, the government has been rather successful to date in adjusting the fee schedule to keep overall expenditures relatively low. A more common approach has been formally imposing an overall cap or global budget on provider reimbursement. This payment approach retains the many benefits of FFS while attempting to constrain overall costs within a predetermined budget. The key to such a system is adjustment of the fees, so that when quantity increases, the price per unit is reduced to keep overall spending within the budget.

Most prominent among the systems using FFS with a cap is the German point system. In this system, medical procedures are assigned a certain number of points rather than a direct price or fee. More complicated and time-consuming procedures receive higher point values. The reimbursement to the provider results from multiplying the quantity of points billed by the monetary conversion factor for a point. For example, if a physician bills for a 200-point procedure and the conversion factor is $1 per point, the reimbursement is $200. The relative value of various treatments is preserved (indeed, these fee schedules are often called relative value scales[24]); yet the total reimbursement can be adjusted to stay within a budget through adjustment of the monetary conversion factor, even if quantity changes considerably. The fee per point is inversely proportional to the quantity of services provided collectively by all the physicians. An increase in overall quantity is matched by a decrease in the price per unit quantity.

Such a system attempts to dampen the cost-escalation incentives of FFS payment by imposing a hard overall budget constraint. Unfortunately, in the countries applying this scheme, the budget constraint is imposed at a very aggregate level. This leads to somewhat perverse incentives. If all participants cooperate in limiting quantity, they will be better off. But each has an incentive to deviate – in this case, to raise income by increasing the number of points billed, through

---

[24] The fee schedule used by Medicare in the United States is derived from a resource-based relative value scale, that is, a relative value scale that measures the relative levels of resource input expended when physicians produce services and procedures (Hsiao *et al.* 1988).

performing many high-point procedures and billing aggres-sively. Each provider tries to increase his own income at the expense of others. It is not surprising, therefore, that systems combining FFS with a cap, such as Germany and Canada, have experienced significant increases in volume and bill-ings.[25] A similar predictable effect has occurred under Hungary's capped FFS payment for specialist outpatient care: an increase in the number of billed service points and a decrease in the money value per point (Orosz, Ellena and Jakab 1998).

Another method of controlling the quantity of services may be to introduce some explicit amount of supply-side cost sharing, which hardens the budget constraint on the relevant decision-makers – the individual providers (or a small pro-vider group). A provider who is at risk for some of the costs of care has incentive to control those costs.

One common form of provider payment that involves supply-side cost sharing is *case-based payment* (also often called *prospective payment*). This is payment of a fixed fee for treatment of a given patient's case or medical condition. The level of the fixed fee depends upon a pre-determined cat-egorization of cases, often based on the patient's diagnosis. In its purest form, since the payment for a given case is fixed prospectively, payment leaves the provider at risk for the costs of care within a given case category. For example, a pro-vider is paid $x for treatment of a patient who suffers a heart attack, whether the treatment involves surgery or medical management only. If treatment costs less than $x, the pro-vider retains the difference as revenue. If the treatment expense exceeds $x, the provider suffers a financial loss. Such case-based payment is frequently used for reimbursing hospitals. Probably the most well known case-based payment

---

[25] As David Naylor notes regarding Canadian physician payment, "the com-bination of a volume-driven incentive system with a fixed pot of funds has proved to be a prescription for conflict and frustration. Both the public and the medical profession acknowledge that 'practice churning' for revenue maximisation occurs" (Naylor 1999: 18).

system is the US Prospective Payment System (PPS) for hospitals based on Diagnosis-Related Groups (DRGs), which we will discuss in more detail below.

Another form of payment that involves a high degree of supply-side cost sharing is *capitation*, or payment of a fixed amount per enrolled consumer per period (e.g. month or year). Capitation may or may not be combined with some reimbursement of costs for actual services rendered to a patient. The greater the degree of supply-side cost sharing, the harder the budget constraint the provider faces when deciding on appropriate treatment. *Pure capitation*, under which the provider is paid no differently for a patient who uses many services than for one that uses few or no services, is a form of *full supply-side cost sharing*. Capitation payment is most financially rewarding if an enrolled consumer uses no health-care services at all: the provider retains the full capitation amount as profit. The more costly services a patient utilizes, the less the profit or the greater the loss the provider must bear.

Supply-side cost sharing, such as full or partial capitation, thus gives providers an incentive to use fewer services and to produce those services at least cost. This incentive counteracts the insured consumer's preference for overuse, helping to rid the system of moral hazard inefficiency. The incentive for cost control may be too strong, however. Just as FFS may lead to "too many" services, high risk sharing such as capitation may lead to "too few" services, especially for patients who would benefit from costly services. A capitated provider will be financially rewarded for skimping on quality, restricting beneficial services, and discriminating among patients by engaging in risk selection.

The more at risk the provider is, the greater the incentive to control costs. There is a fundamental trade-off associated with supply-side cost sharing: it gives a beneficial incentive for improving efficiency, but simultaneously creates a harmful incentive for skimping and risk selection (Newhouse

1996). As a result, payment that features high levels of supply-side cost sharing may result in access problems for high-risk patients and significant risk segmentation, with the healthy in lower-cost plans and the sick in expensive plans. Of course, if there is only one insurer, risks cannot be segmented between different insurers. But in that case consumers' choice will be severely curtailed.

When there is choice resulting in risk segmentation, less healthy people end up paying considerably more for health insurance than healthier people do. This differential payment for health coverage can be considered both an efficiency and equity concern. To some extent regulations can proscribe the most egregious forms of discrimination, such as pre-existing condition clauses that deny treatment for health conditions that emerged prior to enrollment. Many other forms of risk selection, however, are beyond the scope of regulation yet powerfully influence enrollment and treatment decisions. Caution is therefore warranted in using supply-side risk sharing.

Since the need for health-care services is unpredictable and some services are extremely expensive, capitation payment imposes considerable risk on providers. This risk, and the associated incentive to underprovide necessary care, is lessened when the provider has a fairly large pool of patients to spread out the risk. It is for this reason that capitation payment is usually associated with providers or provider groups that serve relatively large pools of patients. There is also less risk if the providers are responsible for only a limited scope of services, such as primary care.[26]

One way to preserve the beneficial cost-control incentive

---

[26] The book consistently applies the term "primary-care physician" (PCP), current in the United States, to doctors who treat patients directly at the primary level. The term applied to such doctors differs from country to country. It may be house doctor, family doctor, or local doctor. The expression "general practitioner" (GP) is used in the United Kingdom. The expression primary-care physician is replaced only where the intention is to point out the characteristics of a specific country or period.

of provider risk bearing and consumer choice, without the harmful incentive effects for skimping and risk selection, is through a technique known as *risk adjustment*. To understand its logic, consider an analogy with paying a builder to construct a home. If you offer to pay the builder less than what the builder estimates it will cost to construct the house, the builder will probably refuse to build it. The builder will agree to build the house for you only if what you offer covers the expected costs of construction, including the extra costs from bad-weather delays, etc.

The same reasoning applies to providers of health-care services. If you wish a provider to deliver quality care to a patient who will be expensive to treat, you should pay the expected costs of treatment. Otherwise the provider will prefer to treat only less expensive patients and will be financially penalized for improving quality (since high quality attracts needy and unprofitable patients). To give the provider incentive to accept and treat all patients, the payer should adjust payments to reflect the expected cost of *each* patient. Such an adjustment of payment for the expected cost of patients is called *risk adjustment*. The estimation of the expected cost is based on observable and verifiable characteristics of patients that are correlated with health-care use, such as age, gender, and institutional status. These characteristics are known as *risk adjusters*.

Risk adjustment techniques hold the promise of making risk selection unprofitable, thus allowing choice while both protecting solidarity (equal access) and preserving incentives

footnote 26 (*cont.*)
    Capitated PCPs have an incentive to refer expensive patients to specialty providers to avoid liability for their costs. In contrast, if financial responsibility for specialty and inpatient care is included in the capitation payment, such as under "GP fundholding" pioneered in the United Kingdom, then the GP must continue to weigh the patient benefit from referral to such services against its cost. The extent to which capitation gives incentives for preventive care (to avoid future costly illness or injury) and comprehensive coordinated care will therefore depend crucially on the scope of services included in the capitation payment.

for efficiency and quality improvement. Unfortunately, even the sophisticated incentive schemes developed to date in the United States and other developed countries are not quite capable of correcting all distortions.[27] Nevertheless, some form of risk adjustment is a promising – if not indispensable – component of any payment system that seeks simultaneously to promote choice, efficiency, and quality.

A final common form of provider compensation, especially in transition economies, is salary payment. Since a salary is not tied directly to quantity of services provided, it is in a sense incentive-neutral, avoiding both the FFS incentive for overutilization and the capitation incentive for stinting and selection.

Incentives for promotion may encourage quality and effort to establish a good reputation among colleagues and patients. Bonuses tied to number of patients or other specific performance measures will encourage increasing the number of patients or exerting effort along the measured dimensions of performance (perhaps to the detriment of other, unmeasured aspects of quality). To the extent that a salaried physician is affiliated with teaching and research, he or she may even be eager to treat rare and complicated cases (the opposite of risk selection). Yet in many cases the incentives facing a salaried provider will parallel those of a capitated provider. A salaried provider is "at risk" for effort associated with the treatment of difficult cases and sacrifices part of on-the-job leisure. Both salaried providers and capitated ones have incentive to stint on care and to refer complicated cases elsewhere. In other words, when payment is not tied directly to a comprehensive measure of performance, there is little incentive for good performance. Fixed medical pay scales do not reflect adequately the knowledge, experience, and

---

[27] The most accurate forms of risk adjustment are based on a patient's diagnosis or whole set of diagnoses. However, they can predict only a fraction of the variance in individual health spending that an ideal risk adjuster would predict (van de Ven and Ellis 2000).

conscientiousness of individual doctors – in other words, the differences in their individual performance. The more rigid the rules for applying a pay scale, the less it is able to reflect these. In Eastern Europe especially, the rigid and hardly differentiated scales of pay inherited from the bureaucratic mechanism of socialism can be expected to survive. For these reasons, a less-than-scrupulous doctor can enjoy a good living by minimizing the effort put into his or her job.

In sum, specifying the level of supply-side cost sharing is an important policy choice because a health-care provider may make treatment decisions that respond to the form of payment. These supply decisions directly affect policy goals such as efficiency, risk pooling, and cost containment. The financial incentives associated with alternative payment methods can differ drastically. FFS payment with a profit margin on each unit, for example, financially rewards providers for rendering large quantities of services. Capitation payment, in contrast, rewards providers for strictly limiting the number of services provided.

If, as we have seen, FFS encourages overutilization and supplier-induced demand, whereas capitation and (to some extent) fixed salaries encourage stinting and risk selection, then some combination of these two extremes may be preferable. The benefits of intermediary levels of supply-side cost sharing, often called mixed payment, have been emphasized by several health economists (particularly Joseph Newhouse). By sharing risk between the payer and the provider, mixed payment encourages provider effort to control costs while avoiding the extreme incentives for stinting and risk selection associated with full supply-side cost sharing.

One clever variant of risk sharing, implemented to a certain extent in the Netherlands, is prospective, mandatory pooling of high risks. Under this system, insurer–providers are paid a risk-adjusted fixed fee for the majority of patients they treat. To mitigate the incentive to avoid high risks, the insurer–providers are allowed to place, at the beginning of the period in question, a small fraction of their patients in a high-risk pool. The expenses of treating these high-risk patients are reimbursed more generously, perhaps in full.[28]

As for the demand side, the supply-side incentive trade-offs associated with setting the degree of supply-side cost sharing can be summarized with a heuristic diagram (see figure 3.3). As the degree of supply-side cost sharing increases, incentives for cost control increase. This spurs efficiency in production of health services, at the expense of escalating incentives for risk selection and its associated loss of choice and solidarity. Higher rates of provider cost sharing also create incentives for greater constraint on use. At the extremes, FFS payment (illustrated with a negative level of supply-side cost sharing) may induce wasteful overuse and "supplier-induced demand," whereas pure capitation payment may lead to underuse and skimping on beneficial treatment.

Payment system incentives and property rights

There is food for thought in the connection between payment system incentives, property relations, and softness or hardness of the budget constraint, especially in the context of this book. One of the dilemmas of the Eastern European health-care reform is to decide whether to introduce private ownership instead of the public ownership prevalent so far. It is clear from the line of argument above that privatization *as such* does not guarantee incentives for efficiency. For instance, if a hospital is privatized, but all its services are paid for on a FFS basis, the soft-budget-constraint syndrome will appear just as if it had remained in public ownership and

---

[28] This scheme is clever because the providers are reimbursed generously only for the high-cost cases that they *anticipated* to be high cost and placed prospectively in the high-cost pool, rather than being reimbursed generously for *all* high-cost cases (which would sacrifice more incentive for cost control).

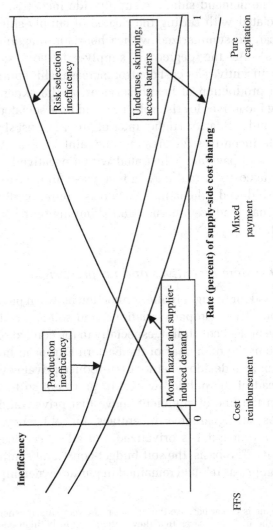

Figure 3.3 Trade-offs in setting the provider cost-sharing rate

the budget constraint were softened by subsidies from the state budget.

This statement can be reversed. If the hospital remains in public ownership, but the settlement system is changed to a rigidly imposed prospective case-based payment system, the budget constraint will harden. It is another matter that a soft budget constraint on the social-insurance fund, which is controlled or strongly influenced by the state (see chapter 5, p. 151), will loosen the financial discipline of state-owned providers such as public hospitals. A purchaser with a soft budget constraint will not show great rigor. It will be prepared to be lenient, so that ultimately the disease of a soft budget constraint affects providers as well.

Advocates of public ownership often argue against forprofit enterprises and privatization by assuming that organizations in public ownership will exclusively consider the public interest, or, more precisely, the interest of patients. In fact, that is not the case. Let us assume that a hard budget constraint is applied with absolute consistency to a publicly owned hospital or clinic. In that case, the heads of the organization, and the other decision-makers subordinate to them, will start to behave like profit-maximizers. Their behavior will be strongly influenced by payment system incentives. If the organization, influenced by these, has a stake in economizing on expenditure, it will be inclined, regardless of public ownership, to let standards of quality fall, and to avoid high-risk patients who are expensive to treat by sending them on to other institutions. On the other hand, if the hospital is on a FFS basis, supplier-induced demand is likely to appear even in the presence of public ownership, as a way of increasing revenues and thereby improving financial performance.

The conclusion to draw is that the prevalent configuration of hardness or softness of the budget constraint and the payment system is usually a factor with as strong an effect as type of ownership.

Empirical evidence

Do health-care providers respond to the financial incentives of different payment systems? Although professional codes of conduct and ethical exactitude may mitigate the effects of monetary rewards on provider behavior, there is nevertheless considerable empirical evidence that providers do respond to incentives. Some has already been mentioned in passing (e.g. increases in volume and billings under FFS with a cap). Statistical investigation of health expenditures in OECD countries has shown that as theory would predict, in ambulatory (outpatient) care "capitation systems tend to lead to lower expenditure on average than FFS systems by about 17 to 21 percent" (Gerdtham and Jönsson 2000: 46).

Further evidence comes from analysis of the impact since 1984 of the US Medicare system for paying hospitals according to DRGs. This case-based PPS is one of the most widely cited and emulated payment systems of recent decades. As noted above, under such a system hospitals have an incentive to reduce costs and improve efficiency, such as by reducing length of stay. But PPS also gives an incentive to stint on care within a diagnosis category, increase admission rates for less severe cases and dump more severe cares, and release patients inappropriately soon (i.e. discharging "quicker and sicker"). These incentives are mitigated by the fact that PPS actually represents a mixed payment system, since it includes many features, such as outlier payments for unusual cases and DRGs defined by procedure, that differ from a purely prospective payment system.[29]

Continuing research has shown that most of the intended beneficial effects of PPS on costs and intensity of care have been realized, while the feared side-effects have been minimal to date (Coulam and Gaumer 1991; Cutler and

---

[29] For example, a hospital receives a larger payment for a patient with coronary artery disease who undergoes a bypass operation than for a similar patient who does not.

Zeckhauser 2000). Admissions declined somewhat, while in many cases inputs to care fell significantly. Studies of the effect on length of hospital stays have almost all found the payment change to be associated over several years with a decrease in length of stay of a fifth to a quarter of pre-PPS levels. The quality of care for the average patient showed little change, although there is lower in-hospital mortality and a compression of mortality rates. Several researchers have uncovered evidence of dumping of high-cost patients from PPS to nonPPS (usually specialized) hospitals. In sum, PPS seems to have contributed to slowing the growth in inpatient costs without severely impacting quality of care, although some adverse side-effects did appear.

Conclusion

Health-care payment systems are set up to fulfill multiple and often conflicting social goals. There is no single "ideal" payment system; any given system will need to find a balance between competing goals.

Since there is considerable evidence that consumers and providers do respond to financial incentives, policy-makers need to be aware of the incentives associated with different payment options, summarized in table 3.3. For example, increasing demand-side cost sharing curbs the wasteful overuse of moral hazard. But it also imposes inefficient risk bearing, making some people underinsured or even uninsured. Raising supply-side cost sharing also curbs moral hazard as well as encourages production efficiency, but it does so at the expense of giving incentives for underprovision (stinting on beneficial services) and risk selection.

Policy-makers should also consider additional factors such as implementing risk adjustment and promoting professional ethics. Improved risk adjustment accuracy serves to prevent risk selection. Professional ethics among health-care providers – defined in terms of fidelity to patient interests rather

Table 3.3 *Incentive effects of payment-system policy instruments*

Policy instrument	Benefit from More of the policy instrument	Cost associated with
Demand-side cost sharing (e.g. patient co-insurance rate)	Constrains overuse (curbs moral hazard)	Inefficient risk bearing Tax on the sick
Supply-side cost sharing (integration of insurance and provision)	Constrains overuse Encourages cost reduction (production efficiency)	Underprovision Risk selection
Professional ethics (provider fidelity to patient interests)	Curbs supplier-induced demand Moderates underprovision Reduces risk selection	Moral hazard
Risk adjustment	Prevents risk selection	
Provider competition for patients	Encourages provider effort (e.g. cost reduction and quality improvement)	Risk selection

than financial reward – may make the problem of moral hazard worse (since doctors may indulge patients' requests for more and costlier services), but can also lead to numerous benefits: curbing "supplier-induced demand," moderating underprovision, and reducing risk selection.

It is clear, then, that incentives matter. Attention should be given to resolving incentive problems, regardless of the other chosen aspects of the economic mechanism (such as the ownership structure). There are inevitable trade-offs: moving in one direction helps fulfill one principle but hurts achievement of another. Extreme solutions can be counterproductive. Policy-makers should search for reasonable compromises, giving some financial and moral incentives to all concerned, patients and providers alike.

4

Some international experiences

This chapter examines international health-sector experiences in only a few respects. It deals mainly with the economic mechanism of health sectors in the OECD countries, which – excluding recent members such as the Czech Republic, Hungary, and Poland – have traditional capitalist, not post-socialist systems. (This is the group we mean when referring to the "developed countries" or "industrialized democracies.") Unlike the discussion on p. 69, which classified the "menu" of institutional alternatives on an abstract plane, this chapter aims to identify, in a somewhat generalized way, some features of the economic mechanisms that actually operate.[1]

The economic mechanisms in the industrialized democracies

Two important features of health-care systems are the form of ownership predominant among health-care organizations

[1] A survey of the state of the health sector in the OECD countries, the mechanisms that apply, its characteristics, and the directions of change can be obtained from the following: OECD (1992, 1993, 1994a); Saltman and Figueras (1997).

As part of the research undertaken before the writing of this book, descriptive and analytical studies were prepared of the welfare sector in Argentina, Australia, Austria, Chile, the Czech Republic, France, Germany, New Zealand, and Poland, and of the reform debates in Hungary. We are grateful to Mária Barát, Róbert Gál, Péter Gedeon, András Nagy, Péter Pete, Judit Rimler, Margit Tóth, and László Urbán for their collaboration. We have used the lessons to be drawn from their (yet unpublished) studies in this book.

(on the supply side) and the predominant source of financing for health care (on the demand side). Table 4.1 surveys the ownership forms found in the health sector of the developed countries. The countries are grouped, beginning with those where the sector operates under state ownership and public financing, and ending with those where private ownership and private financing predominate. The various mixed and combined alternatives are in the middle.

The column headings use the term *predominant*. The real extremes of a *purely* state and a *purely* private-ownership system do not exist in practice. Everywhere there also appear forms decidedly different from the predominant one as well, although in many countries they have only a marginal effect. For some countries there was detailed information available about the role played by nondominant forms of provision and financing. This is summarized in tables 4.2 and 4.3. For the sake of clarity and continuity, the countries are grouped in the same way as in table 4.1, of which columns (1) and (2) (predominant provider, predominant source of finance, respectively) are repeated.

There is an important conclusion to draw from international experience as summarized in these three tables. There is no single model of an economic mechanism in the health sector that typifies even the main features in the developed countries. Nor is it true that there are two models, a strongly "collectivist" or "socialist" European model, and a strongly "individualist" or "capitalist" US model. Europe is heterogeneous, and public financing has great weight in the United States.

Column (3) of table 4.4 shows the proportion of total health-care expenditure financed from state resources. Not even in the United States is this less than 45 percent, while in Luxembourg it is over 90 percent. However, countries are widely dispersed within this band. A comparison between column (3) and column (1) suggests that there is no obvious or ironclad relationship between a country's level of

Table 4.1 *Predominant ownership forms of health-care providers, OECD countries, 1992*

Country	Predominant provider (1)	Predominant source of finance (2)	Notes (3)
Denmark Finland Greece Iceland Ireland Norway Portugal Spain Sweden United Kingdom	Public	Taxation	
Austria Belgium France Germany Japan Luxembourg	Public and private	Social insurance	
Italy	Public	Almost equally social insurance and taxation	
Canada Netherlands	Private	Social insurance and private insurance	
Turkey	Public and private	No dominant source of finance	
Switzerland United States	Private	Private insurance	Coverage of the aged and the poor (23 percent of population) by taxation and social insurance

Note:
The table applies the terminology used in the source. The term "public" mainly refers to state-owned property, but it cannot be excluded that it also covers organizations owned by nonprofit institutions.
Source: OECD (1994a: 11).

Table 4.2 *Supplementary ownership forms in health-care services, selected OECD countries, 1990s*

Country	Predominant provider (1)	Private share of total inpatient care beds, 1997 (2)	Notes (3)
Denmark	Public	0.7	20 percent of outpatient care is provided by private doctors
Finland		4.7[2]	
Greece		29.6[1]	
Italy		21.9[1]	
Norway		0.1	
Portugal		21.7	
Spain		32.5[2]	
Sweden		23.6	8 percent of doctors practice only privately, and 40 percent of dentists work in private practice
United Kingdom		3.7[3]	
Austria	Public and private	30.3	51 percent of doctors practice privately[5]
Belgium		61.9[4]	
France		35.2	
Germany		51.5	
Japan		65.2	
Turkey		5.2	70 percent of dentists and 32 percent of other specialists practice privately
Canada	Private	0.9	
Netherlands		85.0	
United States		66.8	

Notes:
[1] 1996. [2] 1995. [3] 1993. [4] 1992. [5] 1989.
Sources: Information on the predominant provider is taken over from table 4.1. The private share of inpatient beds is from OECD (1999b). The rest of the data have been collected from OECD (1992, 1993: 276–7).

Table 4.3 *Supplementary forms of financing health-care services, selected OECD countries, 1992*

Country	Predominant source of finance (1)	Share of health-care expenditure not financed out of public sources (1992, percent) (2)	Share of the privately insured within the population (percent) (3)	Notes on the conditions of private insurance (4)
Denmark	Taxation	18	26	
Finland		20.7	<10	
Greece		23.9	...	
Iceland		14.8	...	
Ireland		23.9[1]	30	The monopoly public insurer offers private insurance
Norway		5.2	Marginal	
Portugal		30.2	5	
Spain		19.5	10	
Sweden		14.4	Marginal	
United Kingdom		15.6	11	
Austria	Social insurance	34.8	38	
Belgium		11.1	70	
France		25.2	80	
Germany[3]		28.5	10	Full coverage of costs for those with high incomes

			Marginal Marginal	
Japan		28.8		
Luxembourg		8.6[2]		Only against co-payment and for abroad
Italy	Almost equally social insurance and taxation	24.8	...	
Canada	Social and private insurance	27.3	...	
Netherlands		23.4	32	
Switzerland	Private insurance	32.1	35.2	
United States		54.3	70.1	Primarily employment-based; 16 percent of population uninsured
Turkey	No dominant source of finance	34.3[2]	0.5	

Notes:
[1] 1991. [2] 1990. [3] Data excludes the former GDR.

Sources: Information on the predominant source of finance is taken over from table 4.1. Column (2): OECD (1994a: 38). Columns (3) and (4): data collected from OECD (1992, 1994a), and for the United States, US Census Bureau, cited in Kuttner (1999).

Table 4.4 *Real GDP per capita, health expenditure as percentage of GDP, and public share of health expenditure, 1992, an international comparison*

Country	*Per capita* GDP[1] (USD 000) (1)	Health expenditure as percentage of GDP (2)	Public health expenditure as percentage of THE[2] (3)
Luxembourg	33.1	7.0	91.8
United States	29.4	13.9	46.4
Norway	26.8	7.5	82.2
Switzerland	26.0	10.0	69.9
Denmark	25.5	8.0	83.8
Iceland	24.9	7.9	83.8
Japan	24.6	7.2	79.9
Canada	23.7	9.2	69.8
Belgium	23.2	7.6	87.6
Austria	23.1	8.3	73.0
Netherlands	22.6	8.5	72.6
Australia	22.6	8.4	66.7
Germany	22.1	10.7	77.1
France	21.3	9.6	74.2
Italy	21.3	7.6	69.9
Finland	20.5	7.4	76.0
Ireland	20.4	6.3	76.7
United Kingdom	20.4	6.8	84.6
Sweden	20.4	8.6	83.3
New Zealand	17.9	7.6	77.3
Spain	16.0	7.4	76.1
Portugal	14.6	7.9	60.0
Korea	14.5	6.0	45.5
Greece	13.9	8.6	57.7
Czech Republic	13.1	7.2	91.7
Hungary	9.9	6.5	69.1
Mexico	7.7	4.7	60.0
Poland	7.5	5.2	90.4
Turkey	6.5	4.0	72.8

Notes:
[1] Measured by purchasing power parities. The purchasing power parity (PPP) adjustment compensates for differences in the cost of living across countries by comparing prices using a fixed basket of goods. The basket of goods used for this adjustment is a broad measure of the goods that compose GDP rather than just health goods. Thus the differences in health spending reflect differences in the *resources* devoted to health spending rather than differences in the *quality of health goods*. Resource differences are an imperfect indicator of quantity differences when the relative price of health goods varies across countries.
[2] THE = Total Health Expenditure.
Source: OECD (1999b).

economic development and the proportion of public financing for health spending among OECD countries. Analysis of world-wide trends in the era following the Second World War, however, reveals that higher-income countries tend to have larger shares of public financing for health expenditures.[2]

There seems to be no simple, obvious explanation for the wide dispersion in the proportions of the ownership forms and of the various economic mechanisms. Table 4.1 has countries that resemble each other culturally and in development level featuring in different categories (for instance, Belgium and the Netherlands), while countries that differ culturally and in development level appear in the same category (e.g. Denmark and Greece). Perhaps the most plausible hypothesis to explain this heterogeneity is that the course of each country's history, the dynamics of competition between political parties and movements, trends in its economic development, the struggles and coexistence between its classes and social strata, the relations between employers and employees, and many other circumstances have all contributed to the specific system of institutions and organizations in the health sector. Once a country has taken a certain path, it becomes difficult to depart from it. It is not impossible to change direction, but earlier conditions always limit the next step closely.[3] It would be hard for Germany or France to abandon the idea of universal social insurance, but it would be no easier for the United States to introduce it.

Bearing this diversity and "path-dependence" in mind, it is nevertheless useful to consider the primary features of

[2] According to World Bank data for the mid-1990s, the income elasticity for the public share of health spending is 1.21, suggesting that the proportion of health financing from public sources increases as national income increases (Schieber and Maeda 1999: 199). Also see Kornai and McHale (in print). The question will be returned to in chapter 8 (p. 318).

[3] This view is held by the current of opinion in economic history and economic theory that emphasizes the "path-dependence" of development on the previous stage. It is not just the initial state and the destination that count. What happens along the "path" also plays a decisive role. See Arthur (1989), Krugman (1994); Stark (1992).

several health-care systems that have been particularly influential, either as examples or counterexamples for policy-makers in other parts of the world. We introduce here a typology of six "models." Each has a characteristic config- uration of attributes, and can be identified with a country.[4] Although the countries referred to in the typology have each changed their health-care mechanisms several times in their history and are still undergoing reforms, they, primarily, are the countries that embody the main attributes of the six models. They were the pioneers, which seems to justify naming the models after them.

Five of the six models are summed up concisely in table 3.2 (p. 72).

1. *The national health service model: the British model*
   Pioneered in the United Kingdom, this system in its pure form combines state-owned health-care facilities on the supply side with state general-revenue financing on the demand side. Emphasis is on universal and equal access to basic health services. Public hospitals and out- patient facilities are generally funded through budgets and salaries. The government serves a dual role as the purchaser of services on behalf of patients and the owner–operator of provider organizations. Such a system is also called a "public integrated model" to highlight this combination of *public* financing with *integrated* purchaser and provider roles (OECD 1992).[5] Such a system may characterize a national health sector or only subcomponents of it,[6] and may be combined with voluntary supplementary insurance for uncovered services.

---

[4] This section draws upon OECD (1992) and Hsiao (1999).
[5] Beginning with reforms introduced in 1989, the United Kingdom has moved away from a pure public integrated model toward a public con- tract model (discussed below) with separation of purchaser and provider.
[6] For example, the US Department of Veterans' Affairs represents a public integrated system within the broader pluralistic US health-care system.

2. *The national health insurance model: the Canadian model*

   This features a national health-insurance standard-benefit package with public financing, a (regional) single-payer institution, and private delivery of services. Unlike the national health-service model, the purchaser and provider functions are separate, although the sponsor and insurer functions are integrated into regional single purchasers (under provincial governments). Each Canadian province operates a compulsory insurance program for its residents under federal guidelines, paying independent providers largely on a fee-for-service basis. This system also emphasizes universal and equal access to basic health services and can be combined with voluntary supplementary insurance for uncovered services.

3. *The social insurance model: the German model*

   Developed in Germany under Bismarck in the nineteenth century, this health-care system combines compulsory insurance financing on the demand side with pluralistic delivery of services on the supply side.[7] The insurance function is more decentralized than under the national health-insurance model, in that there are multiple sickness funds that pool risk by industry or region and in some cases may compete for enrollees. To assure solidarity, the package of services covered is standardized across sickness funds. Patients generally have free choice of providers, with sickness funds acting as insurer–purchasers *vis-à-vis* public and private providers. Systems such as this that combine *public* (social insurance) financing with *contracting* between purchaser(s) and providers (rather than

---

[7] Before the socialist period, a system of social insurance similar to the German one had operated in some Eastern European countries for several decades. That was the case, for instance, in the territory of the present-day Czech Republic (OECD 1998a), in Poland (Koronkiewicz and Karski 1997), and in Slovenia (Tóth 1997).

integrated provision) are also known as "public contract models" (OECD 1992). Like most systems, social insurance can be combined with voluntary insurance for uncovered services or for the full gamut of services for those allowed to opt out of the mandatory system (such as high-income residents in Germany).

4.   *The voluntary insurance model: the American model*
A health-care system can be based on voluntary purchase of health insurance, creating increased scope for individual freedom, choice, and responsibility, at the expense of assuring universal access and social solidarity. The primary example is the United States health-care system. However, we would like to point out that the expression "American model" is not really accurate. Although the proportion of voluntary insurance is very great and this is a distinguishing mark of the US system, almost half of the financing comes from public sources. The specific problems of the US health sector are considered in more detail on p. 122.

It is worth noting that the Netherlands, in recent years, has introduced a reform that has brought the Dutch health-care mechanism closer to the American model in terms of choice and incentives (van de Ven *et al.* 1994), although the compulsory character of health insurance has been retained. The reforms were based on the theory of managed competition, a concept originated by American health economist Alain Enthoven (1978), but not truly implemented in the United States.[8]

5.   *Medical savings accounts: the Singapore model*
Singapore has pioneered a system combining a particu-

[8] Managed competition envisions active "management" by a sponsor acting on behalf of consumers, including choosing participating health plans, fostering price-elastic demand, and mitigating adverse selection and risk selection through a standardized benefit package and risk-adjusted payments. The failed Clinton health plan (see p. 128) was based on managed competition. Colombia has also sought to implement managed competition in its health sector.

lar variant of public financing, mandatory contributions to individual medical savings accounts, with a pluralistic delivery system.[9] Patients use funds in their medical savings accounts to buy health services from competing private and public providers. This system also heavily emphasizes individual responsibility and choice. Since risk pooling is essential for large catastrophic expenses such as hospitalizations, Singaporeans are also mandated to buy catastrophic insurance, paying the premium out of their medical savings accounts. To curb the tendency toward inequity that such a system of "individual purchaser–insurers" entails, Singapore heavily subsidizes some classes of public providers (e.g. certain wards in public hospitals) to promote equitable access to basic services.

6. *Public provision of medical care: the Soviet model*
   This is discussed in detail in chapter 5, p. 135 and is listed here only to complete the typology.

There are lessons for the transitional economies from this diversity, even at first glance.

First, there is no "model country" to represent the "developed West," whose example might be followed without hesitation. Even the identification of a country that might be seen as a pattern or example to follow is based on a value judgment. Policy-makers would be well advised to consider adopting different aspects from different systems to construct a coherent whole most appropriate for their own country.

Secondly, close attention must be paid to each post-socialist country's historical starting-point: the health-care mechanism established under the socialist system. This can only be transformed; it cannot and must not be torn asunder before an alternative system can evolve to take its place. This

---

[9] China has also adopted a system of medical savings accounts for its ongoing health-sector reforms, and experiments with such accounts are taking place in the United States as well.

warning ties in with principle 7, which requires that organizations and individuals receive time to adjust to the new situation.

Tables 4.1–4.4 present a still picture of the state of the health-care mechanism in the developed countries in the early 1990s. The picture looks fairly complex. The recent and ongoing reforms of health-care systems in almost all industrialized democracies differ from each other in many respects. One question to ask is whether there has been any movement in a common direction. Do the current or envisaged reforms converge towards a common model?

Although some observers might answer decisively in the affirmative (e.g. Besley and Gouveia 1994), it would seem more prudent to say that there are some widespread tendencies, but they are far from uniform or ubiquitous. From this point of view it is worth separating the developed European countries from other OECD countries, particularly the United States.

For the great majority of European industrialized democracies, a keen sense of social solidarity for health care has upheld a predominant role for the state or quasi-state sector both in financing and provision. Nevertheless, in recent years various forms of private provision and private insurance are appearing and to some extent strengthening and spreading. They are far from becoming dominant, but ceasing to be wholly marginal. In France, for instance, where state activeness has deep historical roots, two-thirds of the hospitals and a third of the hospital beds are not run by the state, and 83 percent of the population has supplementary medical insurance (OECD 1993). In Germany, 48 percent of the hospitals are in public ownership, and the rest owned by nonprofit or privately owned organizations (see table 4.2).

"Quasi-market" and "quasi-private" forms are gaining strength in the public sector. For instance, PCPs may receive a fund from the health service, from which to "manage" the entire spending on the patients entrusted to them.[10] While a public hospital may remain in state ownership, the independence of its management may increase. Meanwhile restrictions are being put on the expenditure of state-owned institutions to harden their budget constraints. Table 4.5 provides at least an outline view of various quasi-market reforms implemented in OECD countries.[11]

Other trends have been organizational, such as separating the roles of purchaser and provider or stipulating that PCPs act as "gatekeepers" for patients into the health-care system. Under the latter, patients are required to obtain a referral from their PCPs before seeking care from any specialists (except in emergencies).[12] Statistical analysis of OECD health-care expenditures both at a point in time and over time reveals that primary care "gatekeeping" seems to be associated with lower health expenditure, controlling for *per capita* income and other demographic and institutional features of health-care systems (Gerdtham and Jönsson 2000: 46).[13]

Payment incentives have also exhibited some convergence. Most developed countries require limited patient co-payments to address the dilemma of demand-side incentives

[10] See the discussion of "GP fundholding" in chapter 3 (p. 89, n. 26).

[11] This all arouses a strong sense of *déjà vu* in the Hungarian, Polish, or Czech generation that observed or participated in the reform debates under the socialist system, and witnessed the quasi-reform experiments. They will already have encountered every form and every reform variant earlier in their lives, if not in the health sector, then in the business sphere of the economy.

[12] As explained in chapter 3 (p. 88), high supply-side cost sharing for a broad range of medical care, such as capitation payment for both outpatient and inpatient services, gives providers incentive to control costs, such as by establishing "gatekeeping" requirements to reduce duplicative or unnecessary care.

[13] This is consistent with evidence from the United States, where HMOs (that almost always employ gatekeeping) have been found to reduce health expenditures by about 10 percent relative to fee-for-service (FFS), adjusting for differences in the underlying health of the patient population in the two kinds of plan (Cutler and Zeckhauser 2000: 604).

Table 4.5 *Selected reforms implemented in OECD countries since 1984*

Country	Changes	Cost sharing for health-care services, 1993 (if not indicated otherwise)
Australia	Introduction of demand-side cost sharing[1]	16 percent of health expenditure from direct payments by users in 1989–90
Austria		Inpatient care USD 6/day, an average of 21.5 percent of the price of drugs
Finland[4,5]		Primary-care maximum charge FM 50/visit, with cap or FM 100 annual deductible; outpatient care FM 125/day; 20 percent of THE from direct payments (1997)
Iceland		Primary care max. USD 9/visit; outpatient specialist and outpatient care USD 17 + 40 percent of the rest of the cost/visit
Japan		Cost-sharing as a percentage of the bill: Employees 10 percent Dependents 20 percent Self-employed 30 percent
Luxembourg		Primary care and outpatient specialists 5 percent, drugs 20 percent
Norway		Primary care USD 11/visit, outpatient specialists USD 16/visit
Portugal		Primary care and outpatient specialists 10 percent
Sweden		10.7 percent of health expenditure from direct payments by users in 1989
Switzerland		Primary care and outpatient specialists maximum USD 6–19/visit, inpatient care USD 8/day
Denmark Finland[4] Ireland Italy Netherlands New Zealand Norway Spain	Payment of primary-care doctors partly on a capitation basis, instead of full FFS compensation[2]	

Table 4.5 (*cont.*)

Country	Changes	Cost sharing for health-care services, 1993 (if not indicated otherwise)
Sweden United Kingdom		
Australia Austria Norway Portugal Sweden	Payment of hospitals by case-related payment systems, like DRG instead of annual budget or *per diem* payments	
Denmark Greece Norway Sweden	Reliance on private hospitals to reduce waiting periods for hospital admission[3]	

Note:
FM = Finnish Mark; THE = Total Health Expenditure.
Sources: [1] OECD (1994a: 18). [2] OECD (1994a: 24, 42). [3] OECD (1994a: 20).
[4] Finland Ministry of Social Affairs and Health (1996). [5] OECD (1999b).

for efficiency versus risk spreading and solidarity. In the aggregate, consumer out-of-pocket spending usually accounts for a small but nontrivial percentage of a nation's total health expenditures (see table 4.6). Only a few countries such as South Korea, Portugal, Turkey, and Switzerland require large amounts of demand-side cost sharing.[14] Table 4.7 lists the provider payment systems for selected countries, illustrating that many have introduced supply-side cost sharing (risk sharing) and mixed payment systems.[15] A few

[14] Note that since table 4.6 lists out-of-pocket spending as a percentage of total spending, it includes not only patient co-payments for basic services but also out-of-pocket payment for discretionary services (such as cosmetic surgery) for which there is less conflict with the principle of solidarity.

[15] That a DRG-based mixed-payment system has wide appeal is evident by its adoption (or serious consideration for adoption) in many countries besides the United States, including Germany, France, the United Kingdom, Canada, Australia, Austria, Belgium, Denmark, Finland, Hungary, Ireland, Norway, Portugal, Spain, Sweden, and Switzerland (OECD 1994a: 46).

Table 4.6 *Out-of-pocket payments, selected OECD countries, 1997*

Country	Out-of-pocket payments as percentage of THE
Austria	25.1[1]
Canada	16.5
Czech Republic	8.3
Denmark	12.6[1]
Finland	19.9
France	12.6[1]
Germany	10.8[2]
Hungary	15.1[1]
Iceland	16.2
Ireland	12.9[2]
Korea	52.0[2]
Luxembourg	7.0
New Zealand	23.5[1]
Portugal	44.6[2]
Switzerland	29.8[2]
Turkey	31.7[1]
United Kingdom	2.7[2]
United States	17.2

Notes:
THE = Total Health Expenditure.
[1] 1996.
[2] 1995.
Source: OECD (1999b).

countries have implemented risk adjustment, primarily in the 1990s and using simple risk adjusters such as age and gender, often in combination with various risk-sharing arrangements (see table 4.8).

Public opinion in the industrialized democracies seems to be fairly divided on the subject of health-sector reform. Table 4.9 gives an instructive picture of this. Only a minority of respondents in the five countries surveyed, between 9 and 25 percent, feel that the existing mechanism is basically satisfactory and needs only minor adjustments. The rest see a need

Table 4.7 *Provider payment systems, selected countries, late 1990s*

Country	Primary care	Outpatient specialists	Inpatient care
Australia	FFS	FFS	Budgets with indexed cost caps, some states adopting case-based payment
Canada	FFS, with global budget to physicians' association, negotiated by province	FFS, with global budget to physicians' association, negotiated	Budgets and salary
Denmark	28 percent capitation; 63 percent FFS; 9 percent allowances	Capitation and FFS	Global budgets
Germany	FFS, with global budget to physicians' association; point system of assigned points per service, with the value per point lowered if budget exceeded	FFS, with global budget to physicians' association; point system of assigned points per service, with the value per point lowered	Target budgets and case-based payment
Japan	FFS	FFS	FFS (demonstration project of case-based payment)
Korea	FFS	FFS	FFS
Netherlands	FFS if higher income; capitation (age-adjusted) if lower income; *ex ante* high-risk pooling	FFS and salary	Global budgets, regionally negotiated
New Zealand	FFS, capitation, budget-holding	Contracts and FFS	Contracts and FFS
Norway	Capitation, salary, and FFS	FFS and salary	Global budgets
Spain	Salary and capitation (age-adjusted)	Salary	Global budget for social security hospitals; *per diem* for other hospitals
Sweden	Salary for public; mixed payment in some counties	Salary + budget	Budgets

Table 4.7 (*cont*)

Country	Primary care	Outpatient specialists	Inpatient care
United Kingdom (after 1989 reforms)	Capitation (age-adjusted) and FFS; GP fundholders after 1989 reforms; GP-led Primary Care Groups as purchasers/ fundholders after 1999 reforms	Contracts and FFS	Contracts and FFS
United States	FFS (resource-based relative-value scale); capitation with risk-sharing arrangements, etc.	Primarily FFS	Primarily case-based (DRGs)

Sources: Greiner and Schulenburg (1997); Hakansson and Nordling (1997); Krasnik and Vallgarda (1997); Maarse (1997); Saltman and Figueras (1997); Scott (1997); Hall (1999); Ikegami and Campbell (1999); Liu and Jakab (1999); Naylor (1999); OECD (1999b).

Table 4.8 Risk adjustment and risk sharing, selected countries, 1972–2000

Country (program)	Year began	Mandatory/ voluntary	Risk adjusters	Risk sharing
Belgium	1995	Mandatory	Age/gender/region/disability/ unemployment/mortality	Proportional risk sharing, at least 85 percent
Colombia	1994	Voluntary	Age/gender/region	No (full supply-side cost sharing)
Czech Republic	1993	Mandatory	Age	No (full supply-side cost sharing)
Germany	1994	Mandatory	Age/gender/disability	No (full supply-side cost sharing)
Ireland	1996	Voluntary	Age/gender/hospitalization, weighted with current expenses	Partial; see risk adjusters
Israel	1995	Mandatory	Age	Severe diseases (6 percent of expenses)
Netherlands	1991	Mandatory	Age/gender/region/disability	Outlier and proportional risk sharing
Russia	1993	Mandatory	Many different regional experiments	
Switzerland	1993	Mandatory	Age/gender/region	No (full supply-side cost sharing)
United Kingdom	1991	Voluntary	Age/gender/prior utilization/ local factors	Outlier risk sharing
United States				
Medicare HMOs in 1997	1972	Voluntary	Age/gender/region (county) Institutional status/welfare status	No (full supply-side cost sharing)
HMOs starting in 2000	2000	Voluntary	Age/gender/region (county)/welfare status/Principal Inpatient Diagnosis	No (full supply-side cost sharing)

Table 4.8 (cont.)

Country (program)	Year began	Mandatory/ voluntary	Risk adjusters	Risk sharing
New York Medicaid	1993	Voluntary	Age/gender/region	Condition-specific risk sharing
Health Insurance Plan of California	1992	Voluntary	Gender/number of children/ 120 Marker Diagnoses	No (full supply-side cost sharing)
Minnesota Buyers Health Care Action Group	1997	Voluntary	Diagnosis-based	Stoploss for catastrophic cases
Colorado Medicaid	1997	Voluntary	Age/gender/region; diagnosis-based (Disability Payment System)	No (full supply-side cost sharing)
Washington (state) Health Care Authority	1989	Voluntary	Age/gender/employee status since 1989; diagnosis-based starting 2000	Limited

Sources: Bertko and Hunt (1998); Dunn (1998); Knutson (1998); Wilson *et al.* (1998); van de Ven and Ellis (2000).

Table 4.9 *Public opinion on health care, selected countries, 1998*

	Australia	Canada	New Zealand	United Kingdom	United States
Satisfaction: percentage of respondents who said					
On the whole the system works pretty well, and only minor changes are necessary to make it work better	19	20	9	25	17
There are some good things in our health-care system, but fundamental changes are needed to make it work better	49	56	57	58	46
Our health-care system has so much wrong with it that we need to completely rebuild it	30	23	32	14	33
Access: percentage who reported difficulties seeing specialists and consultants when they needed to					
Extremely or very difficult	14	16	17	10	15
Somewhat difficult	21	30	18	19	24
Not too difficult	25	22	26	30	24
Not at all difficult	29	25	30	25	32
Cost: percentage who reported having problems paying medical bills in last year					
	10	5	15	3	18

Source: Donelan *et al.* (1999: 208, 210), based on data from the Commonwealth Fund's 1998 *International Health Policy Survey* which surveyed a nationally representative sample of about 1,000 adults in each country during April–June, 1998.

for fundamental reforms or a radical rebuilding of the system. The phrasing of the questions did not allow the responses to reveal what *direction* the public wants the changes to take. The five countries covered by the research represent at least three "models," according to the classification presented earlier in this chapter. The ratio of satisfied to dissatisfied differs little from country to country, but the criticism could well come from the "right" in one country and the "left" in another.

Although the public-opinion survey suggests that many people support a strong change, the actual rate of change is low. Most of the measures do not bring a radical change, only cautious, evolutionary alterations.[16]

Even if similar changes occur in all the developed European countries, the picture will remain strongly heterogeneous. However, a prediction can be risked. The developed European countries as a whole will probably come closer to a "mixed," multi-pillar mechanism where (1) public ownership not only has no monopoly, but has declining weight; while (2) public financing remains the predominant but far from exclusive source of funds for health care; and (3) payment incentives are given more attention in aligning consumer and provider interests with policy goals.

A special case: the US health sector

It is not a task for this book to analyze the economic mechanism of the US health sector in detail.[17] However, the debates in post-socialist economies include repeated references to it, often by defenders of the status quo quoting it as a counterexample. So it is important to outline a few of its characteristics.

---

[16] The course of the reforms in the industrialized democracies suggests that the caution urged in principle 7 is being exercised perhaps all too fully, probably because of political difficulties.

[17] There is a very extensive literature on the subject; readers wishing an introduction may consult Fuchs (1996), Newhouse (1996), and Iglehart (1999).

Table 4.10 *Ownership composition of the health sector,
United States, percent*

Service	Units/Date	Public	Nonprofit	Forprofit
All hospitals	Admissions/1997	18	70	12
Short-stay hospitals	Beds/1997	17	69	14
Psychiatric hospitals	Beds/1991	91	3	6
HMOs	Enrollees/1996	0	42	58
PPOs	Plans/1995	0	20	80
Outpatient dialysis facilities	Facilities/1997	..	..	65

Sources: Rose-Ackerman (1996: Table 4: 710); National Center for Health
Statistics (1999); for all hospitals and PPOs, Claxton *et al.* (1997: 12); for
overall HMO enrollment, Gabel (1997: 135); for dialysis facilities,
Nissenson and Rettig (1999:172).

First let us take the supply side. One well founded public
belief in many transitional economies is that the US health
sector is extremely decentralized. It has no powerful hierarchical, bureaucratic organization to run it from a single
center. On the other hand, it is wrongly held that US health-
care delivery comes almost entirely from profit-oriented, privately owned bodies. Data on the forms of ownership in the
US health sector are presented in tables 4.10 and 4.11. They
show that nonprofit ownership is predominant in much of
the US system, particularly for inpatient care, where there are
numerous hospitals owned by churches, foundations, and
nonstate universities. The weight of the forprofit private
sector is sizable but not overwhelming. Interestingly, the proportion of public hospital beds rose over the period covered
by table 4.11 (1980–96). The ownership structure has not
become rigid. More detailed figures show that many hospitals have changed hands, with private hospitals becoming
public ones or vice versa (see Needleman, Chollet and
Lamphere 1997; Melnick, Keeler and Zwanziger 1999).

Table 4.11 *Changing ownership of hospital beds, United States, 1980–1996*

Type of hospital	Percent of inpatient beds in each ownership category in		
	1980	1990	1996
Public	21	18	33
Private	79	82	67
Nonprofit	..	74	57
Forprofit	..	8	10

Source: OECD (1999b).

The situation with financing is far less extreme than many people believe. Looking back to table 4.4, it emerges that about 46 percent of health spending is public expenditure. The two main components of public financing are the health-insurance programs for the elderly and the poor officially in need of welfare assistance (Medicare and Medicaid). Apart from that, the administration also contributes directly to medical research and to medical training of doctors. However, it is certainly true that private sources provide a much higher proportion of health-care financing in the United States than they do in the developed European countries (see table 4.4).

One less known, but important feature of the American financing system is that various specific redistribution processes take place. The insurance schemes run by the government have important redistributive features. Some employers do not deduct a flat sum from their employees' wages as an insurance premium, but a pay-related contribution in bands or on a sliding scale. This also implies a redistribution in favor of the lower-paid employees, although in general the employment-based insurance system is regressive – i.e. imposing a greater proportional burden on lower-income employees.[18] Many hospitals apply cross-subsidies, using part of the revenue collected from the insured and patients paying privately to cover spending on patients without insurance or on research.[19] Increasing competitive pressures, however, limit the ability of providers to continue this practice.

For a long time, provision and insurance in the United States were quite separate parts of the health-sector mechanism. The latter largely took place through private insurance companies who reimbursed patients for their medical bills. Nominally, some of the premiums were paid by the insured and some by employers. In national terms, this employment-based traditional indemnity insurance arrangement covered a very high proportion of workers.

Various integrated or semi-integrated forms have been gaining ground in recent years (see, for instance, Feldstein 1994; Glied 2000). The common feature of these is that the insurer supervises or "manages" treatment to eliminate expenditure it considers superfluous, hence the name "managed care." The organization either has doctors of its own, or has contractual relations with specified providers. These are known in American parlance as "managed care organizations." Table 4.12 shows the main types and their prevalence.

One integrated form, the HMO, traditionally dominated and represented managed care. As mentioned in previous chapters, an HMO combines the function of an insurer on the financing side, with that of primary care on the provision side. Many HMOs also have their own specialist physicians, at least in the main specialties, and own or contract with one

[18] The regressivity of US employment-based insurance stems from two factors: the large proportion of employers who deduct a *fixed* premium contribution from wages (akin to a fixed-head tax which is a greater burden on lower-income employees), and the tax exemption of employer-provided health insurance (which bestows greater benefits on higher-income employees with higher marginal tax rates). See Reinhardt (1998).

[19] This is not a specifically American occurrence, of course. The same often applies in many other countries.

Table 4.12 *Distribution of employees among types of health plans, United States, 1987–1995, percent*

Types of plan	1987	1990	1993	1995
Unmanaged FFS	41	5	Marginal	Marginal
Managed FFS	32	57	49	27
HMOs	16	20	22	28
PPOs	11	13	20	25
Point-of-service plans	..	5	9	20

Notes:
The difference between managed and unmanaged forms and the conditions for HMOs are explained in the text.

PPO stands for Preferred Provider Organization. Under such a plan the insurer contracts with a network or panel of providers to provide medical services. Providers are often paid on a discounted FFS basis in exchange for a guaranteed flow of patients. Enrollees usually have the freedom to see physicians outside the plan network if they are ready to pay the difference in costs out of their own pocket.

A point-of-service plan is a managed-care plan that allows enrollees to choose physicians not affiliated with the plan if they are willing to pay substantially more out of their own pocket for such care.

Sources: Iglehart (1992: 745) for 1987 and 1990; Jensen *et al.* (1997: 125) for 1993 and 1995.

or more hospital(s). Members can choose only doctors belonging to the HMO group. Apart from that, the HMO physician (primary-care doctor or HMO specialist) decides what further outpatient or inpatient care the patient is to receive – or, more precisely, what outpatient or hospital treatment the HMO is prepared to finance. In this sense HMOs are an integrated form, but they are still decentralized; treatment decisions are not governed by a nation-wide centralized organization. Instead, the HMO relies on organizational and payment incentives to align individual providers' interests with that of the larger organization.

More recently, forms of managed care that give patients a wider scope of choice, such as "preferred provider organiza-

tions" and "point-of-service plans," have been gaining substantial market share (see table 4.12). HMOs and these other
"managed," integrated insurer–provider organizations
compete with each other and with other forms of insurance.

What are the achievements and shortcomings of the
present American health-care system? The most adverse
feature is that in recent years a substantial proportion of
Americans, estimated at about 15 percent or over 40 million
people, have no medical insurance. Moreover, there is a less
well known but also serious problem of "under-insurance,"
exposing millions more Americans to high levels of financial
risk from medical expenses. In cases of life and death or other
extreme emergencies, there are public and private providers
that treat the uninsured as well, but treatment for less serious
conditions is often inappropriately postponed. For routine
nonemergency services, such people can rely at most on
charitable institutions or public hospitals and clinics that are
often overcrowded. Studies have shown that the uninsured
"receive on average only about 60 percent of the health services received by insured Americans," after adjusting for
other factors that might explain the difference, such as
income and demographics (Altman, Reinhardt and Shields
1998: 5).

The stratum of uninsured does not coincide with the group
of poor officially registered as needing assistance, because
the latter, as mentioned earlier, are entitled to subsidized
medical care through the Medicaid program. The majority of
the uninsured are "working poor." Only 16 percent of the
uninsured in 1992 were in families in which the head of the
household did not work; the rest were in families supported
by full-time or part-time workers (Rowland, Feder and
Keenan 1998: 28). Most are above, yet not far from, the official poverty line. The high cost of private health insurance is
a substantial barrier to their obtaining coverage. Others have
earnings that could afford them and their families insurance,
but they fail to buy insurance for some reason. They may

hope they will not need health care and prefer to spend their limited money on something else.[20] A few lack the basic educational level necessary to grasp the need for medical insurance, or consider it against their religious beliefs.[21] And others truly in need are held back by modesty or pride from accepting the "welfare" stigma associated with official assistance to the poor. Whatever the reasons, it is a disgrace to a rich society like America's for a wide stratum of the public to have no medical insurance. This is a serious breach of the second ethical postulate, principle 2, the principle of solidarity. It offends the specific egalitarian sense mentioned earlier, which requires that everyone have access at least to basic health care.[22]

There has been a long-standing debate in American society and the political arena about how to overcome this serious shortcoming. President Clinton, at the beginning of his first term, was ready to introduce some form of universal entitlement to health care. That intention ran up against such opposition in Congress that he had to retreat from it. In his second term, universal entitlement, or compulsory general medical insurance (which amounts to the same thing) was not even placed on the agenda, although incremental changes have proceeded apace.[23]

There have been several analyses of why the Clinton plan failed. Opinions differ (see, for instance, Skocpol 1996). It is

---

[20] Many people do not take out voluntary insurance because they know that the law obliges the health-care network to provide free care in emergency cases. They trust that the doctors will interpret "emergency treatment" sufficiently widely in their case, and that they will not need further treatment in any case.

[21] In 1993, 7 percent of uninsured adults reported that they were uninsured by choice or because they did not believe in insurance (Rowland, Feder and Keenan 1998: 29).

[22] Table 4.9 shows that the United States, the richest of the five countries surveyed, was the one with the highest proportion of respondents who had trouble paying their medical bills.

[23] For example, the State Children's Health Insurance Program, passed as part of the Balanced Budget Act of 1997, provides over $20 billion in grants over several years to states to expand health-insurance coverage for children.

certainly worth noting the main argument advanced by the opponents of the Clinton proposals. The introduction of universal entitlement, they said, would involve establishing a vast, centralized bureaucracy, and so raising taxes. This would be incompatible with American tradition, which is imbued with the spirit of decentralization, competition, individual enterprise, restricted federal powers, and relatively low rates of taxation.

Many people, even of those on Clinton's side politically who support his aims in public welfare, argue that it does not require universal health care financed by the state to tackle the problem of the uninsured 15 percent. The problem could be resolved by targeting state intervention specifically at them.

The failure of the Clinton plan exemplifies how a reform program, however well intentioned, cannot be divorced from initial conditions – in this case, a decentralized existing mechanism and nonstate financing of most expenditure. Pragmatic reformers must pay close attention to established traditions and expectations.

It would be misplaced, of course, to assess a country's health sector simply in terms of one feature, in this case the specific egalitarian criterion of "equal access," important though that criterion may be. The performance of the American health-care system also should be reviewed and judged according to other criteria.

Decentralization and competition within sectors give individuals great freedom of choice, upholding principle 1, individual sovereignty. Most Americans have the chance of withdrawal: they can go to a new doctor, a new hospital, or a new insurer if they are dissatisfied. This freedom is limited, of course, by geographic considerations such as local monopolies. A stronger constraint is that many people's insurance is arranged by their employer, which normally contributes financially to the cost, and accordingly restricts the choice of insurance in its own interest. A firm may offer its employees

only a single, relatively cheap alternative.[24] However, in spite
of these constraints, many people still have various opportunities to choose, which is something American citizens value
highly.

Here as in other sectors of the economy, competition
induces quality improvement and technical development, in
accordance with principle 4, requiring incentives for efficiency. The wide freedom of initiative engenders unpar-
alleled scientific achievements. The United States is
undeniably the leading country in the world for medical
research with practical applications.[25]

Surveys of public satisfaction reveal the ambiguity with
which the American public views the health sector, usually
considering their own personal care excellent but the system
as a whole flawed. In the most recent comparisons with
several other industrialized democracies, however, public
discontent in the United States does not seem to be strikingly
higher or lower than in many other countries (see table 4.9).

It is remarkable that the United States has by far the highest
volume of health spending *per capita*, and the proportion of
GDP it spends on health is also the greatest by far (see column
2 of table 4.4). This proportion has grown particularly since
1975. Table 4.13 compares the growth in the proportion of
health expenditure in the United States and other OECD
countries between 1960 and 1997. This shows that the
American proportion has risen much faster than the OECD
average, and faster than that of any other OECD country
except Spain. There, however, health spending in 1960 was

---

[24] A 1997 survey of a representative sample of nonelderly insured adults
found that 42 percent were given no choice of health plan, and of those
who had some choice, 20 percent complained of not having enough
variety (Gawande *et al.* 1998: 187).

[25] In the words of Donna Shalala, the longest-serving secretary of health and
human services in US history, "at the top, ours is the best health care in
the world. There is no substitute for the great American academic health
centers . . . At the low end, though, our system can be lousy, particularly
for people who are not treated early enough" (Shalala and Reinhardt
1999: 47).

Table 4.13 *Growth of health expenditure, OECD countries,
1960 and 1997*

| Country | Share of total health expenditure in total domestic expenditure (percent) | |
	1960	1997
Australia	4.8	8.4
Austria	4.3	8.2
Belgium	3.4	8.0
Canada	5.3	..
Denmark	3.6	8.7
Finland	3.8	8.2
France	4.3	10.0
Germany	4.9	10.9
Greece	3.4	7.8
Iceland	3.2	8.0
Ireland	3.6	7.7
Italy	3.6	7.9
Japan	3.0	7.2
Luxembourg	..	7.8
Netherlands	3.9	9.2
New Zealand	4.2	7.6
Norway	2.9	8.1
Portugal	..	7.3
Spain	1.6	7.5
Switzerland	3.1	10.5
Sweden	4.6	9.3
Turkey	..	3.8
United Kingdom	3.9	6.8
United States	5.3	13.7

Source: OECD (1999b).

a mere 1.6 percent of GDP, and after an almost fivefold
increase it is still only 7.5 percent, hardly more than half the
proportion in the United States.

The high level and growth rate of health spending in the
United States results from a combination of several factors, a
few of which merit enumeration.

First, when citizens themselves largely decide how much of their household budget to spend on health, they give health spending much higher priority than politicians usually do when they decide the structure of budget expenditure. So one reason why the US proportion of health spending to GDP is higher than elsewhere is that consumer sovereignty applies more fully.

A second factor, mentioned already in another connection, is that the United States is the world's foremost country in the development of medical technology. Here as in other fields, pioneering technology is the most expensive to apply. It usually becomes cheaper per patient later, when the process has spread widely and the new device or drug can go into mass production, although per-unit cost reduction may be offset by a higher volume of users. Much of the research and development (R & D) costs of scientific advance are met by American society, notably the patients paying the most for their medical treatment. And policies promoting widespread diffusion and access to the latest technologies tend to put upward pressure on overall health expenditure.

A third factor is the high level of physicians' earnings. American doctors earn about five times the national average, which is even higher than in Germany, where the proportion (although very high) is only four times higher than average (see table 5.12, p. 167).

A fourth reason for a high level of US health spending is administrative costs associated with decentralized insurance and competitive markets. These costs include the marketing expenses and contracting costs of competing insurers and providers, as well as the transaction costs of patients and providers required to file different claims forms for different payers.

A fifth cause of the high proportion of health spending is that some of the services are extravagant, superfluous, and even harmful. The output of the health sector has risen faster than was justified. Particularly before HMOs and other forms of managed health-care organizations became widespread, no one in the decentralized economic mechanism had sufficient incentives to keep costs down. It served the interests of some physicians, in fact, to order more tests and perform more operations than were necessary.

The patient and the doctor passed the costs of expensive treatment on to the insurer, who in turn passed it on to the payers (employers and insureds) as higher premiums. In most European countries, on the other hand, the majority of the health-care costs were financed directly or indirectly out of the state budget, so that fiscal pressures ultimately limited the scope for spending.

This ties in with a sixth factor: the frequency of medical malpractice lawsuits, in which courts often award very high damages, putting further pressure on premiums to cover the associated legal costs. Furthermore, the likelihood of such lawsuits may encourage providers to order superfluous tests and consultations (called *defensive medicine*), to defend themselves against possible allegations of malpractice.

It is not yet possible to say definitively whether fiscal pressure from a system of state financing is the only possible way to constrain runaway health-care expenditure. It seems as if managed-care organizations may be able to curb the process of jacking up and passing on costs, by simultaneously giving patients, doctors, and insurers an interest in cost reduction. Patients are given an incentive to be sparing by the co-payments (although demand-side cost-sharing requirements in managed-care organizations are often minimal), and because they are offered a choice between cheaper and dearer insurance plans. Almost surely of greater significance is the incentive given to doctors and other health-care providers to keep down costs (see chapter 3, p. 88). In addition, the organization directly intervenes in the expenditure – manages care – in various ways. For instance, under some circumstances it calls for a second medical opinion before hospital admission or certain kinds of surgery. It monitors the length of stays in hospital. It checks after the event whether treatment has been appropriate, and so on. Such stricter control on expenditure can have harmful side-effects as well. Patients may be denied on cost-cutting grounds the tests, treatment, or medicines they really need.[26] Providers have an incentive to shun the most severely ill, which leads to risk selection and inequitable access. There are many justified complaints, so that there is a search to find better ways of reconciling patients' requirements, raising the quality of care, and curbing the rise in costs.[27]

The spread of HMOs and other forms of managed care, the controversy and criticism over their practices, and the first pragmatic steps to remedy blatant faults all show the dynamism and the willingness to experiment and innovate, characteristic of the American health sector.

---

[26] For other negative consequences, see chapter 3 (p. 88).

[27] Legislation can be expected, and has in fact been widely debated, to regulate what kinds of provision an HMO or other managed-care organization may deny and what it is obliged to finance. As noted, more flexible practices are already widespread, whereby extra treatment requested by the patient can be prescribed so long as the patient makes a co-payment towards the extra expenditure, as in preferred provider organizations and point-of-service plans.

5

The health sector in Eastern Europe: the initial state

As with the political structure and with other spheres of the economy, the health sector in the various Eastern European countries inherited from the socialist system situations that differed in many respects. However, this chapter concentrates on similarities rather than differences. Most of the common attributes are described here, while some others will be clarified later, when the reform proposals are discussed.

The economic mechanism of "classical socialism"

The socialist system underwent many changes over several decades of history. The model of the Stalin period, before the reforms oriented towards "market socialism," is referred to as the "classical" socialist system.[1] Of course, there were differences between countries even in the classical period. This account confines itself to the main common characteristics. We omitted from chapter 4 (p. 111) a description of the sixth model, "Public provision of medical care: the Soviet model," which now ensues.

The health sector is an integral part of the command economy. It does not differ in the least from the other sectors in its economic mechanism. All the sector's activity is centrally controlled. At the peak is the health minister, who is in

---

[1] For the distinction between classical and reform socialism and the main characteristics of the two periods, see Kornai (1992b).

turn directed by his superiors in the communist party and the state. Orders filter down from him through the bureaucratic hierarchy to the functionaries controlling the lowest-level organizations: hospitals, outpatient clinics, and district doctors' offices providing primary health care. They in turn direct the doctors, nurses, and other medical personnel under their command (in smaller units directly and in larger ones via a further level of bureaucracy).

All institutions providing medical care are state-owned. Whether they are owned by central or local governmental organizations differs from country to country. All those who work in the health sector are state employees. The requisite superior functionary decides who shall be assigned where, who shall be promoted, and who shall be dismissed. Pay-scales are determined centrally.

All health-care-related buildings and equipment are state-owned as well, with the resources and equipment required to run them being allocated to the health sector by the central organization for the management of materials. There is central decision-making about investment projects, which largely decide the capacity of each health-care institution (e.g. hospital or clinic).

Development of the health sector is decided when a decision is made, at the highest political level, about how much of the aggregate resources of the economy to allot to the sector. The dictator and his immediate associates, or formally the Central Committee or the even narrower circle, the Politburo, decide what weight the sector should receive relative to the other sectors. Ordinary citizens have no say at all.

The political leadership in the classical Stalinist period gave different priorities to the different branches of the economy. For instance, high priority always went to heavy industry, especially the arms industry, while the health sector was always among the low-priority branches. Although the total resources devoted to the health sector increased as the economy grew, its share in the allocation remained consistently low. The constant neglect of the health sector is a typical example of how classical socialism infringed principle 8, the requirement of harmonious growth. This, along with the faulty incentives present, was a big factor behind the poor quality of the provisions and the technical backwardness.

The classical socialist system is the ultimate manifestation of paternalism: the ideology and the practice of the system conflict strongly with principle 1, the idea of individual sovereignty. The communist party's philosophy is, "We will look after you. You will receive free health care. We, on the other hand, will decide what care you receive and how much of it." So one of the main characteristics of the classical Soviet model is a universal entitlement to free health care.

Patients have no freedom of choice. For example, in Hungary and Yugoslavia, physicians worked in territorially organized district doctors' offices, and each patient was clearly assigned to one and only one doctor. This district doctor (equivalent to PCP, in US parlance) acted as a "gatekeeper," deciding whether to diagnose and administer the treatment or send the patient on to a specialist or a hospital for further examinations, and also decided which polyclinic or hospital it would be. If the doctor referred the patient on, there would again be one doctor responsible who decided on the further measures. In such a system, there is no room for appeal.

In other countries, such as Bulgaria, the Czech Republic, Slovakia, Poland, and Romania, a network of polyclinics has developed to combine primary care and outpatient specialist care. However, the situation does not differ from the one just described: the individual still has no freedom of choice. The polyclinic doctor is responsible for the patient's treatment and referrals.

The classical socialist system is a "semi-monetized" economy. Input–output transactions are settled in money, but very broadly, for economic organizations as a whole. There are accounts to show whether the budget revenues exceed or fall short of expenditure. However, the difference between an organization's income and its expenditure does not hold great significance. At no level in the hierarchy do decision-makers act as "profit-maximizers" or "cost-minimizers." As mentioned before, resources are distributed mainly in a direct, physical form, as centralized bureaucratic decisions, input quotas, material allocations, and staffing quotas (with assignment of employees to specific jobs in certain countries and at certain periods). The real action concerns the allocation of physical inputs and outputs, to which the budget allocations in money and the money transactions are at most an accompaniment.

With this mechanism, the integration of provision and financing discussed in chapter 3 (p. 76) is difficult to interpret, because the financing is not attached to specific health-care transactions and its role is not essential in any case. However, provision and the input allocations required for it can be said to be linked; to that extent, the Soviet model is an integrated system.[2]

Chronic shortage appears in the health sector, just as it does in other branches of the classical socialist system. The mere fact that all citizens are entitled to free care engenders shortage. The phenomenon of "moral hazard" appears in an extreme form; patients have no incentive whatever to moderate their demands. The usual symptoms of a shortage economy are especially obvious: crowding in clinics and hospitals, long queues in waiting rooms, and waiting lists for hospital beds, examinations, treatments, and long-postponed surgery. Forced substitution is common: the specialist or

---

[2] This in itself means it would be inaccurate to equate the classical, Soviet-type mechanism with the centralized, tax-financed British type. (On the latter, see chapter 4, p. 108.) There is a similarity in that both are centralized and under state control – both are "integrated." However, apart from the dissimilar political contexts, they differ in that state financial allocations are distributed in the British type, while these play only a secondary role in the Soviet type.

medicine really required is in short supply, so that lower-quality substitutes are consulted or prescribed instead.

Two circumstances blunt or obscure the appearance of shortage phenomena. One is the lack of health information. The vast majority of patients have no idea what is being denied them. The other important factor concerns the "gate-keeper" role. Strict conditions are imposed on those who refer patients for tests or for outpatient or hospital treatment or specific procedures in a hospital (such as an operation). The doctors know how scarce the capacity is in clinics and hospitals, so they are sparing with referrals, which somewhat reduces the overcrowding in the clinics and hospitals.

Under the conditions of a command economy and chronic shortage, all spheres of the economy lack the incentives that impel the discovery and introduction of new products, procedures, and technologies. This general observation applies fully to the health sector. Except for a few exceptionally devoted and talented innovators, the scientific and technical development found under the classical Soviet model tended to be of an imitative character. The object was to duplicate the innovations developed in the health sectors and pharmaceutical industries of developed Western economies, legally or by infringing patent rights, and usually after a substantial interval.

Let us sum up what has been said so far. The causes are state monopoly and bureaucratic centralization, coupled with the shortage economy. The effects are the total defense-lessness of patients, a low quality of care, and sluggish scientific and technological development. There are heavy negative items weighing on one side of the scales.

On the other hand, it would be a mistake to omit the items on the other side: security, solidarity, and equality, albeit at an extremely low level. One aspect of this is a relatively comprehensive and effective system of basic public health services, such as immunizations. More generally, the state itself operates as a comprehensive, general insurance institution.

The public becomes used to this and considers it natural. People expect the state to perform this role. This expectation is one of the underlying legacies of the socialist system, with which every later policy has to reckon as a political reality.

However, the paternalist security and equal access to care in the classical, pre-reform period are significantly discredited by manifestations of corruption and privilege. It is possible to obtain more attentive care, treatment out of turn, services that would otherwise be denied, or more expensive medicines, by having personal connections, occupying a high place in the hierarchy, doing doctors a favor, or even bribing them with money or presents. There are special hospitals (or wards within hospitals) for the high-ranking members of the "nomenclature," with less crowding and better equipment. In many places there are several grades of privilege, with the best hospital reserved for the highest stratum of the elite, a less good, but far above-average hospital for the rest of the elite, and so on. There is no reason to expect health care to be immune to the corruption and privilege that imbues every transaction in society under the classical socialist system.

It should be emphasized, at the end of the description of the "classical" socialist health-care mechanism, that the mechanism has not survived unchanged in any Eastern European country. However, remains of it can be perceived in many respects.

Redefining the right to provision

The shift away from the classical system has not been uniform. When and where reforms have been introduced differs from country to country.[3] The book does not provide

[3] Goldstein et al. (1996) and PHARE (1998) provide a general review of health-care reform in the Eastern European countries. The summary that Saltman, Figueras and Sekallarides (1998) gives of health-care reform in Europe includes much notable information and analysis to do with the specific problems of Eastern Europe as well. Summary references appear

an up-to-date report on reform, because the situation is constantly changing, in ways that differ from country to country.

The intention instead is to outline the general tendencies. The beginnings of notable changes before the political turning point of 1989–90 were largely confined to former Yugoslavia, Hungary, and Poland. The process accelerated in the 1990s in several countries, but it has remained far less dramatic than the reforms achieved in other sectors of the economy.

The next few sections provide only a brief, initial survey of some main directions in the shift. We will return to each of these tendencies later. This chapter is descriptive in character. Critical analysis of the present mechanisms will appear in later chapters that describe the reform proposals.

The first aspect to examine is how the legal system in Eastern Europe defines the right to health care. Every citizen was entitled, under the classical socialist system, to free care (as defined by the state) and to nothing else. At least according to the letter of the law, patients could not buy extra provisions for money.[4] No country retained this unlimited, universal entitlement after the change of system. Table 5.1 reveals how the rights were altered: (1) Most countries specifically defined the circle of those entitled. Citizenship is not a sufficient condition. Provision is due primarily to individuals and their family members who have paid social-insurance contributions. The

in Orosz, Ellena and Jakab (1998) and Mihályi (2000) for Hungary, WHO (1999a) for Bulgaria, WHO (1999b) for Croatia, OECD (1998a) for the Czech Republic, Chawla, Berman and Kawiorska (1998) for Poland, WHO (1996b) for Slovakia, and Toth (1997) for Slovenia.

The authors received great help in gathering information about the Eastern European countries from Andrea Despot (Croatia), Matjaz Nachtigal (Slovenia), and Christian Pop-Eleches (Romania), all three of them students at Harvard University, and from Ventsislav Voikov (Bulgaria, Agency for Economic Analysis and Forecasting).

[4] In most socialist countries, the constitution declared that citizens had the right to health care. In two countries, Bulgaria and Poland, the constitution stipulated that *free* health care was a civil right, and in a third, Czechoslovakia, there was separate legislation stating the same. For an international comparison of such constitutional rights, see Hofmann *et al.* (1998).

Table 5.1 *Right to health care, Eastern Europe, late 1990s*

Country	Basis of entitlement[1]	Basic coverage[2]
Bulgaria	Citizenship until June 1999, since then contributions	Almost universal
Croatia	Contributions	Co-payments for house calls by a doctor or nurse, all visits to a doctor's office, and certain preventive examinations/tests
Czech Rep.	Contributions	Universal except for dental care and cosmetic surgery
Hungary	Contributions	Universal except for dental care and cosmetic surgery
Poland	Citizenship until 1998, since then contributions	Almost universal
Romania	Citizenship until 1998, since then contributions	Almost universal
Slovakia	Contributions	Universal except for dental care and cosmetic surgery
Slovenia	Contributions	Almost universal, with universal copayment

Notes:

[1] Wherever the German model was introduced, it was stipulated in principle who pays contributions for whom. Countries differ as to whether children are insured through their parents' contributions (as, for instance, in Hungary and Bulgaria) or through contributions paid by the state (for instance, in the Czech Republic and Slovakia). The contributions covering the health care of old-age pensioners are generally paid by the state or by the pension fund. In practice, the state in several countries (in the Czech Republic, Hungary, and Slovakia) has pruned its contribution payments, thereby reducing the central budget deficit and raising the deficit of the social-insurance organization.

[2] Pharmaceuticals have ceased to be prescribed free of charge everywhere. On this, see table 5.6 (p. 155).

Sources: WHO (1996a, 1996b, 1999a, 1999b, 1999c); Toth (1997); NERA (1999); OECD (1999a).

state undertook to pay the social-insurance contributions of some other, large groups of nonemployed.[5] (2) Several countries have removed certain services (such as dental care) from the scope of free treatment. In other words, they have begun the process of distinguishing between *basic care* available free (or almost free) under the social-insurance scheme and *supplementary care* that can be bought with money, although this remains within a relatively narrow range. (3) Several countries have ceased to offer various services entirely free of charge. They have introduced co-payments, to augment the social-insurance contributions.

Despite these restrictions, a very wide range of the public still receives health care almost free of charge. The man in the street, who has not followed the detailed measures, has the feeling that the universal entitlement remains, and most of them continue to expect it. This is one of the most important starting conditions for all further health-care reform. The majority of people will consider they are being deprived of their rights if there is a more radical restriction of the universal entitlement than has occurred already.

The separation of financing from provision

The command economy broke down in the 1990s, in every country in Eastern Europe, even where the change had not occurred much earlier, as it had in Yugoslavia, Hungary, and Poland. That inevitably brings an increase in the role of money and financial settlement of resource allocation. To apply the typology introduced in chapter 4 (p. 72), the change in the health sector can be described, in settlement terms, as a shift from the Soviet model ("public provision")

---

[5] Ensuring compliance with this measure is quite difficult even among the active population. Usually there is only a superficial check on whether patients applying for treatment have a social-insurance number. There is no check on whether they have actually paid contributions, whether they pay what the law stipulates, etc.

to the British model (the "National Health Service").
However, in every case the change has been inconsistent:

- Many specific health-care services have no price that
  the buyer (whether some state institution, the social-
  insurance apparatus, or the patient) can recognize and
  pay and the provider can receive. Instead, the individual services are paid for as part of the compensation for
  some aggregate service.
- The compensation is set so that it more or less covers
  the provider's operating costs, but it does not cover the
  costs of renewing and developing fixed assets. The calculation does not include depreciation. This ties in
  with the fact, mentioned before, that gross investment
  activity in the health sector is strongly centralized. One
  reason why the institution receiving the compensation
  for health-care delivery (for instance, the hospital or
  clinic) cannot make investment decisions is that it does
  not receive the revenue to fund them. The financial
  cover for its investments has to come from a central
  organization; it has to bargain for state subsidies. If it
  decides on such expenditure nonetheless, it will have
  to secrete the money for it – in defiance of the law – out
  of the funds received for its current inputs. For instance,
  it may fail to pay its doctors and other medical staff for
  working overtime so that it can buy a new instrument.
  This practice seriously distorts all the calculations
  required for resource allocation.
- Rational calculation is impeded by an impenetrable
  web of various differentiated subsidies.

This brings us to a problem familiar from the debates about
market socialism. At a level of sterile theoretical economic
reasoning, it is conceivable for there to be an economic mechanism that retains public ownership, but the agents in it
behave *as if* they were profit-maximizing private owners. This
makes it possible to apply a market mechanism that helps to

ensure an efficient allocation of resources. The problem with this idea (not just in the economy as a whole, but in the health sector) is that it does not take account of the actual behavior patterns induced by specific forms of ownership. Real owners would not tolerate a situation in which the compensation for their output did not cover depreciation and provide the funds for asset renewal and development. The health-care institutions of Eastern Europe, on the other hand, tolerate this, because that is what is required of them. If at least some of the services were provided by institutions in private hands, eventually that would force a radical change in the payment system, bringing in a health-care-pricing regime that allowed rational calculations to be made. That is called for even if most of the providers remain in public ownership.

The Eastern European countries usually turn from an integrated mechanism to a system that separates provision and financing. They develop a mechanism that resembles the German model, from two points of view. First, the social-insurance fund for health care has its own, separate source of revenue – a contribution that citizens are legally obliged to pay expressly for the purpose.[6] Secondly, the fund stands as a *purchaser* paying money to the provider as *seller*, from which it is institutionally distinct.

The settlement method before the separation combined the Soviet and the British models (see the typology in chapter 4, p. 72) in different proportions in different countries. The proportions depended on how far and how long the central allocation of inputs remained, and how long and how consistently the monetization of the economic processes – the application of payment in money – were being realized.

The years that appear in table 5.2 signify when each country shifted towards the German model. This leaves open the

---

[6] This book usually omits the attribute "health care" from the phrase "health-care insurance fund," as it is clear from the context whether the argument refers to the health-care fund or the pension and health-care funds as a whole.

Table 5.2 *Shift toward the German model of social insurance, Eastern Europe*

Country	Year of introduction	Autonomy	Controlled by the government	Notes
Bulgaria[2]	1999–		Yes up to 2000	
Romania[2]	1999–	Yes		Since 1999, geographically decentralized SIFs[1]
Poland	1999–	Yes		Since 1999, geographically decentralized SIFs
Albania	1994–		Yes	Restricted SIF finances only drug reimbursement and PCPs
Czech Rep.	1992–	Yes		Since 1993, decentralized, competing, nonprofit health-insurance funds
Slovakia	1994–	Yes		Since 1993, decentralized, competing, nonprofit health-insurance funds
Hungary	1991–	Yes up to July 1998	Yes from August 1998	
Croatia[2]	1945– (1993)	Yes		
Macedonia[2]	1945– (1991)		Yes	
Slovenia[2]	1945– (1992)	Yes		

Notes:
[1] SIF stands for Social Insurance Fund (for an explanation, see discussion in the text, p. 147).
[2] For an explanation of the dates see main text.
Sources: WHO (1996a, 1996b, 1999a, 1999b, 1999c); Toth (1997); OECD (1999a); personal communication by the Romanian Ministry of Health.

question of what legal status the purchaser, the social-insurance fund, has in each country. It may be some institution separate from the government and its central budget, with its own governing body. Alternatively, it may be subordinate to the central government and operate as part of the governing bureaucracy (while remaining separate, within the government apparatus, from the bureaucracy controlling and inspecting the "sellers," the health-care providers). The columns of table 5.2 describing legal status, read "yes" where this distinction can be established clearly. In Hungary, for instance, the social-insurance fund has acted as an independent purchaser since 1991, and most of its revenues form an earmarked fund. To that extent, it resembles the German model. The fund was autonomous until mid-1998, since when it has been subordinate to the government (WHO 1999b).

In Tito's Yugoslavia, each republic ran its own health sector, which operated in a territorially decentralized form. Unlike other socialist countries, Yugoslavia did not discontinue the occupation-based social-insurance funds from before 1945. To that extent, the settlement system could be said to have resembled the German model, although it was otherwise a fairly fragmented and inefficient mechanism. Croatia, Macedonia, and Slovenia replaced this, at the beginning of the 1990s, with a national social-insurance fund.

After several years' preparation, Poland introduced in 1999 a mechanism that resembles the German model in its financing and payment procedures. Romania and Bulgaria were planning in 1999 to introduce the German model, but its introduction is likely to be delayed, although legislation separating financing from provision has come into effect.

Financing

We will first consider the demand side. Let us go through the possible sources of financing, according to the system of classification presented in chapter 3 (p. 74).

(A) State budget

As the post-socialist health sector in Eastern Europe shifts away from the mechanism applied under the classical social-ist system, it has adopted the German model to a greater or lesser extent, and radically reduced the proportion of health care financed directly by the state budget. However, the state does not withdraw from financing: its role varies from country to country, but remains very appreciable.

The central state budget continues to finance public health care (such as immunizations and chest screening). It still sup-ports or heavily subsidizes large, specialized national insti-tutions (such as cancer-research and transplantation institutes), much of the medical research, and medical train-ing. Central state financing of these activities is usually defended on the grounds of their strong external effects (externalities or aspects of public goods).

It has already been mentioned that the central state budget remains the main source of finance for larger investment pro-jects.

A bigger role in health-care financing than under the clas-sical socialist system goes to the decentralized regional insti-tutions financed by the state budget: to higher (provincial, county) and lower (town, village) levels of local government. This also entails the transfer of some property rights. However, the process is ambivalent. It increases the respon-sibility of local-government organizations for providing health care to the population and their powers to intervene, but the financial resources for doing so do not always increase proportionately. In the health sector, as in other spheres, strong tensions between central and local or regional government prevail.

(B) Compulsory social insurance

Once social insurance has been introduced, all employers and employees are obliged to pay social-insurance contributions.

Table 5.3 *Size of the health-care contribution and distribution of the contribution between employers and employees, Eastern Europe, late 1990s*

Country	Size of contribution (percentage of earnings)	Distribution of the contributions between employers and employees, percent
Albania	3.4	50:50
Bulgaria[1]	6.0	50:50
Croatia	16.0	50:50
Czech Rep.	13.5	66:33
Hungary[1]	14.0	79:21[3]
Macedonia	3.6	100:0
Poland[1]	7.5	0:100
Romania[1]	14.0	50:50
Slovakia	13.7	66:33
Slovenia[2]	12.8	50:50

Notes:

[1] From 1999.

[2] The size of the contribution has steadily fallen from 18 percent in 1992.

[3] In Hungary, employers pay a fixed amount every month as health contribution for each of their employees to the health insurance fund. The amount to be paid in 2000 is the equivalent of about 5 percent of the average wage.

Sources: Saltman and Figueras (1997); NERA (1999); WHO (1999a, 1999b, 1999c).

The size of these and the nominal split between employers and employees differ from country to country (see table 5.3).

The compulsory contributions form the main source of revenue for the social-insurance fund, including the health-insurance fund, although not usually the sole source. For the health sector as a whole, the social-insurance funds had become, by the end of the 1990s, the main sources of finance for health care in Eastern Europe.

At first sight, it appears that the social-insurance fund has to cover its expenditure out of its revenues, in other words that there is a budget constraint. How hard or soft is that budget constraint? Figure 5.1 shows the deficit of the social-

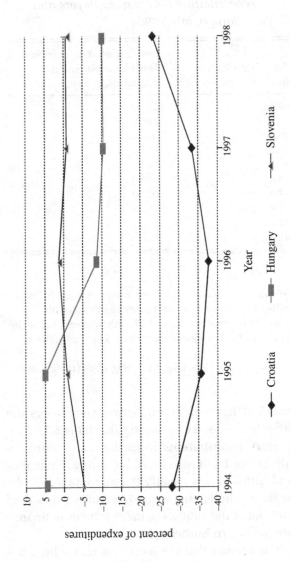

Figure 5.1 Deficit of social health insurance funds, Croatia, Hungary, and Slovenia, 1994–1998

Sources: PHARE (1998: Appendix), Statistical Office of the Republic of Slovenia (1998), Banka Slovenje (1999), Central Bureau of Statistics (1999), OECD (1999a).

Table 5.4 *State guarantees for maintaining the solvency of social health-insurance funds, Eastern Europe*

Country	Guarantees
Bulgaria (2000–)	In case of financial deficit, the SIF[1] will be allowed to use short-term, interest-free credits from the state budget or from extra-budgetary accounts and funds
Croatia (1993–)	Legal guarantee for paying the deficit of the SIF
Czech Rep. (1993–)	The Parliament can vote for providing credit in case of deficit of the SIF; not for other nonprofit health-insurance funds
Hungary	Legal guarantee for paying the deficit of the SIF
Poland (1999–)	SIFs must create a reserve fund, which can be used only with the approval of the Supervisory Board of the SIF; local government may also provide the territorial fund (unlimited) loans
Slovakia	Legal guarantee for the SIF, the IF[2] of the Ministry of Internal Affairs, Ministry of Defense, and Ministry of Transport and Communication, not for other nonprofit health-insurance funds
Slovenia	No guarantee

Notes:
[1] SIF stands for Social Insurance Fund (for an explanation, see discussion in the text, p. 147).
[2] IF stands for Insurance Fund.
Sources: WHO (1996a, 1996b, 1999a, 1999b, 1999c); Toth (1997); OECD (1999a).

insurance fund for health care in three countries. This is noticeably high in two countries and very low in the third, Slovenia. The explanation becomes obvious from careful study of table 5.4, which shows where there is legislation obliging the state to cover the health-insurance deficit automatically. Slovenia is the only one of the three countries featuring in figure 5.1 where there is no law obliging the central or local budget to bail out the health sector.[7] The

[7] Table 5.4 reveals that a bailout is not obligatory in the Czech Republic, but not prohibited either. The deficit can be covered if a parliamentary majority (i.e. the governing parties) can be convinced of the need to do so.

social-insurance funds in the other two countries – Croatia and Hungary – enjoy one of the most extensive of soft budget constraints. As table 5.4 shows, the situation is similar in several other post-socialist countries. Other spheres have to lobby to be rescued and put pressure on superior organizations. In the health sector, the law guarantees that the state will bail out an institution that runs a deficit. This rule itself encourages the toleration of waste, and it casts doubt on whether financing through social insurance is really separate from direct financing from taxation, since a deficit brings an automatic call on the latter.

(C) Voluntary insurance

There are several versions of this. Where it is compulsory for employees, including the self-employed, to have social insurance, other groups in society may be given the option of joining. They will be able to use the services covered by social insurance only if they have paid the required contributions.

Almost all post-socialist countries have seen the appearance of private commercial, forprofit insurers and nonprofit insurers offering medical insurance. The situation is outlined in table 5.5. Private insurance policies may be taken out by those who do not qualify for health-care social insurance (such as certain categories of foreigners resident in the country), and by those who want to cover supplementary services not funded by social insurance. We will return in more detail to this distinction later.

Column (3) of table 5.5 is worth noting: the role played by private insurance is still minimal.

(D) Direct payment by patients

All the Eastern European countries have begun to introduce a co-payment system. Social insurance continues to finance the bulk of the cost of care, but this is augmented by direct

Table 5.5 *Share of private health insurance, Eastern Europe*

Country	Provided by (1)	For what (2)	Expenditure for private health insurance (3)
Bulgaria	Commercial insurers	Amenities	Minimal
Croatia	Commercial insurers Nonprofit insurers	Amenities excluded from basic package, co-payments	Minimal
Czech Rep.	Nonprofit insurers Commercial insurers Foreign managed-care companies	Amenities excluded from basic package, care in private hospitals	Minimal
Hungary	Commercial insurers Voluntary health funds Foreign managed-care companies	Amenities, care in private hospitals, loss of salary during sickness, gratuities[1]	Minimal
Macedonia	Commercial insurers Voluntary health funds		Minimal
Poland	Commercial insurers Foreign managed-care companies	Amenities excluded from basic package, care in private hospitals	Minimal
Romania	Commercial insurers		Minimal
Slovakia	Commercial insurers Foreign managed-care companies		1 percent of THE (1995)
Slovenia	Slovenian Health Insurance Fund Commercial insurers on voluntary basis	Co-payments, drugs, emergency care abroad	12 percent of THE (1997)

Notes:
[1] The unofficial term "gratuity insurance" is common for some of the health-insurance policies available on the market.
THE = Total Health Expenditure.
Sources: PHARE (1998: Appendix); WHO (1999b).

contributions from patients. Table 5.6 shows the services for which a co-payment has to be made in each country, how much the co-payment is, and whether it is uniform or differentiated according to some criterion. However, the principle that patients should make a small contribution to the costs of certain services has begun to apply everywhere.

Within social insurance, patients have a choice of primary-care physician (PCP) in all Eastern European countries except Bulgaria. These act as "gatekeepers": social insurance will cover only the cost of a specialist or hospitalization if the PCP has referred the patient. However, there is a way in most countries of avoiding the gatekeeper and going straight to the chosen specialist or hospital, if a special co-payment is made. This co-payment is quite high in some countries, such as Bulgaria, Hungary, and Slovenia.

It is worth emphasizing that the introduction of co-payments in Eastern Europe as a whole and in the health sectors of individual countries is still quite sporadic and applicable only to a small proportion of health services. Patients pay directly for legal private care, for instance from a doctor, nurse, or physiotherapist in private practice or in a private hospital, etc. The giving of semi-legal or illegal gratuities to doctors and other medical providers is also common. These will be discussed in a later section.

Figure 5.2 presents an overall picture of the structure of financing by sources. It records the situation in 1997. It emerged earlier that Bulgaria, Poland, and Romania have introduced or are preparing to introduce reforms, so that the financing by 2000 will certainly have shifted towards the middle column. The upper part, by definition, contains the whole contribution paid by the public in the form of co-payments, through the mediation of private insurance, as fees for legal private practice, or as semi-legal gratuities. These figures are published for want of better information, but our impression is that they grossly underestimate the direct expenditure by the public.

Table 5.6 *Presence, absence, size, and sphere of co-payments, Eastern Europe, late 1990s*

Country	Pharmaceuticals	Outpatient care	Inpatient care
Albania	Yes, different reimbursement categories[1] On average 25 percent	No	No
Bulgaria	Yes, for all outpatient care, and in practice in hospitals as well	Appreciable except in cases of referral. Planned: 1 percent of the minimum wage/visit	Appreciable except in cases of referral. Planned: 2 percent of the minimum wage/day, for max. 20 days annually
Czech Rep.	Yes, different reimbursement categories[1] On average 10 percent	No, except for the material costs of one or two dental treatments	Yes, in institutions for chronic bed-ridden patients and for extra hotel services
Croatia	Yes, appreciable	10 percent	Yes, appreciable
Hungary	Yes, different reimbursement categories[1] On average 30 percent	Appreciable except in cases of referral	Yes, in institutions for chronic bed-ridden patients and for extra hotel services
Macedonia	20 percent	20 percent	10 percent
Poland	Yes, different reimbursement categories[1]	No	No
Romania	Yes, appreciable	No	No
Slovakia	Yes, different reimbursement categories[1]	No	No
Slovenia	Yes, different reimbursement categories[1]	Family doctor, 0–25 percent Dental care, 0–85 percent Other outpatient care, 0–85 percent	5–15 percent

Note:

[1] Most countries have introduced a differentiated system of subsidies for pharmaceuticals. The co-payments may vary according to the type of drug and according to the patients' social situation. Some must be paid for by the patient entirely and some receive state subsidies according to a set amount.

Sources: Chen and Mastilica (1998); NERA (1998a); PHARE (1998: Appendix); personal communication by Ventsislav Voikov, Bulgaria.

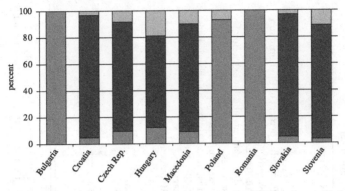

■ Central and local state budget (based on taxes)   ■ Social-insurance funds (based on contributions)
□ Households (direct expenses)

Figure 5.2 Sources of health-care financing, Eastern Europe, 1997

Sources: Tóth (1997); Bútora and Skladony (1998); OECD (1998a, 1999a); PHARE (1998: Appendix); WHO (1999a, 1999b, 1999c); personal communication by the Romanian Ministry of Health.

Delivery: public institutions

Having outlined the situation on the demand side, let us describe the supply side. As far as ownership relations are concerned, the vast majority of the institutions providing health care (hospitals and clinics) have remained in public ownership even in the countries where the reforms are most advanced. However, it should be considered that economics draws a distinction between ownership in the legal sense and actual exercise of various property rights, including rights of control. If this approach is taken to the situation of hospitals, clinics, and other institutions in public ownership, they are found to have shifted considerably since the classical socialist period. Here too the collapse of the command economy has made itself felt.

It is worth recalling the situation of state-owned enterprises in Hungary, and later in Poland, the Soviet Union, and China, in the period when experiments were being made with market socialism. (This is still occurring in the Chinese state-owned sector.) A curious hybrid emerged of centralized bureaucratic control and market coordination. Enterprises won a measure of independence, but there remained a dependency on a superior organization, which intervened in their activity in hundreds of ways. The ownership relations of publicly owned health-care institutions in Eastern Europe today, with their curious combinations of independence and dependency, are reminiscent of the market-socialist period.

Take, for instance, the responsibilities of hospital managers. (The same applies to the heads of other public health-care institutions as well.) They have wide powers in many partial decisions, just as the factory managers of market socialism did, but there remain superior organizations with great power over them:

- State organizations make the appointments. It varies from country to country whether this is the province of the health ministry or of the local (or regional) government. Whatever the case, the career of a health-sector manager is in the hands of the bureaucracy.
- State organizations decide about investment in the hospital. The centralization here is even stronger than it was in other sectors under market socialism. It bears a closer resemblance to the extreme centralism of the classical, command economy, before the market-socialist reforms. Essentially, all investment decisions are concentrated in the hands of central or local government. The power to decide lies mainly with the former, as local government has little money available for such purposes. Some investments attract a contribution from the social-insurance fund. There is almost no chance of the hospital or facility for self-financed investment.
- Either state organizations or social insurance set the budget for current expenditures. (Table 5.7 reviews the state's powers over investment and current spending.)

Table 5.7 *Responsibilities for budget allocations, Eastern Europe, 1998*

Country	Budgets covering operating costs	Budgets covering capital costs
Albania	SIF + MoF	MoF
Bulgaria[1]	MoH, other ministries	Municipal government, MoH
Croatia	SIF	Municipal government, MoH
Czech Rep.	SIFs	Municipal government, MoH
Hungary	SIF	Municipal government, MoH
Macedonia	SIF	SIF
Poland[1]	MoH	Municipal government, MoH
Romania[1]	MoF	Municipal government, MoH
Slovakia	SIFs	MoH, SIFs
Slovenia	SIF	MoH

Notes:
MoF = Ministry of Finance; MoH = Ministry of Health; SIF = Social Insurance Fund.
[1] From January 1999, in Poland, budgets for operating costs are allocated by the territorial SIFs. Covering capital costs will remain the responsibility of the MoH. In Bulgaria and Romania, from 2000, operating costs will belong to the SIF.
Sources: PHARE (1998: Appendix); WHO (1999b).

- Where stricter payment procedures have been adopted, the state body (or possibly the professional association of doctors, as a providers' "cartel") usually decides the relative "prices" or point scores of the various medical procedures.[8]
- In most countries, doctors working in hospitals and other public institutions qualify as public servants, ranked in the bureaucratic hierarchy according to their position and seniority[9] (see table 8.3, p. 302). Their sal-

---

[8] For the point system applied in the German model, see chapter 3 (p. 86).
[9] However, PCPs in Hungary do not qualify as civil servants, and neither PCPs nor other doctors dealing with outpatients so qualify in the Czech Republic and Slovakia.

aries depend in general on the budget allocation for paying health-care personnel, which is influenced by the fiscal position of the state, and in particular on the rank assigned to individuals in the bureaucratic pay structure.

- Although the manager in principle enjoys independence in operative decision-making, his superiors intervene in various ways. From time to time, they employ the customary method in a planned economy, of imposing "physical" targets. In Hungary, for instance, it turned out that there were many superfluous hospital beds. If an appropriate economic incentive had been provided, hospitals themselves would have had a vested interest in reducing the number of beds (and the proportionate costs of maintaining them). Instead, an administrative order was issued in 1994, designating how many beds each hospital had to eliminate, and when this campaign failed, ceilings for each county were set in 1996 (OECD 1999a: 121–2). Similar administrative interventions occurred in Bulgaria and the Czech Republic in 1997–8.

- It is laid down in principle that hospitals have to cover their expenditure out of their revenues; they have no right to exceed their budget allocations. In practice, this occurs repeatedly. A hospital runs into debt, having spent all its money for the year some months in advance. If it finds a source of credit, it may become deeply indebted. The outcome is usually a bailout, in which the deficit is covered and the debts are paid out of the central or local (or regional) state budget. Attempts to deny such assistance result in enormous pressure on the superior organizations, which eventually relent. The Polish health sector had amassed debts equivalent to several billion dollars by the end of 1998. The Finance Ministry then carried out an extensive bailout. Some of the debt was converted into state bonds and some transferred to banks by agreement, while some of the sums owed to suppliers were paid in cash (OECD 2000: 151). It was mentioned earlier in relation to financing that the social insurance fund usually has a soft budget constraint. The same clearly applies to provider organizations. The budget constraint of public health-care institutions is quite soft – the state does not require financial discipline of the sector. That leaves the way open for waste.

All these items will be familiar to those who studied the market-socialist experiments in reforming socialist countries, when attempts were made to place state-owned enterprises in a quasi-market environment.

Delivery: legal private activity

The first nonpublic hospitals, polyclinics, clinics, and other health-care providers have appeared in some countries, such as the Czech Republic, Hungary, Poland, Slovakia, and Slovenia. Some are owned by churches and private foundations and run on a nonprofit basis. Others are commercial, forprofit institutions. Of the latter, it is worth mentioning that most capital cities now possess foreign-owned health-care institutions with up-to-date equipment and doctors who speak foreign languages, mainly to cater to foreign residents. In the Eastern European region as a whole, the share of the nonpublic sector in the total volume of services provided by hospitals and other institutions is estimated to be very small, a couple of percent at most (as measured, for instance, in hospital beds or number of cases treated).

The one exception is the Czech Republic, where 9.4 percent of all the hospital beds were in private hospitals in 1997. Hungary also has a high private-sector proportion for certain special diagnostic and therapeutic treatments. By 1996, 80 per cent of the 5.4 billion Hungarian forints earmarked for kidney dialysis was paid to the private sector, and

Table 5.8 *Nonstate sector of health-care services, Hungary, 1996, selected data*

Types of service	Description	Percentage
Inpatient care	Ratio of the payments made to private hospitals for inpatient care by social insurance, to the total expenditure on inpatient care by social insurance	1.3
Dialysis	Ratio of the private sector in the HUF 5.4 billion budget	80
CT diagnostics	Ratio of privately owned machines to the total number of machines	75
MRI diagnostics	Ratio of privately owned machines to the total number of machines	57
Ambulance	Ratio of the payments made to private providers by social insurance to the total expenditure on ambulance services by social insurance	8
Specialist care in the home	Ratio of the payments made to private providers by social insurance to the total expenditure on home care by social insurance	0.8
Dentistry	Ratio of the payments made to private dentists by social insurance to the total expenditure on dentistry by social insurance	6.5
Primary care[1]	Ratio of self-employed primary-care doctors contracted by social insurance to the total number of primary-care doctors paid by social insurance	76

Note:
[1] The data on primary-care doctors refer to May 1997. The rest of the data are for 1996.
Source: The table was compiled by Virág Molnár, based on data provided by the National Health Insurance Fund.

75 per cent of the CT scanners and 57 per cent of the MRIs were in private hands (see table 5.8).

There has been a much bigger change among doctors practicing individually. Three categories can be distinguished here:

Primary-care physicians

Before the reforms, PCPs paid by social insurance were state employees, just like their colleagues in hospitals or specialist clinics.[10] In some Eastern European countries (the Czech Republic, Hungary, Romania, and Slovakia), the service has been "privatized," in other words, the doctors have been converted from state employees to self-employed professionals, working under contract from the insurer and from the local (or regional) government, which provides the premises and equipment.

Dentists

Privatization of dental care is quite extensive in most Eastern European countries.

The proportions of privatization in these two categories appear in table 5.9.

Other physicians in private practice

In most countries under the classical socialist system doctors were not allowed to practice privately, although it occurred illegally or semi-legally.[11] By the early 1990s private practice had been legalized in the Eastern European countries, making private practice widespread everywhere. This applied especially where there was a campaign for privatization, as there was in the Czech Republic in 1993, Slovakia in 1995, and Croatia in 1996.

Comprehensive data for the whole region were not access-

---

[10] The term "district doctor" was used on p. 137 for physicians to which patients were assigned compulsorily under the socialist system, on a territorial basis. Once this function is transferred to the private sector, it is more apposite to adopt the term current in the developed market economies.

[11] Individual private practice persisted in the Stalinist period in some countries, such as Hungary and East Germany, although only sporadically.

Table 5.9 *Share of private health-care providers, Eastern Europe, 1997,[1] percent*

Country	Primary-care physicians	Dentists	Pharmacies
Bulgaria	Minor	82	70
Croatia	Minor	96	~100
Czech Rep.	95	~100	~100
Hungary	76	40[1]	~100[1]
Poland	Minor	~100[1]	93
Romania	Minor	~100	75
Slovakia	98	~100	100
Slovenia[2]	14	37	68

Notes:
[1] Share of private inpatient beds is insignificant in all countries, except the Czech Republic, with 9.4 percent in 1997.
[2] 1998.
Sources: Bútora and Skladony (1998); Gyenes and Kastaly (1998); Institute of Health Information and Statistics of the Czech Republic (1998); Health Insurance Institute of Slovenia (1999); National Statistical Institute (1999a); WHO (1999b, 1999c); Romanian National Commission for Statistics (1999).

ible, but the partial information obtained suggests that the proportion of specialist care given through legal private practice is low in most countries, with some exceptions. Data about specialist services in private and public sectors in the Czech Republic and Budapest, Hungary are presented in tables 5.10 and 5.11. Table 5.11 shows that in some specialties the proportion is over 50 percent, though the Hungarian data are not directly comparable to the Czech ones (see notes to table 5.11). The spread of private activities is presented in terms of the time expenditure of physicians, in a survey taken in Krakow (Chawla *et al.* 1999: 10). This shows that 1,096 specialists spent an average of 10.8 hours a week on private practice, while in each case holding a job in a public organization. Mention will be made shortly of the semi-legal,

Table 5.10 *Distribution of health employees, by sectors, Czech Republic, 1997, percent*

Health employees	Central government	Municipal governments	Private sector
Physicians	39.4	5.8	54.8
Pharmacists	10.1	n.a.	89.9[1]
Paramedical personnel with higher education	55.8	8.3	35.9
Health employees, total	52.7	n.a.	47.3[1]

Note:
[1] Also includes those employed by the municipal government.
Source: Institute of Health Information and Statistics of the Czech Republic (1998).

concealed private practice that becomes tangled up with the activity of public employees.

Having looked at the privatization of medical care, it is worth mentioning the ownership of pharmacies. This side of health care has been wholly or overwhelmingly privatized in most countries (see table 5.9).

The picture that emerges is rather mixed. The main outlines are these: privatization of health services that are provided in small-scale organizations is quite extensive (in some countries, strongly so). Most large, hospital-scale activity remains in public ownership. The ownership structure in the health sector of the 1990s also resembles the situation found in industry and commerce during the market-socialist reforms of the communist period.

Doctors' earnings and gratuities

There is another, final resemblance between the market-socialist period and the health sector of the 1990s, and that is the tension apparent between legal and illegal (or semi-legal) earnings. The market-socialist period saw a strong

Table 5.11 *Share of private specialist providers, Hungary and Czech Republic*

Specialty	Budapest[1] Number of specialist licenses issued in 1999[2] Total	Budapest[1] Number of specialist licenses issued in 1999[2] Private	Private licenses/ all licenses[3] (percent)	Czech Republic Specialists[4] in nonstate sector/ specialists in both state and nonstate sector, 1997 (percent)
Internal medicine	1,892	1,217	64	48
Surgery	726	166	23	42
Obstetrics/gynecology	485	289	60	62
Pediatrics	478	324	68	76
Lung	155	38	25	…
Ear, nose, and throat	188	107	57	56
Ophthalmology	228	131	57	59
Dermatology and venereology[5]	176	132	75	64
Psychiatry[6]	278	69	15	64
Urology	131	59	45	33
Primary-care dentistry and special dentistry	1,974	1,877	95	…
Remedial gymnastics and massage	129	82	64	…

Notes:
[1] National data were not available.
[2] Licenses were issued under several categories: physician in private practice, health-care entrepreneur, private clinic, unit of a public or private, nonprofit, or private forprofit hospital.
[3] Following from the licensing mechanism, this ratio does not reflect the number of patients treated in the private sector, nor the number of doctors working there.
[4] Including specialists working in both outpatient and inpatient units.
[5] In the Czech Republic, only dermatologists.
[6] Neurology excluded.

Sources: Institute of Health Information and Statistics of the Czech Republic (1998); personal communication by István Felmérai of the National Public Health and Medical Officers' Service of Hungary (2000).

development of an economic sphere that remains important to this day, known variously as the "second," "shadow," "gray," "informal," or "hidden" economy. Most people have a "first," official, entirely legal income: earnings from work, or perhaps a pension, childcare benefit, unemployment benefit, or sick pay. They also have a second income. They are paid for certain services, but do not declare this for tax purposes or pay a social-insurance contribution on it.[12]

This duality appears in its strongest (and furthermore, least palatable) form in the health sector in Eastern European countries. This phenomenon also affects nurses and other health workers, but attention here will be focused on the physicians, where it is most prevalent.

One aspect of the phenomenon is that the pay of doctors employed by public institutions is disproportionately low. Tables 5.12 and 5.13 show that physicians are among the best-paid professionals in the traditional market economies of developed industrial countries. In Eastern Europe, medical earnings at the official work place in the mid-1990s were only 1.3 to 2 times the average earnings. This relatively low proportion understandably embitters and annoys the medical profession. The depressed state of doctors' pay seems to them less and less supportable as the development of the capitalist market economy causes progressive differentiation of earnings in other fields.

The other side of the coin is the system of what are known as "gratuities." Let us begin by clarifying what is meant here by gratuities.

(a)   The term "gratitude money"[13] in its strict sense means payments made by a patient or relative to a doctor or other health-care provider for services available free of charge under the prevailing mechanism. These services

---

[12] Many people live entirely on income from the second economy and have no official earnings at all.

[13] The term current in the Hungarian medical profession is the Latinate *parasolvencia*. The Polish term translates as "envelope money."

Table 5.12 *Physicians' earnings compared with earnings by all employees, 1992–1999, an international comparison*

Country	Year	Average earnings of all employees = 100
Czech Rep.	1998	170
Hungary	1998	127
Poland	1996	133
Romania	1997	121
Slovakia	1998 ˙	165
Slovenia	1997	211
Austria	1997	169
Finland	1998	208
Germany	1992	404
Sweden	1997	170
United Kingdom	1999	243
United States	1993	496

Note:
The most recent data available for each country have been given.
Sources: Compiled with help from János Varga. The data were collected from Physician Payment Review Commission (1996); US Bureau of the Census (1996); Czech Statistical Office (1999); Office for National Statistics (1999); ILO (1996, 1998, 1999a, 1999b); OMMK (1999); Romanian National Commission for Statistics (1999); Statistical Office of the Slovak Republic and VEDA (1999a, 1999b).

are financed by the state or by social insurance. The public institution in which the treatment takes place (for instance, a hospital) has already compensated the doctor and other medical personnel for the labor involved, usually in the form of salary. The person accepting the gratuity does not pay an extra fee or rent for use of the premises, equipment, drugs, and so on; these are also financed out of public funds.

The closest parallel to a health-sector gratuity is a tip given to a waiter in a restaurant. Or there was the case of car drivers during the shortage economy under the

Table 5.13 *Physicians' earnings compared with those of other serving as the basis of comparison = 100),[1] 1996–1999, an*

Occupation	Czech Rep. 1998	Hungary 1998	Poland 1996	Romania 1997	Slovakia 1998
All professionals[2]	90	98	113	..	128
Accountant	..	44	77	26	86
Architects[3]	101	106	85	..	..
Computer programmer	121	90	104	118	97
Economist[4]	91	55	..	..	..
Legal professionals[5]	80	51	61	..	94

Notes:
[1] Latest data based on average gross earnings. The US data show the median, as the middle scores for the population. US data in the category Professional specialty.
[2] Czech Republic: University-level study. Slovenia: Employees with university attainment. United Kingdom: Professional occupations. United States: Data in the category Professional specialty.
[3] Sweden and Poland: Architects, engineers, and related professionals.
[4] Slovenia: Economist–analysts–planner. Sweden: Social science and linguistics professionals.
[5] Czech Republic and Finland: Lawyers. Hungary: Lawyers, legal advisors. Slovakia: Lawyers excluding advocacy and jurisdiction. Slovenia: Basic law

socialist system who gave "black-market rides," carrying private passengers in a state-owned vehicle and pocketing the fare received. These are the most appropriate analogies, however undignified they may sound.

(b)   At least conceptually, gratuities are distinguishable from the proportion of the fees paid to doctors and other health-care providers in private practice (home nurses, physiotherapists, masseurs) that recipients fail to declare, mainly to evade tax. The provider in such cases does not offer an invoice and the patient does not request one. This is simply the customary "gray-economy" method of tax evasion, analogous with what many taxi-drivers, self-employed artisans, and other service providers do.

professionals (earnings of the profession or occupational group
international comparison

Slovenia 1997	Austria 1997	Finland 1998	Germany[7] 1998	Sweden 1997	United Kingdom[9] 1999	United States 1998
101	..	..	..	132	185	152
205	95	140[6]	132	..	165	172
155	..	137	214[8]	120	179	133
127	92	154[6]	144	..	187	137
97	..	129	..	122	..	128
77	..	116	140[8]	104	133	95

court judge. United States: Lawyers and judges. Germany: Attorneys.

[6] Data for 1995.

[7] Data refer to the provinces of the former Federal Republic of Germany.

[8] Data for 1989.

[9] Data for April 1999.

Sources: ILO (1996, 1998, 1999a, 1999b); Bureau of Labor Statistics of the United States (1999); Czech Statistical Office (1999); Office for National Statistics (1999); OMMK (1999); Romanian National Commission for Statistics (1999); Statistical Office of the Slovak Republic and VEDA (1999a; 1999b); Statistical Office of the Republic of Slovenia (1999).

(c) Phenomena (a) and (b) may combine in a specific way, mainly in the doctor–patient relationship. A patient arrives at a doctor's private office and pays the doctor, formally as a fee for the visit. In fact, the patient wishes to purchase a privilege by making the payment. He/she expects special attention from the doctor at the latter's main place of work, a state hospital, or clinic – help in jumping the queue for an examination, a more comfortable ward, and so on.[14] In the rest of the book we use the term "gratuity" in its wider sense, to cover both (a) and (c).

---

[14] The Czech payment system precludes a semi-legal linkage between the two types of ownership. The insurer will only pay a private physician who is not in state employment.

Phenomenon (b), tax evasion, is not specific to Eastern
Europe; it occurs all over the world.[15] On the other hand phenomena (a) and (c) are probably specifically socialist and
post-socialist – Eastern European (and also post-Soviet and
Chinese) – habits, or at least are much more pronounced
there than elsewhere.

Experts on the subject consider that semi-legal payments to
doctors are very widespread in Hungary, Romania, Poland,
and Bulgaria, and much less so in the Czech Republic,
Slovakia, Croatia, and Slovenia. Research in Poland found
that the amount of gratuity doctors received in Poland in
1994 was roughly equivalent to their official gross salary.
About 60–70 percent of those receiving treatment in hospital
gave gratuity to physicians (Chawla, Berman and Kawiorska
1998: 8).

There was wide research into the size and frequency of gratuities, and attitudes towards them, in Hungary in 1998,
using two samples, one of the population and the other of
physicians.[16] As expected, the frequency of gratuity payments depends on the type of medical service received. Let
us look at the situation in which gratuities are most common.
In the survey of the population, more than three-quarters of
the respondents said it was customary to give a gratuity for a
surgical operation, a childbirth, or if an on-call doctor paid a
house call at night. When the physicians were asked, their
responses were exactly the same: surgeons receive a gratuity
from 73 percent of patients and gynecologists from 85
percent.

---

[15] Tibor Scitovsky, the distinguished economist, describes in his autobiog-
raphy an example of (b) – the prevalence of tax evasion among French
doctors. The professional body representing French doctors is prepared
to defend its members on tax charges provided they have not understated
their income by over 30 percent. More than that and they are on their own
– enough is enough. See Scitovsky (1997: 187–8).

[16] The findings of the survey, undertaken by the TÁRKI research institute
and headed by Géza Bognár, Róbert Gál, and János Kornai, were summed
up in Bognár, Gál and Kornai (2000). All the Hungarian data in this
section has been taken from that study.

Table 5.14 *Average gratuity "prices" of medical care, Hungary, 1999, HUF*

Service	Estimate by the public	Estimate by doctors
Night call by on-call physician	857	763
Routine gynecological examination	860	1,231
Injection administered at the doctor's office	206	146
To surgeon, for appendectomy or gall-bladder operation	6,001	8,879
To obstetrician, for childbirth	10,982	19,340
If the doctor places a healthy patient on the sick list	..	2,063
If the doctor certifies that an able-bodied patient qualifies for a disability pension	..	32,086

Note:
Members of the public and the medical profession were asked, "How much gratuity do people give?", not "How much did you give?", or "How much were you given?" This was to encourage respondents to give more honest answers. The last two questions would have referred to acts that could be construed as bribery, and so they were not put to members of the public.
Source: Bognár, Gál and Kornai (2000: 307).

The survey also inquired into the customary amounts of gratuity given or received. Table 5.14 gives a rather revealing selection of the responses. Childbirth, ostensibly free, involves a gratuity ranging between about HUF 11,000 and 19,000, according to the public and the physicians, respectively. As a comparison, the net average earnings of employees in that year were HUF 45,162 a month (KSH 1999: 93).

Based on the responses of the population, the researchers made an estimate of the aggregate amount of gratuity received in the health sector. There are inevitably several uncertainties about any such estimate. However, the conclusion that the macro-level gratuity total received by practicing physicians was more than one-and-a-half times bigger than their official aggregate earnings is more likely to have been distorted downwards than upwards. The proportion in Hungary may have been the highest in the region. Thorough micro-estimates of gratitude payments have not been elaborated in other countries.

The two sides of the gratuity system explained in this section – intolerably low official pay and the prevalence and astonishing size of the semi-legal gratuity payments made – are inseparably linked.

The majority of the public is convinced that doctors expect gratuities. However, this can be stated with certainty only of a minority of doctors; there are many who do not share this expectation. They are prepared to be equally attentive and careful with every patient, irrespective of any gratuity or fee for a visit to the doctor's private practice. However, the mere fact that patients *think* they can buy extra attention from the doctor by method (a) or (b) or (c) has a demoralizing effect. Table 5.15 sheds light on how the ethically problematic phenomenon of gratuities is viewed by the public and by the medical profession in Hungary.

Gratuities are unfairly distributed among health-sector personnel.[17] For instance, a patient receiving surgery (or a relative) will hand the gratuity to the directing surgeon, even though the operation is teamwork. There are surgeons who share their gratuities with the members of their team, but not all of them do so. There are whole specialist professions, such as radiologists, anesthetists, and laboratory personnel, who are left without gratuity income.

Gratuities cause confusion among patients. The market is not transparent and the prices are unclear. Everyone is hesitant about giving too much or too little. Patients vie with each other, which pushes up the prevailing rates of gratuity.

---

[17] Losonczi (1997: 23) quotes some staggering findings of a survey at a large provincial hospital. For instance, only about 10 percent of the doctors working in the hospital receive gratuities, and within this group, about 2 percent of the doctors receive 80 percent of the gratuities.

Table 5.15 *Opinions on medical gratuities, among doctors and among the public, Hungary*

Opinion	Agree		Disagree	
	Wholly	Partly	Wholly	Partly
Giving gratuities reassures patients, because they feel they are buying extra attention:				
Physicians	19.4	44.2	19.5	16.9
Public	26.1	28.4	19.8	25.7
Gratuities make no difference in treatment:				
Physicians	32.0	17.6	23.7	26.7
Public	14.4	17.1	30.0	38.5
Gratuities erode the confidence essential in the doctor–patient relationship:				
Physicians	17.8	17.6	31.9	32.7
Public	15.1	21.7	33.2	30.1
Gratuities are a necessary evil:				
Physicians	58.0	22.2	9.8	10.1
Public	52.3	30.1	9.2	8.4
So long as the state does not pay them properly, doctors have a right to accept gratuities:				
Physicians	54.4	27.5	11.0	7.1
Public	39.1	28.4	17.5	15.0

Table 5.15 (*cont.*)

Opinion	Agree		Disagree	
	Wholly	Partly	Wholly	Partly
It is morally reprehensible for doctors to accept gratuities:				
Physicians	3.6	7.5	29.4	59.6
Public	16.6	17.7	33.3	32.4
Gratuities are unpleasant and demeaning to both doctors and patients:				
Physicians	68.0	21.8	7.1	3.1
Public	30.0	32.4	22.6	15.0
The existence of gratuities shows that society considers doctors to be underpaid:				
Physicians	72.6	17.5	6.7	3.2
Public	41.6	28.1	17.0	13.3
Gratuities are not a moral issue:				
Physicians	42.2	29.1	18.1	10.7
Public	33.5	29.3	19.4	17.8

Source: Bognár, Gál and Kornai (2000: 295).

The prevalence and demoralizing effect of gratuities are one of the main brakes on the emergence of straightforward private activity and respectable business relations in the health sector.

Economic indices for the health sector and population health status

To recapitulate, substantial changes can be said to have occurred in the health sectors of the Eastern European countries compared with the pre-1990 mechanism inherited from the socialist system. Some countries have taken few steps along the road to reform, while others have made great strides. However, the results everywhere have been inconsistent, and there is great need of further reform.

Although it points beyond the immediate subject of this book, it is worth concluding this outline of the starting position with a few words on the economic scope and performance of the health sector. This will reveal a picture that is disturbing in several respects. However, it is simply a picture of the present situation, which reformers need to keep in mind when drafting reform proposals. No causal analysis will be attempted here. It would be good to know to what extent the incompleteness of institutional and incentive reform can explain the ambiguous performance of the health sector. A causal link can be suspected, but the task of clarifying that cannot be attempted here.

One approach to summarizing the economic scope of the health sector is to look at data on national health expenditures. Table 5.16 shows *per capita* health spending in Eastern Europe, using prices that adjust for cost-of-living differences and therefore are comparable across countries. As a comparison, table 5.17 contains data for the OECD countries in 1970–94, at prices comparable with those in table 5.16. Only in the Czech Republic and Slovenia did *per capita* health spending in 1994 exceed the OECD average in 1970. In the

Table 5.16 *GDP and health spending, Eastern Europe,*
1990–1994

	GDP *per capita*, USD 1990 (PPP)[1]				
Country	1990	1991	1992	1993	1994
Bulgaria	5,296	4,157	3,764	3,812	3,914
Czech Rep.	9,754	8,363	7,970	7,623	8,058
Hungary	6,514	5,657	5,535	5,605	5,756
Poland	4,504	4,234	4,206	4,260	4,605
Romania	4,433	3,706	3,321	3,363	3,454
Slovakia	7,315	6,273	5,977	5,829	5,986
Slovenia	..	8,920	8,191	8,520	8,979
	Health spending *per capita*, USD 1990 (PPP)				
Bulgaria	275	226	256	196	185
Czech Rep.	527	443	430	556	612
Hungary	436	385	398	415	455
Poland	230	246	265	..	309
Romania	124	122	116	101	114
Slovakia	393	310	304	371	422
Slovenia	..	461	608	653	700

Note:
[1] PPP = purchasing power parity (for an explanation, see note to table 4.4,
p. 106).
Source: Kornai and McHale (2000: 383).

other countries, it was below that average, around the level
of spending in the poorer OECD countries 24 years earlier.
Comparing the situation in the two groups in 1994, the
Eastern European countries show a wide dispersion in *per
capita* health spending: between 8 and 52 percent of the
average for the industrially developed countries.

The main reason for the disparity between the two groups
of countries, of course, is that Eastern Europe has a substantially lower *per capita* GDP. The left block of table 5.18 presents health-sector spending as a percentage of GDP.

How does Eastern European health-care spending, measured in this way, compare to what would be considered

Table 5.17 *Health spending* per capita, *OECD countries, 1970–1994*[1]

Country	1970	1982	1994
Australia	672	1,077	1,453
Austria	512	926	1,432
Belgium	425	1,009	1,471
Canada	813	1,267	1,791
Denmark	690	1,237	1,496
Finland	531	894	1,153
France	662	1,198	1,671
Germany	566	1,059	1,765
Greece	189	294	565
Iceland	445	1,027	1,408
Ireland	316	688	1,011
Italy	502	924	1,402
Japan	419	904	1,330
Korea	45	141	386
Luxembourg	475	976	1,753
Netherlands	653	1,098	1,481
New Zealand	568	777	1,068
Norway	428	994	1,529
Portugal	141	445	839
Spain	263	542	909
Sweden	869	1,390	1,364
Switzerland	814	1,313	2,052
Turkey	72	107	170
United Kingdom	464	733	1,083
United States	1,159	1,880	3,246
Mean	508	916	1,353

Note:

[1] All values are measured at 1990 US prices, adjusted for GDP PPPs.

Source: OECD (1998b).

Table 5.18 *Actual and predicted health spending, Eastern European countries, 1990–1994*[1]

Country	Actual health spending, percentage of GDP					Predicted health spending, percentage of GDP					Difference between actual and predicted spending				
	1990	1991	1992	1993	1994	1990	1991	1992	1993	1994	1990	1991	1992	1993	1994
Bulgaria	5.2	5.4	6.8	5.2	4.7	4.7	4.2	4.2	4.2	4.2	0.5	1.3	2.7	0.9	0.5
Czech Rep.	5.4	5.3	5.4	7.3	7.6	6.2	5.8	5.9	5.8	5.8	−0.8	−0.5	−0.5	1.5	1.8
Hungary	6.7	6.8	7.2	7.4	7.9	4.8	4.5	4.7	4.7	4.7	1.9	2.3	2.5	2.7	3.2
Poland	5.1	5.8	6.3	..	6.7	4.0	3.9	4.0	4.1	4.2	1.1	1.9	2.3	..	2.5
Romania	2.8	3.3	3.5	3.0	3.3	3.9	3.6	3.5	3.6	3.5	−1.1	−0.3	0.0	−0.6	−0.2
Slovakia	5.4	5.0	5.1	6.4	7.1	5.2	4.9	5.0	5.0	4.9	0.1	0.1	0.1	1.4	2.1
Slovenia	5.6	5.2	7.4	7.7	7.8	..	5.7	5.7	5.9	5.9	..	−0.5	1.7	1.8	1.9

Note:
[1] The predicted figures are based on regression estimates. The explanatory variables in the regression are *per capita* GDP, the elderly dependency rate, and the female/male labor force ratio.
Source: Kornai and McHale (2000: 384).

"normal" for market-based economies? We can obtain a reasonably precise answer to this important question by pursuing the following line of thought. First, let us assume that an Eastern European country, say Slovakia, had a political and economic system similar to that of "normal" market economies. In that case, its "normal" ratio of health spending to GDP could be predicted based on (a) Slovakia's own economic and demographic characteristics, and (b) how those characteristics relate to health-care spending in market economies. The latter relationship – how health spending in market economies is associated with GDP growth and changes in other variables (such as the age structure of the population) – has been the topic of much econometric research.[18] Reference will be made here to the analysis done by the first author of this book and John McHale. That study explored the validity of many different econometric specifications. Let us focus on results from a regression using a pooled time-series, cross-section sample for the years 1970–94 and 25 OECD countries (the current OECD members except the Czech Republic, Mexico, and Poland). In addition to GDP *per capita* the other explanatory variables are age structure and female labor-force participation. The relationship is allowed to shift over time in response to new technology-induced increases in health spending. Taking the experience of these countries as a benchmark, the "normal" ratio of health spending to GDP for an Eastern European country such as Slovakia in 1994 can be predicted by plugging into the regression equation Slovakia's 1994 GDP, population age structure, and female labor-force participation.[19]

---

[18] Gerdtham and Jönsson (2000) comprehensively survey the extensive literature on these investigations.

[19] A detailed account of the research appears in Kornai and McHale (2000). Table 5 in the study is reproduced here as table 5.18.

There are many statistical uncertainties about the Eastern European data employed in the research. There is also a debate occurring in the literature about the appropriate econometric techniques for international comparisons. Although these difficulties are a warning to be cautious, the calculated results given here seem to be appropriate for drawing qualitative conclusions.

The result can be seen in the central block of table 5.18; for Slovakia, it is 4.9 percent. In other words, the central block presents the values predicted by the regression equation.

The right block in table 5.18 shows the difference between the values in the left and the middle blocks, for the same country and at the same time. It can be seen that in 1994 Romania is the only country for which the actual proportion falls short of the proportion predicted by the regression. For the other Eastern European countries in the table, the actual number exceeds the predicted number. Hungary is especially worth noting, because here the divergence between actual and predicted spending is greatest, as table 5.18 and figure 5.3 show.[20]

This difference between the predicted "normal" pattern and actual health spending in Eastern Europe is closely tied to the unprecedented social and economic transformation of the past several years. The massive fall in production in Eastern Europe in the 1990s was the deepest recession so far in economic history in these countries. However, spending on the welfare sector, including health spending, decreased less than GDP. This was one of the attempts made by all governments in the region to alleviate somewhat the severe decline in living standards caused by the recession.[21] So at the trough of the recession, health-sector spending grew as a proportion of GDP. Whether this proportion will remain high (or grow even further) or not will depend to a large extent on reform policies, both those of the health sector and those promoting overall economic growth.

It is worth recalling principle 8, the requirement that the

[20] It was recognizing this difference that prompted the first author to call Hungary a "premature welfare state" in his (1992a) study. Various historical circumstances led the Hungarian government, before the collapse of the socialist system, to go further in developing the welfare sector than other countries at a similar level of economic development.

[21] In the period 1991–4, Croatian health expenditure decreased much slower than GDP. More strikingly, in Bulgaria, Romania, Slovakia, and Slovenia health expenditure actually increased while GDP declined (Kanavos and McKee 1998: 33).

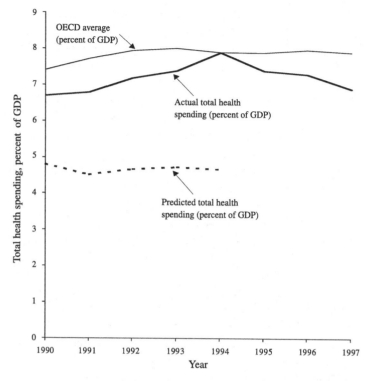

Figure 5.3 Hungary, actual and predicted health-spending data during the transition, 1990–1997

Source: Kornai and McHale (2000: 385).

proportions between welfare-sector spending and spending to promote economic growth should be harmonious. There can be some departure (to follow the vocabulary of the regression calculation just described) from the "normal" proportions, from the proportion of GDP customarily spent on health care in other countries with similar characteristics, but it is risky to deviate too long or too far. There are too many other pressing concerns to allow health spending to absorb an increasingly disproportionate share of society's resources. The fact that positive numbers appear for 1994 in the right-hand block of table 5.18 (except for Romania) shows that these countries spent as much as (or in some cases more than) would be spent in a market-based economy at a similar level of economic development. Changes that have occurred in more recent years require further studies.

This argument will probably seem convincing to a macroeconomist, who is used to considering the relative proportions of each sector in the whole economy, as a measure of opportunity cost and efficiency of resource allocation. The trouble is that neither patients nor doctors think of it in that way. They are more concerned with what tables 5.16 and 5.17 illustrate: how Czech, Polish, or Slovenian citizens today receive only a fraction of what their more fortunate Western European counterparts receive. *That* relative proportion is the one that fuels public dissatisfaction. It is not alleviated by the other, more sobering thought that they receive no small amount compared with the economic strength of the country.

Since the total proportion of economic resources devoted to the health sector is by no means "small" in Eastern Europe, yet health problems abound, there is an acute need for policies to increase the "value per dollar" of health-care spending. This need for greater efficiency is further underscored by the legacy of socialistic planning in the region's health-care delivery system. One of the well known symptoms of the chronic shortage economy under the socialist system was that shortage and surplus existed side by side throughout the economy. For instance, a company might complain of a constant labor shortage while exhibiting unemployment on the job. Inventories might be building up in warehouses while customers queued for the goods they sought. In this respect as in others, vestiges of socialism can be discerned in the health sector. It is astonishing to find, as illustrated in figure 5.4, that a relatively poor country such as Bulgaria or Slovakia has more doctors or hospital beds *per capita* than the OECD average! At the same time, doctors' waiting rooms are overcrowded. There are long queues for certain kinds of

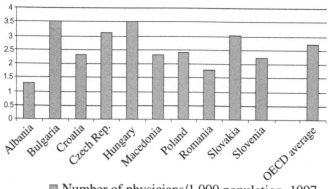

Number of physicians/1,000 population, 1997

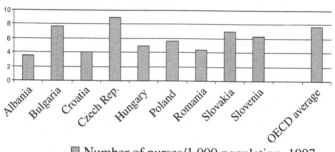

Number of nurses/1,000 population, 1997

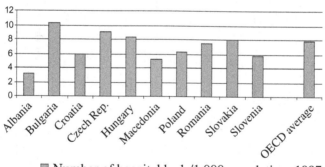

Number of hospital beds/1,000 population, 1997

Figure 5.4 Resources in health-care provision, Eastern Europe, 1995–1997

Source: WHO (1999d).

Table 5.19 *Infant mortality, life expectancy at birth, and crude death rate, Eastern Europe, 1990–1997*

Country	Infant mortality rate (deaths per 1,000 live births)			Life expectancy at birth, in years			Crude death rate[1] per 1,000 population		
	1990	1994	1997	1990	1994	1997	1990	1994	1997
Albania	30.9[2]	32.9	..	72.6	73.0	..	5.5[2]	5.3[4]	..
Bulgaria	14.8	16.3	14.4[6]	71.5	70.8	72.8[6]	12.1	13.2	14.7
Croatia	10.7	10.2	8.2	72.6	73.2	72.6	10.9	10.4	11.4
Czech Rep.	10.8	8.0	6.1	71.5	73.2	74.1	12.5	11.4	10.9
Hungary	14.8	11.6	9.9	69.4	69.5	70.8	14.1	14.3	13.7
Macedonia	31.6	22.5	15.7[5]	71.8[3]	71.9	72.5	7.7[2]	8.1	8.3
Poland	16.0	15.1	12.2[5]	71.0	71.8	72.4	10.2	10.0	10.0[5]
Romania	26.9	23.9	22.0	69.8	69.4	69.1	10.7	11.7	12.4
Slovakia	12.0	11.2	8.8[6]	71.1	72.5	..	10.2	9.6	9.8[5]
Slovenia	8.3	6.5	5.2	74.1	74.2	75.3	9.4	9.7	9.6
OECD median									
male	7.9	6.2	5.9	72.6	73.5	74.5	7.6	7.1	7.1
female				79.0	79.7	80.6			

Notes:

[1] Crude death rate is the death rate not adjusted for differences in the composition of the population that would explain differences in death rates, such as gender and age. The OECD median death rates are based on age-adjusted mortality data, and therefore are not directly comparable to those for Eastern Europe.

[2] 1989; [3] 1991; [4] 1993; [5] 1996; [6] 1998.

Sources: Central Statistical Office (1998); OECD (1998b, 1999b); Statistical Office of the Republic of Slovenia (1998); WHO (1998, 1999d); Central Bureau of Statistics (1999); National Statistical Institute (1999a, 1999b); Statistical Office of the Slovak Republic and VEDA (1999c).

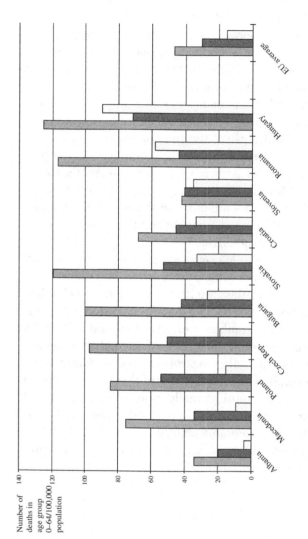

Figure 5.5 Standardized male mortality rates (ages 0–64/100,000), Eastern Europe

Notes: Standardized death rate represents what the crude rate would have been if the population had the same age distribution as the standard European population. Data for Albania: 1993, Bulgaria: 1994, EU average: 1995, all other: 1996.
Source: WHO (1998).

tests and long waiting lists for certain kinds of treatment (for instance, various surgical procedures). There is much unused capacity and scope for more effective use of both physical and human capital.

The symbiosis of shortage and surplus should further spur reformers to devise an economic mechanism in the health sector that encourages efficiency, better use of resources, and a closer balance between supply and demand.

Mention has only been made so far of a few features of the state of the health sector. To complement this, we would like to offer readers a glimpse of the state of health found in the population of the Eastern European countries. This is provided in table 5.19 and figure 5.5, which reveal that the Czech Republic and Slovenia are the only countries in the region whose health indicators are close to those of the European Union. The situation in the other Eastern European countries is worse to an alarming degree.

Table 5.19 and figure 5.5 serve exclusively as background information. We do not attempt to explain how the state of health in any country ties in with the economic mechanism governing its health sector. The state of health in a population depends on the combined effects of several factors. Its economic mechanism is only one of several explanatory factors and not necessarily the strongest of them (Adler *et al.* 1993). However, it can certainly be said that if the operation of the health sector could be made more efficient, it would help to improve the health status of the population, in conjunction with other favorable changes. There is definitely a great need for improvement, as the disturbing picture presented by table 5.19 and figure 5.5 makes plain.

Part II

Guidelines for reform

Introduction to part II

Part I of the book covered the starting points for reform: guiding principles, attributes specific to the health sector, international experiences, and initial conditions found generally in Eastern Europe. Even if reformers in every Eastern European country embraced identical principles, their actual plans of action at any time would differ, because each country would face a different situation – legally, structurally, and economically, and in terms of public attitudes and political preferences. That is one reason why this book cannot present practical programs that go into detail.

Part II is confined to describing the general approach and broad outlines of the reforms that the authors consider reasonable and desirable. It is appropriate to reiterate here a point first made in the general introduction to the book (p. 61): we consciously acknowledge that the reforms we recommend reflect our values. This is not an *à la carte* list of reforms from which people may choose randomly or selectively – this for conservatives, that for centrists, the other for left-wing socialists. If the system of values expressed in chapter 2 is acceptable, readers can make good use of the package of interdependent reforms that follows in the rest of the book. If it is unacceptable, all they will gain from part II is knowledge of what practical changes would follow from the principles expounded earlier. Consequently, there will not be a comprehensive analysis, issue by issue, of all the substantive alternatives discussed in the literature on the subject. If there appears to be only one solution in line with that set of principles, only that one will be recommended. Alternatives will be given only where they, too, accord with the guiding principles, such as alternatives that strike different balances between principles that may require trade-offs (e.g. between individual choice and social solidarity).

Chapters 6 and 7 and the first half of chapter 8 disregard temporarily what support the people concerned would give to the reforms being recommended and what stance the various political forces would take towards them. This aspect, the political economy of health-care reform, is discussed in the second half of chapter 8 and in chapter 9. To put it another way, chapters 6, 7, and the first half of chapter 8 are confined to recommendations. Chapter 9 ends by adding predictions of the extent to which the reform process is likely to succeed, and what political and social difficulties it is likely to encounter.

6

The demand side: financing, benefits, and organization of insurance

The guiding ideas behind the recommendations

This section sets out to sum up concisely the ideas that guide the recommended reforms of the economic mechanism on the demand side. Later, the proposals will be broken down systematically and the details and necessary qualifications discussed.

Health services are divided into two parts: basic and supplementary care. All citizens should have access to basic care. This right has to be enshrined in law. Apart from that, the state should ensure, economically and organizationally, that this legal guarantee is upheld.

Supplementary care, in contrast, has to be purchased by patients. There should be the legal and organizational conditions for this to develop legally under conditions of commercial purchase and sale.

The main source of financing for basic care is the tax paid by citizens and/or the compulsory contributions levied on them like a tax. In other words, basic care is financed out of public money. This is the dominant, if not the exclusive source.

The main financing source for supplementary care is the individual's or family's own money. Another important source might be a voluntary employer contribution (over and above the employer's health-care contribution required by law). In both cases, the source is private money.

Where is the dividing line between basic and supplementary care? The discussion will return to this several times. Suffice it to say here in advance that the dividing line is not health-care needs or medical possibilities, which are insatiable. The macro-allocations of public money used to finance basic health care, like those for education, defense, or environmental protection, should be decided in the political sphere. The amount available for basic health care is what the constitutionally authorized organizations, the central and local legislative bodies, allocate for the purpose. Those complaining that total spending on basic care is not enough, whether they are patients or doctors or anyone else, have to battle on the political front.

However, the political sphere does not directly determine spending on supplementary care. This is predominantly determined by whatever households and employers are willing and able to spend on such care.

Chapter 2 highlighted several serious dilemmas caused by conflicts between principle 1, individual sovereignty, and principle 2, solidarity. Reforms need to strike a sober compromise between these two.

The proposal here is that principle 2 and its application to health care – the principle of specific egalitarianism – should apply at the level of basic health care. There should be universal and equal access to a basic benefit package. This basic level of health care should accord with the country's level of economic development (principle 8). The financing should be sustainable (principle 9) both fiscally and politically. The state revenues and budget allocations required should be acceptable not only to present-day taxpayers and legislators, but, so far as can be envisaged, to future taxpayers and legislators as well.

Only the macro-budget for basic care is decided in the political sphere. The micro-allocation – who receives what and when – consists of millions of detailed decisions, reached primarily and in most cases by decision-makers in the health sector itself – i.e. by providers and patients. However, there needs to be an appropriate mechanism to ensure, so far as possible, that the total cost requirement for all the micro-decisions fits into the overall budget for basic care. This book does not define basic care with a list of specific medical interventions or medicines. Instead, it suggests a *procedural* definition of the two fundamentally important categories of basic and supplementary care and presents recommendations regarding what institutions and individuals should be authorized to determine and update the basic benefit package (p. 216).

In contrast to basic care, there is no guaranteed universal and equal access to supplementary care. Rather, services falling outside the basic benefit package are available to those willing to pay for them. Services deemed supplementary are therefore distributed unevenly among the members of society. There is quite a strong correlation with income and wealth, in other words, with how much households can afford to spend on health care. However, it does not just depend on this. It is also a matter of individual or family preferences and of how much income people want to devote to this purpose, at the expense of other types of expenditure.

Inequality in the distribution of health-care expenditures offends many people's sense of justice, including, there is no denying, the authors'. On the other hand, it would also be ethically injurious to bar anyone from spending his or her own money on personal health and that of their loved ones. If a market economy allows all consumers to spend the money on food, housing, cultural pursuits, or entertainment that they see fit, what right does the state have to prevent them from spending what they see fit on health care? That would be a grave breach of principle 1, individual sovereignty. Furthermore, it would be hypocritical, because affluent patients will purchase additional services anyway, if not legally, then in the "gray" or "black" economy. Therefore, legal and efficient forms for allowing individual choice of supplementary care should be created.

By the same principle, employers should not be denied the right to spend more than the compulsory minimum on their employees' health.

The moral concerns regarding inequity are lessened by the realization that the willingness of the affluent to purchase health care beyond basic care can have favorable external effects. It may help doctors and other health-care providers to gain experience in applying new, initially more costly procedures; it may translate into extra revenues for obtaining more expensive equipment, which may then be used more widely by those who otherwise might not have such access; and it allows public financing to be targeted more effectively on the less fortunate. In coordination with policies designed to assure that differential use of supplementary services does not undermine the integrity of universal equal access to the socially defined basic benefit package, and some attention to enforcing an overall constraint on total health spending, allowing supplementary care is a straightforward requirement of individual sovereignty. Citizens should be allowed to choose, not only whether or not to spend their own money on supplementary health care, but also which insurer or provider will give the best value for their money.

In sum, then, the proposals for reform are based on public financing for basic care, private financing for supplementary care, pluralistic delivery of services, and managed competition, with attention to incentives and regulation to impose a constraint on overall health spending (basic and supplementary, public and private). The rest of this chapter discusses reform of the demand side of the health sector in more detail, including financing, scope of benefits, and organization of insurance. Financing comes first, and merits considerable discussion (pp. 195–216), because it is a critical, and often underappreciated, policy instrument for designing a system that simultaneously upholds principles of solidarity and sustainability as well as choice and efficiency. Although it may seem out of order to discuss financing basic care before defining the basic benefit package (pp. 216–227), this is in fact the essence of our proposal: that the scope of basic care should be defined primarily through its financing – i.e. by how much society, through its democratic institutions, decides to spend on basic care. Who receives what health services as basic care is determined in three interdependent ways: first, by the mechanism for determining *total spending* on basic care (p. 196), with the redistribution that it implies (p. 200) and influenced by some financing from patient co-payments (p. 213); second, by the institutional process that decides *which health services* are in the basic benefit package (p. 216); and, third, by doctors and other health-care providers (in conjunction with patients themselves) when they decide *who receives what services*, under the constraints imposed by the limit on total spending, the scope of the benefit package, and the influence of organization and incentives (pp. 227–261 and chapters 7 and 8).

The financing of basic care

Who should determine the amount of society's resources that will be spent on basic health care? This book recommends that setting the total level of spending or macro-allocation for basic care should not be left to health-care providers (the "sellers") nor to patients (the "buyers"). The state has an obligation to guarantee a reasonable macro-allocation for basic care and the individual a citizen's right to make use of it.[1] In this respect, the mechanism recommended bears a closer resemblance to the German system, or more generally, to the

---

[1] It is worth considering whether the right belongs to citizens who break the law by not paying their health contribution or tax. Not even they can be denied emergency care; obviously children cannot be punished for the sins of their parents. It seems more appropriate not to deny "free-riders" their citizen's right, but to improve the efficiency of tax or contribution collection.

European and Canadian pattern, than to the American one. It retains the acquired rights enshrined in law in most East European countries during the socialist period and not withdrawn so far during the post-socialist transition in the region.

How does the suggested method of financing basic care differ from the one employed before the change of system? The main difference is that the political process has become *democratic*. The decision-makers are no longer the leading group in the communist party, but legitimate legislative institutions: the freely elected Parliament and local authorities.

There is no intention of idealizing this decision-making process. The "will of the people" cannot be said to manifest itself in the legislation governing the revenues and expenditures of the health sector. There is a great deal of friction in the transmission that connects citizens with the legislature. The real preferences of the public are often distorted in the decisions of central and local assemblies. This issue of basic health care also gets into the political fray surrounding all parliamentary decisions. Legislators and the governmental bodies devising legislative proposals are influenced by party interests, pressure groups, and lobbies, and tempted by cheap popularity and demagogy. Even so, there is a legitimate political mechanism at work, which can be described by echoing what Churchill said in the House of Commons in 1947, "No one pretends that democracy is perfect or all-wise. Indeed, it has been said that democracy is the worst form of Government except all those other forms that have been tried from time to time."[2]

To encourage the wishes of the public to crystallize and be applied more fully, principle 6, *transparency*, should be fulfilled more consistently. There are several techniques for doing so:

1. It is expedient to collect as large a proportion as possible of the revenues required in the form of earmarked

[2] *The Oxford Dictionary of Political Quotations,* Anthony Jay (ed.), Oxford University Press, 1996, p. 93.

tax or compulsory contributions. Let it be guaranteed by law that the sums citizens pay for basic health care may be used only for that purpose. Empirical investigations show that people feel more inclined to pay taxes if they know the exact purpose for which their money is used.[3]

In practice, it is not possible to arrive at a one-to-one correspondence between earmarked revenues and expenditures on basic care. There is no avoiding the use of other sources. Nonetheless, the higher the proportion of earmarked health tax or compulsory contributions employed, the clearer the connection between tax deductions on the one hand and care standards on the other becomes to citizens.[4] The following, simple line of argument has to be suggested: If you are dissatisfied with the current basic benefit package, the main means of changing it (but not the only one) is to pay more health tax. To reduce the tax you pay, accept the consequences: in future, you will have to pay for care that the state has paid for so far.

2. The first problem ties in with some fiscal illusions that affect the ideas of much of the population. Although the spread of compulsory co-payments and gratitude money have shaken their belief that health care is free, many people still do not understand that the promise of free care is not belied solely by direct contributions. The main reason is that basic care is ultimately financed by the tax and contributions collected from citizens. Many people are insufficiently aware of how much basic

---

[3] An American investigation based on a public-opinion poll in Maryland (Haynes and Florestano 1994) found that many more people agree with earmarking taxes for specific purposes than oppose it. The strongest support was expressed for earmarked taxes for health care.

[4] This idea particularly induces many health economists in developed industrial countries to support the introduction of an earmarked health tax. Victor R. Fuchs, for instance, the 1995 president of the American Economic Association and one of the foremost economists dealing with health care, expressed support for a general health tax in his inaugural address. Fuchs (1996: 16–20).

health-care costs, and of who contributes to what extent, through their contributions and tax payments.[5] A strengthening of tax awareness is essential if citizens are to express informed opinions about health taxation and expenditures.

3. Even if earmarked taxes or contributions are dominant, the financing of basic care takes place through a very complex web of channels. This makes it all the more important that revenues and expenditures should be accounted for in as transparent a way as possible, open to scrutiny.

4. Politicians in all countries, when competing for votes, are fond of promising, on a level of general rhetoric, more abundant and better-quality care *simultaneously* with tax reductions. It is not easy for voters to find their bearings. The task of asking hard questions to elicit greater transparency belongs to the medical profession, the media, the press, the academic world, and, not least, economists dealing with the health sector. Politicians have to be made to reveal, as specifically as possible, what they are preparing to do and support their arguments with figures that can be checked.

Let us now survey the sources that make up the macro-budget of basic care.

(a) Where suggestion 1 is accepted as just described, the biggest item is the earmarked health tax or health-care social-insurance contribution, which the law has to stipulate can be used only for health purposes.

(b) There are expenditures earmarked for health-care pur-

---

[5] As mentioned in n. 6 of chapter 2 (p. 161), a Hungarian research group under the auspices of TÁRKI set out to measure the population's tax awareness and the extent of its fiscal illusions. About 14 percent of the public do not realize that social insurance contributions are deducted from their wages or are not certain about it. Of the group whose members are aware of the deduction, 16–24 percent do not know the rate of contribution. TÁRKI repeated the survey in 1999 and found a similar distribution.

poses in the central budget. The structure of the budget differs from country to country, but in most of them, such items appear under several headings – in the budgets for the health ministry and those of other ministries and programs as well. Unfortunately, this makes the situation harder to categorize in detail.

(c) The same comments can be made about local-government authorities, whose health spending likewise appears under several headings.

(d) Contributions to the health sector also come from extra-budgetary public institutions, such as the state pension fund.[6]

(e) Patients make direct co-payments for basic care. These come from the patients' own pockets but count toward total financing of basic care.

(f) Private donations are made for basic-care purposes by individuals, companies, and foundations. As with the previous item, these come out of private pockets, but go into the common purse. Such payments are still only sporadic in Eastern Europe, but not unknown. It would be desirable for the scale of these to increase.

Adding up all these items yields the macro-budget for basic care. This cannot be spent at will, as the health sector sees fit, if for no other reason because some of its sources already have obligations attached to them. The money for the pension fund should be spent on providing basic care to pensioners, local-government money has to be spent locally, co-payments go towards covering the bill of the patient who paid them, and so on. Nonetheless, it is possible to make several kinds of rearrangements, constrained by the ultimate upper limit of the macro-budget.

---

[6] Items (a)–(d) may overlap with each other. Separating them out depends on the budget structure of the country concerned. From the viewpoint of the economic content of the items, the only point to emphasize is that *over and above* the main source (a), there may exist other sources that count as public financing.

The main actor in the decision-making process of allocating the total budget for basic care is the health-sector apparatus, in which the medical profession sets the tone. However, as public money is concerned, there is justification for having state and civil society bodies capable of exercising supervision over the distribution. These would be institutions, committees, and ad hoc working groups formed at higher and lower levels, containing doctors, employers, insurers, lawyers with knowledge of the health sector, health economists, and representatives of various groups of patients. (Examples of such bodies in other countries are given in the discussion of institutions for prioritizing basic care on p. 225)

The scope for supervision and influence by civil society is one way in which the allocation of public financing for basic care under democratic conditions differs (or, rather, should differ) from what went on during bureaucratic disaggregation of central quotas under the socialist command economy. Both allocation processes involved jostling among various groups for public money, but under democratic conditions this should receive greater publicity and occur under stronger social control.

Of course, the participants in decision-making about micro-allocation will not accept the macro-allocation with resignation. There is a great need for them to make their voice heard. They can try to put pressure on legislators, to alter the total budget for basic care, but they have to acknowledge that they do not decide that budget. The decision is made by the legitimate bodies in the political sphere, representing the interests of taxpayers and others in society.

Redistribution through financing

Guaranteed universal basic care cannot be provided by an insurance scheme run on a purely commercial basis. It was mentioned in chapter 3 (p. 59) that the financing method has to combine insurance with elements of redistribution among social groups. The latter is essential, in at least three ways:

1. Some people suffer from a congenital disease or susceptibility to a disease, or enter life with some other physical disability. Others succumb during their lifetime to a disease that leaves a permanent disability. People's chances of health or illness – health risks – are unequal. Some people are at a health disadvantage throughout their life or the remainder of their life.

   With a purely commercial insurance system, the disadvantaged would have to pay a higher premium than their more fortunate counterparts. Equal access to basic care can be attained only if there is some redistribution to the benefit of the former, at the expense of those without a permanent health disadvantage. This redistribution represents a specific kind of solidarity, *risk solidarity* (van de Ven and Ellis 2000).

2. The effect of age is connected with point 1, but can be taken separately. The relation between expenditure on health care and age is illustrated by Czech data in figure 6.1, but the relationship is valid generally. The curves begin with higher expenditures: care for infants is much more costly than care for those over four years old.[7] After that, the expenditure curve steadily falls until the age-group 10–14, when it starts to rise, first slowly and then more steeply. The strongest growth occurs after age 64, when very expensive interventions may be made to prolong life.[8]

---

[7] The first column in figure 6.1 represents the age group of 0–4 years. The disbursements in this period are highest where an attempt is made to save a premature baby. The more premature the baby is, the higher the costs of saving it.

[8] This book does not deal with the serious moral dilemma of how far, within the bounds of basic care paid for out of public funds, the curve can and should go on both sides towards the steepest rise in expenditures. The more generous the care covered for some groups, such as the elderly, the more resources are drawn away from care for other age groups.

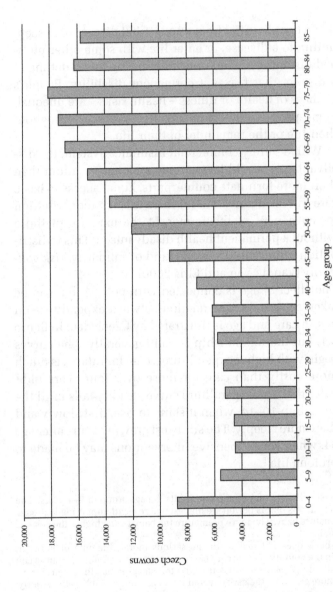

Figure 6.1 Average health-care costs per insured, by age groups, Czech Republic, 1997

Source: Institute of Health Information and Statistics of the Czech Republic (1998).

With a purely commercial system of insurance, the premium would depend on the size and age structure of the family. It would certainly tend to rise with age. In fact, under unregulated free market competition among health insurers, people might be unable to purchase medical insurance at all after a certain age. To ensure that everyone has access to the basic care regardless of age, there will again have to be redistribution, in favor of the aged and of families with dependent children, at the expense of the rest of the population.

3. Points 1 and 2 concerned expenditures that are necessarily unequal, given genetic endowments, the natural aging process, etc. Let us now look at the financing side. With a commercial system, the same premium would be paid by everyone in the same risk category (with the same expected costs of care), irrespective of income or wealth. With a more general insurance scheme, risk can be pooled so that everyone pays the same premium regardless of individual risk, but this may still be problematic if the premium is independent of income. For example, let us assume (calculating with the redistribution outlined under points 1 and 2) that it is established what average premium per insured will be required to cover all medical costs, pooling risk across the entire population. If everyone were required to pay this average premium, irrespective of their income, many would be unable to do so, so that they would be excluded from basic care.

This illustrates why universal care requires further redistribution, to the benefit of the poor at the expense of the rich. This kind of redistribution can be called *income solidarity*, to distinguish it from solidarity regarding health-cost risk, discussed above. An adequate state program will have to be devised for those who cannot pay even the minimum compulsory health-care contribution.

The three items so far do not include all the redistributive measures required to ensure universal basic care. However, they suffice to demonstrate that one of the underlying ideas behind the reform this book recommends, a state guarantee of basic care, can be secured (or if already secured, can be maintained) only if risk and income solidarity are accepted by society. Should the majority of voters, and consequently the majority in Parliament, reject principle 2 (solidarity) and the concomitant specific egalitarian redistribution for basic health care, the reforms outlined in this book could not be introduced or maintained.

The subsequent arguments assume that this rejection of solidarity does not occur and that the specific redistribution embedded in public financing to support risk and income solidarity for basic care is politically acceptable and sustainable. Even so, many questions remain open, of which a few will be considered here.

Tables 6.1, 6.2, and 6.3 provide some insight into how the costs and expenditures of health care are distributed among various population groups in Hungary, Slovenia, and the Czech Republic. Unfortunately, the structures of the three tables differ, so that they cannot be compared directly. Furthermore, the classification of the population is unfortunate. The residual categories include groups that should be observed separately if the distribution is to be studied more deeply. It is not just that the authors of this book or other researchers into this subject do not receive a clear view of the situation. The requirement of transparency is not met: the public is unable to follow who is paying for whom.

For want of a better source of information, let us try to draw a few conclusions from these tables. The data from Hungary and Slovenia support what was said earlier in the section: the *per capita* cost of basic health care of old-age pensioners is much greater than it is for active earners. In light of the arguments propounded earlier, no one will expect the elderly to pay these high costs out of their own

Table 6.1 *Distribution of health expenditures financed by social insurance, Hungary, 1995*

Categories of the insured	Proportion of population (percent)	Proportion of financing (percent)	Proportion of total spending (percent)	Average *per capita* spending (HUF)
Employed	31.1	68.0	24.3	20,708
Old-age pensioners[1]	23.2	21.3	44.8	51,350
Self-employed	7.5	3.3	5.9	20,708
Unemployed	2.2	1.7	1.6	18,474
Other[2]	36.0	5.7	23.4	17,300

Notes:

[1] Contributions of pensioners were not deducted from pensions, but paid by the pension-insurance system out of its budget, in proportion to the pensions. As the book relates, this arrangement ended in 1997.

[2] The "Other" category includes all those insured as dependents of the insured, whose contributions are paid by the budget.

Source: World Bank (1997b).

Table 6.2 *Distribution of health expenditures financed by social insurance, Slovenia, 1998*

Categories of the insured	Proportion of population (percent)	Proportion of financing (percent)	Proportion of total spending (percent)	Average *per capita* spending (SIT)
Employees, employers, and self-employed	63.1		49.2	95,000
Without dependents	39.1	80.2		
Old-age pensioners[1]	26.6		43.8	184,000
Without dependents	23.5	16.7		
Farmers	1.9		1.2	68,000
Without dependents	1.2	0.5		
Others[2]	8.4		5.8	48,000
Without dependents	6.7	2.6		
Total	100			
	70.5			

Notes:

[1] Contributions of pensioners were not deducted from pensions, but paid by the Institute for Pension Insurance system out of its budget, in proportion to the pensions.

[2] The "Other" category includes the unemployed, budget beneficiaries, and those for whom contributions are paid by the municipal government.

Source: Health Insurance Institute of Slovenia (1999).

Table 6.3 *Distribution of social insurance contributions, Czech Republic, 1994*

Categories of the insured	Distribution of the insured population (percent)	Distribution of total income from social insurance contributions, (percent)
Paying for themselves:		
Employees	41.0	73.4
Self-employed	4.5	4.6
Other premium payers	1.7	1.0
Paid for by the government:		
Pensioners	21.5	8.5
Children	24.2	9.6
Unemployed	2.7	1.1
Maternity leave	2.5	1.0
Other	1.9	0.7

Source: NERA (1996).

pockets. However, the redistribution from the working tax-payers to the elderly is nontransparent because only a small proportion of the health expenditures on the elderly is covered by the pension system. The rest of the financing cannot be traced. The program to provide health care for the elderly should be clearly distinguished, so that this program can be financed out of public money, with parliamentary agreement.

It is compatible with the ethical principles advocated in this book, and indeed a requirement for financing basic care to uphold income solidarity, that society should pay the bill for basic care for the poor and unemployed. But the transparency principle requires that these financial expenditures should be accounted for separately. Let it be apparent which authority or which program is covering the care for those in need.

Transparency is not the only problem. The tables reflect,

and sometimes in an exaggerated way, the general distortions of the tax system in the post-socialist countries, particularly regarding the unfair distribution of the tax burden. The income of the population of active age falls into two main sets. One consists of legal earnings from regular employment. This income is easily identified, so that a tax or contribution dependent on income is simple to levy. With this kind of income, it is easy to apply the third of the types of redistribution discussed in this section, through a simple linear payroll tax or an equivalent linear social-insurance contribution. Those who earn more will pay more. The second set consists of all other income, which is hard to tax and may escape taxation altogether. Many people obtain "invisible" income. For instance, the employer, in agreement with the employee, reports only part of the pay to the authorities and pays the rest directly in cash to avoid taxation. Many of the self-employed, who range from destitute casual workers to millionaire business people, disguise their income altogether, or declare only part of it. The agricultural population is a special case, whose members partly overlap with the self-employed. The agricultural population in all Eastern European countries contributes proportionately less than its share to the common purse, and that applies to its payments of health-care contributions as well.[9] For instance, the employer, in agreement with the employee, reports only part of the pay to the authorities and pays the rest directly in cash to avoid taxation.

Universal entitlement means not only that *everyone* receives basic care but also that everyone has a responsibility to pay the health tax or compulsory contributions, unless social solidarity dictates otherwise. In the latter regard the universality of the basic-care entitlement in Eastern Europe is

[9] In Albania, for instance, self-employed people living in rural areas comprise 54 percent of the active population. Only a tenth of this group paid contributions for health care in 1997. (Health Insurance Institute of Albania 1998.)

distorted. Not everyone who receives sufficient income *contributes* to financing basic care. There are many free-riders. Public opinion would be content with the existence of free-riders if they were all desperately poor, but in fact many free-riders have an acceptable standard of living or are positively prosperous. This division into two income sets is reflected in an exaggerated form in the rows of the three tables that have to do with employees (tables 6.1–6.3). Employees make up 30–40 percent of the population, but they bear 60–80 percent of the financing load. That financing load would be far more acceptable if it were spread out among a larger percentage of the population, who in fact are employees in many cases but do not pay taxes on their income.

Some recommendations can be formulated in the light of what has been said.

A broader base

Expanding the financial resources for basic health care is part of a more general task that is on the agenda of every Eastern European country: expanding the base of contributions. Efforts must be made to convert activities in the tax-evading, informal, semi-legal or wholly illegal economy into parts of the legal, taxed economy, which joins in bearing the burden of public spending. That includes measures against the free-riders of basic health care.

The expression "health-care contribution," used hitherto, leaves open the question of whether the compulsory payments are to be a tax or a social-insurance contribution. At this point, however, the choice narrows. If the intention is to expand the base for compulsory payments for health-care purposes, to cover, for instance, earnings not associated with work, it becomes essential to introduce a comprehensive, general health tax and merge the present social-insurance contributions into it. Broadening the base of the health tax and not an increase in tax rates, is a preferred method for increasing revenue.[10] If the tax base were widened, contribution rates could be reduced while retaining the present standard of basic health care, or alternatively, the standard of care could rise without raising the tax rates.

A simple, transparent rule is recommended: let the health tax be "neutral"; let earnings be treated the same regardless of source. Wherever the earnings come from, on whatever score, let them be liable for the earmarked health tax. There is no need to set up new categories for this purpose or introduce new terms. The requisite definition of taxable income should be adopted from prevailing fiscal practice. A health tax that upholds the principles guiding these recommendations and has the virtue of simplicity could be linear, with a single rate applicable to all taxable income, regardless of source. While it is certainly unavoidable to have exceptions to the general rule, it is expedient to keep their number low.

Minimum requirement

To make health-tax avoidance harder, all citizens engaged in income-producing activity or receiving income in their own right should continue to pay a fixed, minimum tax, for the right to basic health care for themselves and their dependents. In other words, there should be a fixed sum payable up to an income ceiling, beyond which proportional tax should be paid, perhaps again up to a given threshold (discussed below).

---

[10] A similar idea has been advanced during the debates in France on reforming the welfare sector. Several experts recommended that as with tax, the liability to pay contributions should be extended. Their argument ran that health care had been extended to the whole of society, so that there was no justification for having only the wage and salary earners financing that care through their contributions. See Nagy (1997: 34).

The objection that the present welfare system bears too heavily on the active, wage and salary-earning population has also been voiced during the debates in Germany. This means that the active working population is supporting, for instance, those who do not need it, because they are living on the income from their capital. See Henke (1988: 67).

Similar arguments have been heard in the United States (see n. 4 above).

A uniformity of regulations is recommended to govern the fixed sum and the part of the tax proportional to income. Although taxation through a fixed minimum sum is regressive, as is financing by patient co-payments, such measures are useful for their disciplinary effect in linking financing to scope of provision. In both cases, exemptions would be made for those whose low income precludes paying these contributions without undue financial hardship. The proportion of incomes affected by the exceptions and the size of the concession should be much smaller than the present proportion of total incomes that is exempt from mandatory contributions. This is one of the purposes: to broaden the tax base despite the exceptions. By adjusting the level of the fixed sum and the progressivity of the remaining income-tax financing, the authorized democratic decision-makers in each country can decide what balance to strike between different redistributive and incentive goals of financing.

The idea has been put forward that citizens who wished to do so should be allowed to withdraw voluntarily from the general health-care system. They would not pay contributions and they would not avail themselves of public-financed care. The authors take the view that this right of withdrawal cannot be given at the present level of development in the region. The essential redistribution is on a large scale, so that withdrawal by those paying high contributions would cause serious losses to the system. On the other hand, it is not right to apply to an unlimited extent the formula of linear contributions. Up to a certain threshold of income, the contribution should remain proportionate to income, but thereafter it could be sharply graduated downwards or even be zero. A contribution formula of that kind operates in many Western countries and in some countries of Eastern Europe as well.

Co-payments

Since patient co-payments represent a tax on the sick, regardless of income, they weaken the redistributive effects of basic-care financing through broad-based taxation. As was mentioned in chapter 3 and will be discussed in more detail in the next section, however, universal co-payments are valuable for the incentive they give to limit demand.[11] To balance these considerations, there is justification for setting co-payment levels relatively low, to lessen their regressive effects.

Earmarked contributions

The highest possible proportion of the funds required for basic care should be covered from earmarked health-care contributions (or, where it can be introduced, from an earmarked health-care tax), and as little as possible from general budget revenues. It is easier to gain political acceptance for the former form of financing.

Sector neutrality and risk adjustment

Once all income is being taxed to finance basic health care, everyone has a right to receive it, including those, for instance, who avail themselves of private hospital treatment and doctors. The entitlement to basic care should be "sector-neutral" – available without discriminative restrictions from public or private providers. This subject will be considered in more detail later.

Everything said in this section refers simply to basic care, not to supplementary care, where principle 1, not principle 2, is dominant. As a later section (p. 246) will discuss in more detail, the proposed reform allows all individuals (and all employers prepared to pay part of their employees' costs) to obtain the supplementary insurance that they are able and

---

[11] Rigid rules are not intended here. In cases where co-payments would place great burdens on needy people, exemptions should be made.

willing to buy, subject only to general regulations designed to combat market failures.[12]

Co-payments

This method of payment was referred to earlier as *demand-side cost sharing* or *co-payments*. Already mentioned several times in passing, it is now time to look at this issue more closely.

As noted in chapter 3, one dilemma of payment-system design (as well as financing and benefit design) is the demand-side trade-off between efficient use, risk spreading, and solidarity associated with different levels of patient co-payments. Principles 8 and 9, calling for harmonious spending proportions and sustainable financing, do not really require co-payments. Basic care could be financed entirely by the health tax or compulsory contributions. This would probably have administrative advantages, because collecting and keeping account of co-payments causes extra work. It would also guarantee maximum risk spreading for patients and solidarity among consumers at different risk of needing basic services.

However, principle 4 – the need to encourage efficiency – gives a cogent motivation for introducing co-payments. It is an economic truism that nonpayment breeds waste and shortage. Although moral hazard is associated with any kind of insurance, for supplementary health-care "market-clearing" prices will eventually emerge for both up-front insurance premia and point-of-service co-payments, so that the market mechanism mediates between insurer, provider, and user. This is not the case with basic care, since public

---

[12] If an employer is prepared to contribute financially to the group supplementary insurance it has organized, there may still appear a redistributive element. This can be interpreted as a manifestation of solidarity among workers in the same organization.

financing is used to assure risk and income solidarity. Users of basic health services therefore have a much weaker financial incentive to limit their demand than would be the case if they paid a market price at the time of use. However, although the incentive is weaker, it is not right to avoid demand-side cost sharing altogether. Even a nominal co-payment has a disciplinary effect. It is for this reason that it would be beneficial not only to introduce modest co-payments for basic services, but also to stipulate that patients cannot buy supplementary insurance to cover these payments completely, removing the desired disciplinary effect.

It is worth remarking that the role of co-payments in financing basic care is increasing in many developed countries. In France, for instance, demand-side cost sharing takes the form of co-insurance, patient responsibility for a proportion of what is spent on that patient (rather than a fixed co-payment). Patients have been allowed to purchase supplementary insurance to cover the extra costs. A proposal has been put forward that patients should not be exempt from all demand-side cost sharing even if they have such insurance (OECD 1994b). In Germany, for hospital treatment, the insured pay a fixed sum per day for the first two weeks; after that, the treatment is fully covered by insurance (Pfaff, Busch and Rindsfüsser 1994).

Chapter 5, describing the present position of the reforms in Eastern Europe, gave a short account of where each country stands regarding introduction of co-payments. Table 5.6 shows that several countries in the region do not link many basic services to a co-payment of any kind. Although the first steps towards introducing co-payments have been taken in pharmaceutical supplies, these have not gone far enough in most countries in the region. Here further steps are necessary, in the authors' view.

Policy-makers need to act circumspectly and conscientiously keep the requirements of fair income and cost distribution in mind, while strengthening incentives for efficient use and curbing moral hazard. There are several complementary ways of doing this:

- The most important is for the scale of co-payments to be small, so that they are not a great burden on anyone. It is not for "fiscal" reasons that co-payments need to be introduced, but to act as an incentive to curb costs.

- There has to be careful consideration, from the medical and financial points of view, about the co-payment to prescribe for each kind of service. Haste can easily lead to mistaken measures that harm patients while failing to exert the desired economic effect.

- The co-payments should not be introduced at a time of economic crisis.[13] If possible the system should come into operation in a period of economic expansion, when the additional burden can be offset by increasing real earnings.

- Let there be a ceiling on the amount of co-payment any patient has to make in one year. Many commercial insurance policies include such a "stoploss" feature. Once people reach this ceiling (or once family members reach their combined ceiling) they should not have to pay any more co-payments. This ceiling might differ according to family income.

- The question of setting criteria for making exemptions from co-payments needs thorough consideration. Redistributive measures are justified by principle 2. The way of applying the principle depends on how the welfare sector in general and the health system in

[13] It seems to have been a mistake to try to introduce co-payments for the first time in Hungary as part of the 1995 stabilization and adjustment program. The government had to retreat in the face of the resistance it encountered. See Losonczi (1997: 93).

The co-payments introduced in Croatia in the early 1990s and the exclusion of certain preventive procedures from the basic package led to those in the worst financial situation losing access to preventive and primary care. This may cause damage in the long term (Chen and Mastilica 1998).

particular are going to handle cases of need. If, for instance, the needy are to be given financial assistance, the amount of this assistance will play a role in the decision. As far as economic incentives are concerned, if the assistance is enough to cover the co-payment, the incentives, even within the group concerned, will be maintained. However, paying such assistance is not always feasible, in which case the needy should be exempted from co-payments.

It is not this book's task to devise detailed practical measures. All we have tried to do is to demonstrate what we mean by trying to ease the difficulties caused by a co-payment system. However, while emphasizing this, it bears repeating that abandoning full and general "free" care and introducing co-payments is essential for curbing the rise in costs and overcoming the chronic shortage of funds for basic health care. Introducing demand-side cost sharing even in the face of popular discontent is a good gauge of the courage and principle of the political leadership, and of the government's and Parliament's commitment to reforming the health sector.

The basic benefit package

The previous sections have already clarified the main idea concerning the borderline between basic and supplementary services. The upper limit of spending on basic services is the politically feasible macro-budget. This section addresses the difficult question of how the content of the basic benefit package should be determined (apart from the requirement of some co-payments, just discussed). Who determines what health services are included in the citizen's entitlement to basic care?

Given the scarcity of resources in any society, some method of rationing is inevitable. The fact that it is common for insurance to cover all "medically necessary" services does not obviate the need for rationing. Why would something different be "medically necessary" in Germany and in Albania? "Most of the ways in which we ration care are invisible, obscured by cultural assumptions, political understandings, and economic realities" (Mechanic 1997: 83–4). Coverage of "whatever is medically necessary" shifts all the burden of decision-making onto the doctor or other health-care provider. Yet the provider is most attuned to the needs of individual patients, and far removed from the constraints of the macro-budget. There is certainly no reason for the sum of health-care demand defined according to each patient's "medical necessity" to stay within the macro-budget, unless services are implicitly rationed through such methods as waiting times and adjusted quality of care. Definition of basic care according to "medical necessity" is therefore indeterminate or even misleading. More specific criteria are needed.

We urge consideration of a transparent, socially acceptable process of explicit priority-setting to define a basic benefit package. It must be acknowledged from the outset that the criteria for making inclusion/exclusion decisions in health care can never be complete and unambiguous. There will always be scope and need for medical judgment. No list of priorities, guidelines, or treatment protocols can specify every scenario, every possible contingency. This is precisely the reason why we emphasize throughout the study the importance of incentives. Patients and providers must in the end make decisions about use of health-care resources, and those decisions will be colored by the incentives they face. Nevertheless, the inability to pre-specify everything does not negate the value of establishing a transparent and legitimate process for guiding the social choice of what health-care services should be included in the basic benefit package.

Transitional economies can make use of the diverse experiences of many other countries in this respect. There have been explicit efforts to define priorities for public coverage in many developed countries. For example, Sweden established a Parliamentary Priorities Commission to address this issue. In the Netherlands, the Dunning Committee Report of 1991 recommended priority-setting according to four criteria: medical care must be necessary, effective, and efficient; and there must be some patient co-responsibility. New Zealand established a Core Services Committee (later renamed the National Health Committee) and conducted a series of consensus conferences to help define health-care priorities. The state of Oregon in the United States expanded coverage to more low-income families by limiting the basic benefit Medicaid package to a specific list of services. Israel grappled with how to define basic care when implementing National Health Insurance in 1995.

Let us briefly examine the logic of various approaches to defining basic health care:

(1) As a first approximation, the status quo could serve as the basic package. Patients continue to receive all the services to which they have grown accustomed. In New Zealand, for example, "core services" were defined to include all services currently offered, since they were taken to represent "the values and priorities of past generations of New Zealanders" (Honigsbaum *et al.* 1995: 26). Israeli National Health Insurance adopted as its basic benefit package the comprehensive list of services of the largest sickness fund (Chinitz and Israeli 1997). Although adopting the status quo is far from unproblematic (e.g. it may build in inefficiencies and itself represent ambiguity from coverage of "all medically necessary services"), it nevertheless has social legitimacy and is generally politically feasible. This approach may be a good starting point in Eastern Europe, where much of the citizenry feels entitled to public financing for all available medical services. If the basic package is initiated as the status quo level of expenditure, further discussions

can focus on the micro-allocation of any increase in the macro-budget.

(2) The basic package will be limited by the real capacity of the health sector, in terms of both physical and human capital. The appropriate diffusion of new medical technologies is a particularly important issue for defining basic services constrained by a macro-budget. Most OECD countries have some system of health-technology assessment, including rigorous regulatory programs to assure the safety of new drugs and medical devices. Although detailed discussion of personnel policy and technology assessment are beyond the scope of this study, it must be noted that decisions on investment and medical education will have a critical indirect impact on what services are available and become socially accepted as integral to basic care.

(3) One approach to defining basic care is to develop a prioritized list of included health services. A frequently advocated and logical criterion for the ordering of services on such a list is some measure of "value for money," such as cost-effectiveness. Cost-effectiveness is the net gain in health from a health service (compared to doing nothing), divided by its cost. Ranking services by cost-effectiveness is information-intensive. Although measuring cost accurately presents some difficulties, the more problematic aspect is usually quantifying effectiveness in terms of health outcomes. Some form of adjustment is required for the fact that once illness or injury strikes, a person may never regain full health (i.e. there may be permanent effects on quality of life). Measures of cost-effectiveness with such adjustments include "Quality-Adjusted Life Years" (QALYs) and "Disability-Adjusted Life Years" (DALYs). When data is available, these can be used to rank services according to how much it costs to achieve an additional year of healthy life. That is, the lower the cost per DALY

obtained, the more cost-effective the service is.[14] Planning can start with "filling up" the macro-budget, beginning with the most cost-effective services and moving down the ranking list to cover progressively less cost-effective services.

Such a cost-effectiveness "algorithm" was used in Oregon to prioritize services for Medicaid beneficiaries in the initial (1990) list. The list that was actually implemented in 1994, however, was only loosely based on cost-effectiveness criteria (Tengs 1996). There are 743 medical condition/treatment pairs on the current list. The approved 1999–2001 budget funds condition/treatment pairs from line 1 through line 574 (Office for Oregon Health Plan Policy and Research Homepage 2000).

Although ranking according to cost-effectiveness is appealing in an era of evidence-based medicine, this criterion cannot be applied in a mechanical way to define a final listing of services for a basic package. Flexible deviations from a strict cost-effectiveness ranking are almost invariably needed to take into account other social values. For example, the initial 1990 ordering of condition/treatment pairs in Oregon gave high priority to certain treatments that many considered unimportant, such as treating thumb-sucking and acute headaches. Even more objectionable was the lower ranking given to treatment for certain serious and life-threatening conditions, such as AIDS and cystic fibrosis (Tengs 1996). The Oregon Health Services Commission prepared a revised list that prioritized services first along the dimension of "essential" (e.g. acute fatal) versus services that were "very important" (e.g. chronic nonfatal) or "valuable to certain individuals"

[14] Prioritization according to cost-effectiveness in terms of DALYs, for example, was recommended by the World Bank in its 1993 *World Development Report* (World Bank 1993).

(e.g. infertility services). The ordering was then subject to "hand adjustment" by commissioners, guided by public opinion and professional judgment. This process illustrates the limitations of strictly technical rankings.[15]

Oregon is not the only example of an explicit service list. As noted above, in Israel the basic basket for national insurance was a detailed service list originally used by a large sickness fund. But the Oregon approach stands out for its initial commitment to a cost-effectiveness ranking. Discussion of the Oregon experience often focuses on the ordering of condition/ treatment pairs. Yet this focus overlooks perhaps the most important strength of the Oregon approach, the *process* for defining the list and how it gained legitimacy for those operating under it (i.e. patients, their advocates, providers, and health plans).[16] There was widespread public consultation and open acknowledgment that cost-effectiveness or cost-benefit rankings, although useful, could not constitute the only criteria for decisions of exclusion. There needs to be some sense of broader social acceptability.

It is important to note that a ranking of services need not preclude coverage of additional services, *if* an efficient provider can provide those services for no more than the per-person cost allowed for basic services without engaging in risk selection. In this way, all patients can potentially benefit from efficient care,

[15] New Zealand's Core Services Committee felt that a list "would either have to be so broad as to be meaningless, or so rigid as to be inflexible and unfair"; the British government declared explicit listing of services "an exercise fraught with danger" (Ham 1997: 61–2).

[16] One can object that the Oregon Plan embodies rationing for the poorest segment of the population rather than the entire population and on these grounds is morally objectionable (e.g. Daniels 1998). We are sympathetic to this view, and note that what we are proposing is broader, system-wide reform for transitional economies in which the distinction between basic and supplementary services applies to all social strata.

without compromising the constraint on overall health spending. For example, in Oregon over three-quarters of beneficiaries are enrolled in managed-care plans. These plans receive a capitation payment based on the projected cost of the basic benefits covered on the Prioritized List. Since the plans assume full financial risk, their medical directors can – and do – authorize care for diagnoses "below the line" – i.e. for services not explicitly included in the basic package (Bodenheimer 1997: 654). This further illustrates how payment incentives interact with inclusion/exclusion decisions. By using capitation payment to transfer the risk to integrated provider organizations, the government maintains its hard-budget constraint while still allowing patients to benefit from efficiency improvements that may justify broader coverage. (Caution is nevertheless warranted regarding risk selection.) Several other factors also mitigate controversy over Oregon's Prioritized List.[17]

(4) Often the legal system plays an important role in defining the scope of basic health care. In Oregon, for example, the first list had to be modified because the ranking algorithm seemingly undervalued the quality of life associated with various states of disability and was potentially in violation of the Americans with Disabilities Act. In Israel, a case study of the role of courts in changing a basic benefit package comes from the controversy over Betaseron, a drug used to treat multiple sclerosis, a disease clearly covered by the Israeli National Health Insurance law. In 1995 several patients who were denied access to this drug filed suit

---

[17] Coverage has expanded, both in terms of population covered and in terms of some services (e.g. dental care and organ transplants) that were previously excluded. Moreover, since a diagnosis is required before treatment can be denied, many conditions (e.g. bronchitis) for which treatment is not technically covered can nevertheless be treated during a covered diagnostic visit (Bodenheimer 1997: 653–4).

and obtained court support in their quest to have the insurance pay for access to this drug. In 1996 the Ministry of Health recommended including the drug and, with the approval of the Ministry of Finance and the Committee on Labor and Social Welfare, Betaseron officially became part of the basic benefit package. The Ministry of Health issued guidelines (adopted from the United States) regarding who would have access to the drug. A court later overturned this limitation, in effect ruling that "cost considerations may be used to keep an item out of the basket completely but not to decide who will receive the service once it is in the basket. Only a prescribing physician can determine the use of a covered service" (Chinitz and Israeli 1997: 208).

(5) Clinical guidelines are an increasingly prevalent method for prioritization, usually supplementing one of the other methods for defining a basic benefit package. There are valid reasons for including a service, but only with restrictions. For example, cost-effectiveness rankings of a service may vary widely according to who receives the service (e.g. mammography screening for older versus younger women). In the Netherlands, entire groups of services are rarely excluded; rather, the extent of coverage is limited (Ham 1997: 61). In Oregon, the Health Services Commission developed six clinical guidelines to "clarify the intent of the condition/treatment pairs" (Oregon Health Services Commission 1999: ix). Guidelines can be seen as an attempt to develop an evidence-based link between a provider's professional judgment about an individual patient's needs and the broader social goal of prioritizing use of limited resources.

Well-established insurers (such as large managed-care organizations in the United States) have financial protocols for inclusion and exclusion decisions. These may feature precise instructions for doctors, based on medical practice and financial considerations. This approach to defining benefits can be seen as an organizational fusing of clinical guidelines and provider-payment incentives to influence the scope of services through providers' clinical decision-making.

(6) Another approach is to formulate a list of services that are clearly excluded from coverage. In the OECD, dental and vision care, regular physical exams and inoculations, *in vitro* fertilization, etc. are frequently not covered in public basic benefit packages. A variant on this theme is to define a basic package by considering whether there is precedent for a viable private insurance market for services excluded from publicly financed basic coverage. Although private insurance will tend to spring up naturally for many services, there are some health services which private insurers rarely cover or that present particular difficulty for regulating in a private insurance market. Using this line of reasoning, the Netherlands established a basic coverage tier under the Exceptional Medical Expenses Act for expenses "where the risk is such that it cannot be borne by individuals or adequately covered by private insurance," including long-term care in nursing homes, psychiatric hospitals, etc. (Netherlands Ministry of Health, Welfare, and Sport 1998: 5).

Clearly there are many different approaches to defining basic care. Inclusion and exclusion decisions are often highly controversial and politically charged. Basic benefit package designers are frequently subject to lobbying by specific beneficiary or provider groups that feel that services they value are unfairly excluded.[18] Each society will need to establish an approach compatible with its own cultural, political, and economic circumstances.

---

[18] In Israel, for example, "several high-visibility and costly procedures were added to the basket in the wake of pressure brought by a number of special disease-interest groups" (Chinitz and Israeli 1997).

We urge policy-makers in Eastern Europe to develop a process for prioritization of basic care that supports the principle of *transparency*. Eschewing the difficulties of explicit priority-setting merely leads to nontransparent forms of rationing.[19] Public involvement is critical. New Zealand used questionnaires, public meetings, ethics workshops, and open expert advisory hearings. Sweden and Oregon also used work groups to study and discuss the issues. The Netherlands had an extensive communication plan, including a public information campaign, responses elicited through a simplified report sent to all health professionals, and widespread media coverage (Ham 1997).

Appropriate institutions need to be established for coordinating public involvement and otherwise overseeing the continuing process of defining and updating the scope of basic care. In many countries such institutions already exist; for others, they must be created. Usually legislatures have final authority, but many countries attempt to keep the listing of specific medical services out of the political fray. It may be useful to describe in some detail the institutional arrangements in a few cases.

In Oregon, the state legislature established the Oregon Health Services Commission to develop and review the Prioritized List of Health Services. The Commission is composed of eleven members (five physicians, four consumer representatives, a public health nurse, and a social worker). Modifications to the List currently are made every half-year for coding changes and every year for consideration of new medical technologies. More thorough biennial reviews prior to each legislative session involve surveys of providers and open public hearings. The Health Outcomes Subcommittee (composed of the physician members of the Commission)

---

[19] Philosopher Norman Daniels suggests four conditions for establishing the legitimacy and fairness of limit-setting decisions in health care, including that the rationale for decisions be publicly accessible and subject to appeal (Daniels 1998: 42).

first review the evidence and then make recommendations to the full Commission. An independent actuarial firm determines the fiscal impact of any modifications of the List. If the modifications imply any significant change in cost, the Commission must present the request to the Oregon Legislative Emergency Board. Even if there is no projected change in cost, the Commission must report to the legislative leaders. Prior to the Balanced Budget Act of 1997, Oregon also had to gain approval from federal authorities (i.e. the Health Care Financing Administration). The Commission has also established a subcommittee on process to clarify the methodology of the prioritized list.

In Israel, implementation of the national health insurance law is overseen by a National Health Council, chaired by the Minister of Health and including representatives of the sickness funds, consumers, health-policy experts, and other government officials. Medical councils composed of leading medical practitioners give input on revisions to the basic benefit package. The Minister of Health may recommend additions to the basic basket, but "if these require additional resources, he or she must guarantee, together with the Minister of Finance, their availability. Any removal of items from the basic basket must be approved by the parliamentary Committee on Labor and Social Welfare" (Chinitz and Israeli 1997: 206–7).

Similarly, in the Netherlands, the Health Insurance Funds Council (or Health Care Insurance Board) makes recommendations to the Ministry of Health, Welfare, and Sport, and eventually legislature, regarding inclusion/exclusion decisions. The Council's 38 members include representatives of employers, employees, health insurers, and health-care providers (Netherlands Ministry of Health, Welfare, and Sport 1998).

Slovenia is the only Eastern European country to apply a transparent procedure that establishes priorities. Every year, there are negotiations between the Health Ministry, the providers, and the medical-insurance company, resulting in an agreement on the quantity and price of care and the payments to be made. The agreement covers, for instance, how many hip replacements, cataract and heart operations, MRI tests, and so on the insurer will finance. The likely number of patients is estimated from the previous year's data and the lengths of the waiting lists. (It is worth noting that precise data on these are available.) These data provide the basis on which it is decided how many of each procedure to finance. The providers can apply for funds from the allocations. The insurer does not pay for procedures over and above the agreed numbers.

In 1998, the total number of hospital patients was at 8 percent more than planned, but the aggregate volume of the provisions realized was 95.3 percent of the plan. Hospitals where the performance did not reach the planned figure were given compensation by the insurer, to prevent institutions making efforts to spend at all costs the complete sum they had applied for (Health Insurance Institute of Slovenia 1999).

Organization of insurance: ownership, decentralization, and managed competition

In the rest of this discussion, it will be assumed that those drawing up the reforms have accepted the proposals put forward so far in this chapter. They are ready to treat basic care as a universal right to be financed out of public money. Even so, they still have before them several alternatives, which can be classified from several points of view.

A first choice concerns whether basic care should be provided directly by the state in an integrated national-health service, or whether it should be purchased from separate providers, through a system of social insurance. As noted earlier, the classic case of the first is the original British system and of the second the German one. To give a clear example as a reminder, hospital costs are covered directly by the state budget under the first system (through an administrative authority). Under the second system, most public financing is collected under the heading of a social-insurance contribution from those who are legally compelled to contribute and then goes into the coffers of an insurance institution (or several such institutions), which in turn pays the hospital. Under this system, "money follows the patient" rather than being allocated by the central budget directly to a provider.

This book recommends the second alternative. It is more flexible and transparent, and leaves open more avenues towards further reform variants. (As was noted in chapter 4, even the United Kingdom has moved away from a pure integrated model by separating purchaser and provider roles within the National Health Service.) The most cogent argument, however, is that social insurance is the starting point in most Eastern European countries (see table 5.2, p. 146). These countries have already changed from the Soviet model of integrated, centrally directed provision and financing to the German model of social insurance with separation of provision from financing, which leaves few arguments for reintegration.[20] In terms of the typology introduced in chapter 3 (see figure 3.1, p. 77), Eastern Europe has transformed from "I. Integration" to "II. Separation" and we believe this is a positive first step in reform. This leaves open the question of the remaining degree of integration between sponsor(s), insurer(s), and provider(s) – II.i, II.ii, or II.iii – an issue to which we will return.

A second choice concerns what is often referred to in the literature on the subject as deciding between a "single-payer" and a "multi-payer" system, and the associated degree of centralization or decentralization. Should there be a single health insurer for basic care, who pools risk for all consumers

---

[20] The discussion returns later to the question of whether it is worth considering integration of insurance and provision in small units like American HMOs, in the context of a decentralized system of health insurers and providers. That was an important issue in Poland throughout the lengthy negotiations about the health-care reform (Bossert and Wlodarczyk 2000).

and pays providers for all or most of the costs of basic care? Or should insurance be decentralized, with smaller risk pools and possibly competing insurers?

Under a single-payer system, the roles of sponsor and insurer are naturally integrated (II.ii). The government or noncommercial central fund in charge of disbursing the compulsory contributions for basic care on behalf of consumers (i.e. the sponsor) also acts as insurer. There are many advocates of the idea that insurance for basic health care should remain in such a noncommercial, social-insurance framework, but be broken up into regional bodies to prevent over-centralization. Instead of a single, giant organization, there would be smaller, regional social-insurance organizations that would be easier to monitor (World Bank 1993; Bossert and Wlodarczyk 2000). These would not compete with each other. All those entitled to care, along with their dependents, would automatically pay contributions to and receive insurance from the social insurer for the area in which they lived. The decentralization would therefore retain an insurance monopoly, albeit at a regional rather than a national level. There has been some debate about whether regional decentralization is worthwhile while retaining an insurance monopoly. This is simply an administrative problem, not a delicate issue of social policy. Advocates of regional decentralization cite above all the advantage that it encourages flexible adaptation to local conditions. Where this favorable effect really occurs, there can be no objection to it.[21] The more fundamental policy question is whether an insurance monopoly should be retained, or whether it is worthwhile introducing competition among insurers.

A multi-payer system, by definition, breaks the monopoly

[21] Whether it is worth aiming for territorial decentralization probably depends on the size of the country. The population of most post-socialist countries in Eastern Europe is around 10 million or less. The problem has received greater attention in Poland, which has 38.5 million inhabitants. There territorial decentralization has featured in all the various reform proposals (Bossert and Wlodarczyk 2000).

over insurance: multiple insurers co-exist and compete for consumers; providers may receive payment from multiple payers.[22] Although in theory competing insurers could all be state-owned, in practice multi-payer systems almost invariably feature competing private insurers. There could, however, continue to be a single national sponsor, a central fund, that mediates between consumers and insurers by passing on public health-care financing to insurers in accordance with which consumers have chosen which insurers. In this case, the sponsor function is separate from the insurer function (forms II.i or II.iii in figure 3.1).[23] Private insurers would compete in selling health insurance. They would certainly compete with each other, but how would they relate to the noncommercial social-insurance organization (that originally functioned as both sponsor and insurer)? Would they simply augment its activity, or would they compete with it?

A   Under this alternative, there would continue to be a public monopoly over insurance for basic care, although risk might be pooled at the central or regional level. In contrast to this insurance monopoly for basic care, there would be legal opportunities for competition in insurance and provision of supplementary care. Insurance for supplementary services could be offered by both public and private insurers.[24]

---

[22] With social-insurance monopoly decentralized to a regional level, specialty providers in particular areas (such as hospitals with high-technology equipment in the nation's capital) may receive patients and their associated payments from several different regional insurers, thus introducing an element of a multi-payer system. To distinguish this case from multiple insurers in each region, we continue to refer to the former as a regional single-payer system.

[23] It is also possible for the sponsor to organize its own insurance plan and simultaneously to manage competition among separate insurers, although this may make the sponsor less objective *vis-à-vis* the competing insurers. The redistribution in the Czech Republic is done by a single insurer, the General Health Insurance Institute, so that it has a sponsor function. In Poland, a separate equalization fund has been established, operating independently from the regional single payers.

[24] This raises a terminological problem. The term "social insurance" origi-

B   Under this alternative, the public monopoly over insu-
     rance for basic care would cease. Private insurers would
     be free to offer insurance covering basic as well as sup-
     plementary care. This alternative would turn health
     insurance into a field in which competition was felt in
     every branch.

Figure 6.2 represents schematically how four important
choices regarding insurance organization are classified and
linked together. A stand has already been taken on the first
dilemma; what follows concerns the choices remaining after
separation of financing and provision has been established.

There is considerable debate in the literature about the relative virtues of single- and multi-payer systems.[25] Most of
these issues arise in conjunction with choice 3, the form in
which a multi-payer system would be structured, and will be
discussed in a moment. The primary reason why a multi-
payer system can be recommended to Eastern Europe is its
ability to support the principles of choice, competition, and
incentives for efficiency. If supplementary care is to be
allowed, and consumers are allowed to purchase insurance
for such services, then a multi-payer system follows almost
automatically. A public single-payer could offer consumers
supplementary insurance, but consumers would have little
choice; a more vibrant supplementary-care sector would
allow consumer choice among competing (public and
private) insurers.

nally denoted the "pure" Bismarckian model in which the income of the
insurer would come from the payments of its members and the insurer
had a monopoly over insuring basic care. If private insurers are also
allowed to join in offering insurance for basic or supplementary care, it is
doubtful whether it is worth reserving the concept of social insurance for
noncommercial, publicly owned insurers. To avoid controversies in terminology, from this point onwards the expression "public insurer" will
be contraposed with "private insurer."

[25] On the advantages and drawbacks of centralizing and decentralizing insurance, see Saltman and Figueras (1997: 43–58).

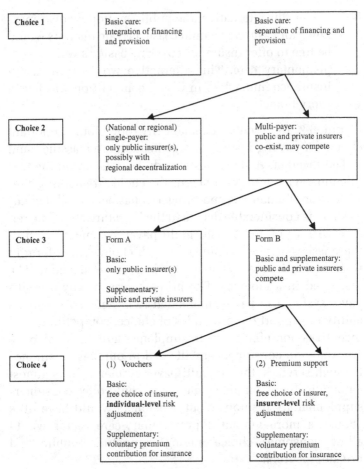

Figure 6.2 Alternative ways of decentralizing the insurance system

What is of practical concern to Eastern Europe is the viability of a multi-payer system, should its citizens prefer such a system. Tempers have not become frayed about whether private insurers should be allowed to offer supplementary insurance packages. The trouble is that the idea has not excited much enthusiasm among the insurers themselves. The opportunities for this have hardly been exploited, in fact.

What would really interest the private insurers would be to participate in basic care. If they could offer their consumers a policy that included both basic and supplementary care, they would face enormous market prospects. Where the insurer interest in providing basic and supplementary care stems from the potential to offer efficient integrated services to consumers, this should be welcomed and encouraged. Caution is warranted, however: one significant reason why insurers may be eager to offer basic as well as supplementary coverage is because they foresee profitable opportunities for risk selection. If private insurers "cream skim" low-cost consumers through marketing attractive supplementary packages, such insurers may be able to make considerable profits, while leaving the public insurer(s) with an adverse selection of high-cost consumers. Policies to avoid the latter scenario feature prominently in the recommendations to follow in this and later chapters.

Prior to summarizing the main arguments regarding forms A and B, it is useful to consider how form B, managed competition for both basic and supplementary insurance, would be structured. True decentralization of insurance for basic as well as supplementary care, with independent, private and public insurers competing with each other, could be administered in several ways. The sums for financing basic care, notably the compulsory contributions of citizens, would flow into a central state fund.[26] Consumers would choose among

---

[26] A continuation of the terminological problem raised in n. 24 has to be mentioned here. What name should be given to the compulsory health-care contributions paid by citizens? Where the German model has entrenched itself, these are known in most countries as "social-insurance contributions." If the proposal on p. 197 is accepted, they should be referred to instead as "health tax." At the same time, it is doubtful, as n. 24 pointed out, that the category "social insurance" can be maintained once there is competition in all branches of medical insurance between publicly and privately owned insurers. For the rest of the book, the umbrella term "compulsory contribution" will be used. In fact the attribute "compulsory" will often be omitted if it can be deduced from the context that this is a question of a contribution that has to be paid, not a voluntary insurance premium.

competing insurers. How would the public financing for basic care, held in the central fund, reach the chosen insurer? Two alternatives are shown under choice 4 in figure 6.2 and illustrated in figure 6.3.

One technique is a *voucher system*. Each year, the central fund, acting as a sponsor, would issue all those entitled to basic care with a voucher, which they would pass on to the insurer of their choice. The value of the voucher would differ, mainly according to age, but also according to sex, occupation, and perhaps other criteria. In other words, the vouchers would be individually risk-adjusted. For instance, the voucher of a 70-year-old consumer would bring the insurer a much bigger payment than the voucher of a 30-year-old. The individual risk adjustment would be calculated so that the total value of the vouchers equaled the macro-budget for basic care. Consumers would choose between a range of insurance policies, which would cover the same basic benefit package but potentially differ in the supplementary care covered (which services were covered, how much demand-side cost sharing the patient would bear, how much choice of doctor the patient would enjoy, and so on). The money derived from each consumer by the insurance company would consist of two items: the risk-adjusted value of the voucher the individual had handed over and a further payment out of his or her own pocket towards the premium for supplementary insurance. Under such a voucher scheme, an insurer would charge different individuals different prices for the same package of services. For example, an individual's premium for basic-care insurance would be the value of his or her risk-adjusted voucher.

Premium support is an alternative way of organizing the flow of funds from the central fund to competing insurers. Each insurer would charge all consumers the same price for a given set of services. The central fund would promise each citizen a fixed sum of money to support the purchase of insurance for basic care. The sum would be the same for all

(1) Vouchers

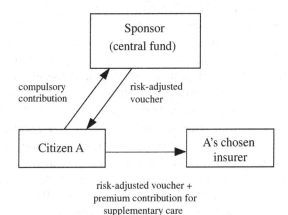

(2) Premium support

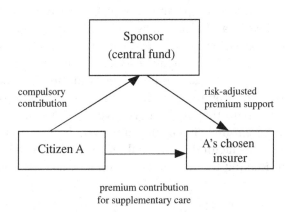

Figure 6.3 Financing flows under different decentralized insurance schemes

Note: For simplicity, only one citizen and one insurer is shown, although all citizens may choose from among competing insurers under either scheme. The premium contribution for supplementary care is voluntary. Providers (not shown) may be integrated with insurers or separate entities paid by the insurer for providing services.

people entitled to basic care. Consumers would compare insurance packages and choose a preferred insurer. If the premium for the chosen insurance package is higher than the defined sum promised from the central fund, the consumer pays the extra amount. This makes the consumer cost-conscious when choosing an insurer, and therefore induces insurers to strive to improve to attract more enrollees. Unlike a voucher scheme, the central fund does not pay the individual the premium support, but rather pays the individual's insurer. To avoid insurer competition based on selecting good risks rather than lowering cost and/or improving quality, the *ex ante* payments to insurers should be risk-adjusted to reflect the risk of their pool of enrollees. Selection could be further mitigated by mixed payment and mandatory high-risk pooling.[27]

An example of managed competition based on premium support comes from Harvard University. Harvard contributes a defined sum to the purchase of insurance and tries to give its employees a choice. There are nine insurance plans to choose from, differing from each other in terms of premium, size of co-payments, scope of services, restrictions on choice of providers, etc. The employer's contribution is fixed, irrespective of how employees choose. Those who choose a more expensive (and they hope more favorable) plan must pay a higher premium. Since the university's contribution is uniform, this factor does not influence the choice of the individual. Making the insurance companies compete has sub-

---

[27] Mixed-payment supplements *ex ante* premium payments from the central fund with some *ex post* payment to an insurer based on the actual use of services by its patients. Under mandatory high-risk pooling, insurers receive additional payment for those patients that they predict in advance will be high-cost. The insurers are required to contribute to a pool of funds to cover the costs of high-risk patients and are allowed to place, at the beginning of the period in question, a small fraction of their patients in the high-risk pool. The expenses of treating these high-risk patients are reimbursed from the pool of funds more generously than others, perhaps in full. These payment concepts were introduced in chapter 3 (p. 92) and will be discussed in more detail in chapter 8 as well.

stantially reduced the costs to the university and to the employees. On the other hand, adverse selection (see chapter 3, p. 56) raised its head. A death spiral developed for the most generous plan and it had to be withdrawn. This removed the most attractive plan from the set of choices available to employees. Despite this negative side-effect, the competition between the insurers seems to have brought favorable results overall (Cutler and Reber 1998).

To avoid such problems of selection, the premium-support payments should be risk-adjusted. (Harvard was not using risk adjustment during the period of the study cited above.) The central fund should predict each citizen's basic care cost. Instead of giving that risk-adjusted sum to the individual as a voucher, the fund would pay that defined amount directly to the individual's chosen insurer. Since the payment is directly to the insurer for all of the covered individuals, risk adjustment for premium support involves predicting costs for a pool of individuals rather than each one separately.

Choice 4, between vouchers and premium support, involves several technical issues for which no definitive theoretical and empirical evidence has yet been collected, particularly since there is little experience with vouchers. Perhaps a voucher scheme may be preferable if high weight is put on principle 1 over principle 2, and premium support if the relative weights are reversed. The question of the most effective strategy for structuring form B certainly merits further study.[28]

Let us return to the third choice, between the alternative forms A and B. This is a far from straightforward choice problem. Opinions in some countries have already clashed,

---

[28] The second author feels that a system of premium support would be preferable to a voucher scheme for assuring choice while avoiding problems of selection. The primary reason is that relying on individually risk-adjusted vouchers when the technology of risk adjustment is limited may lead to severe problems of risk selection, which can become institutionally entrenched and politically difficult to reverse.

while in others the debate is still to come. A notable public-opinion survey was conducted in Hungary on this subject (see tables 9.2–9.4, pp. 332–333). A high proportion of the sample would support a change from A to B even if it meant higher contributions, but many would do so only if the contributions stayed the same, and some dismiss any idea of competition.

Retaining form A also poses problems from the point of view of public law. Who is the legitimate decision-maker in the affairs of the monopoly social-insurance organization, the legislature or the government? Or should there be a separate governing body for the social-insurance system? In the latter case, what procedure should be taken to form the governing body? Should it be elected by the insured, or should it consist of delegates of social organizations (such as employers, employees, or medical associations?)[29] The purpose here is simply to raise these questions, not to go into specific recommendations. All that needs to be underlined, in view of the fact that this is a special monopoly organization run on public money, is that public supervision is vitally needed.

Form A, based on a public monopoly of basic insurance, has two big advantages. It is simple to administer, so that it could be much cheaper to run than having several parallel, competing organizations, each with its own administration, which would also mean that the providers had to collect their

---

[29] The public law status of the centralized social-insurance system in Eastern Europe differs from country to country. In Bulgaria, for instance, the autonomous National Health Insurance Fund began to exercise its statutory rights in 2000. Its governing body consists in equal proportions of representatives of the insured, the employers, and the employees. Legislation was passed in Romania in 1998 granting self-governing powers to the Health Care Fund, which is headed by representatives of the insured and the employers. There is a similarly constituted body heading the social-insurance system in Slovenia. In Hungary, on the other hand, the hitherto self-governing Social Insurance Fund, consisting of employers and employee representatives, was abolished in 1998, when the government took over direct control. The criticism of this change has been that public supervision of the financing of the basic provision is insufficient.

payments from several places at once.[30] The other big advantage is that it covers – pools risk for – the whole population. Especially with a national single-payer rather than regional ones, the public, among whom the risk is spread, is of maximum size. On the other hand, form A has the disadvantages associated with a monopoly: a tendency to make customers defenseless. Monopoly deprives the citizen of the means of exit, which would spur the insurer on to greater performance, innovation, and technical development. There is no economic incentive for a monopoly insurance organization to strive for maximum performance, either in its own administration or in its interaction with health-care providers. There is little reason to be thrifty in its expenditure. This form obviously clashes with principle 3, the need for competition to develop.

This is where the great advantages of form B lie. Here as in any other sphere, competition will induce greater ingenuity, innovation, and attention to consumers' needs. One drawback is the greater administrative expense, but it is clear that if this were the only shadow hanging over form B, the choice would be easy. In any sphere of the economy, the combined administration of several parallel organizations is always costlier in aggregate than the administration of a single monopoly organization. In the case of a forprofit organization, revenues must cover expenses and profits as well. The problem reproduces, within the bounds of a single branch, the well known contrast between socialism and capitalism, central planning and market competition. At first sight, the first element in these pairs, centralization and administrative monopoly, seems "cheaper" from a static point of view. However, the rivalry between the two systems over several decades proved that it was actually more expensive in the

---

[30] With the basic package, the monopoly social-insurance organization in Slovenia devoted 2.2 percent of spending to administration, while its counterpart in Hungary spent 3.8 percent (Health Insurance Institute of Slovenia 1999; National Bank of Hungary 1999). These figures show that the level of administrative spending is indeed low.

long term, because it led to indolence, technical conservatism, and stagnation.

It is much harder to compare the alternative forms from the risk-spreading point of view. Apart from the general arguments brought up in every debate about centralization and decentralization, monopoly and competition, there are some problems specific to the health sector to consider. It has been alluded to above, and discussed in detail in chapter 3, that competition combined with bearing risk leads to powerful incentives for adverse selection, risk selection, and cream skimming. Rival, competing insurers may try to gain an advantage by avoiding high-risk insureds. It is incumbent upon policy-makers themselves to define, and encourage sponsors to carefully monitor, the "rules of the game" for competing insurers, so that problems from selection can be minimized. Discussion will return to this point in chapters 7 and 8, but it may be useful here to delineate a few of the more important policies necessary to combat incentives for selection:

- It has to be stipulated legally that an insurer who wants to participate in the insurance market for basic care may not refuse a policy to anyone who wishes to purchase one. There must be a regular period of open enrollment, and no "pre-existing" conditions clauses (that preclude coverage for patients that contracted a medical condition prior to enrolling in that health plan). All purchasers of a given insurance package must be able to pay the same premium. In contrast, insurance for supplementary care is a voluntary transaction: if the client is unwilling to pay the premium the insurer asks, the contract will not be concluded.
- This will be a regulated industry; entry into it will not be entirely free. Companies wishing to enter the market will have to meet several professional and financial requirements. Ultimately, it would be desirable to have

just a few large, reputable insurers operating in a given market area, each with a large membership.[31] That will make it easier to spread risk, without sacrificing the beneficial incentives of competition for enrollees.

- Employers intending to contribute to the medical insurance of their employees will bring large groups of individuals to their insurers. This will increase the concentration and the size of risk pools, and allow employers to fulfill some of the roles of a sponsor, particularly as a countervailing power for bargaining with insurers. More will be said about the role of employers as sponsors on p. 255.

- The payment system, particularly risk adjustment, will be critical in mitigating incentives for risk selection. Appropriate differentiation of the payment an insurer receives for different insureds will reduce in itself the resistance to accepting insureds who are bad risks. The more risk factors the payment captures, the greater the incentive for insurers to accept, or even seek out, enrollees who are likely to involve greater expenditure. Since risk adjustment is complex and limited, risk-sharing and mixed-payment systems should be encouraged, including mandatory *ex ante* high-risk pooling. These payment policy options, mentioned in chapter 3 (p. 92), will be discussed in more detail in chapter 8 under the linkages between demand and supply. Suffice it to note here that a combination of such policies, carefully

---

[31] In the Czech Republic, where a decision in favor of form B was taken in 1992, several small insurance companies came into being initially. By 1995, there were 27 insurers, of which some had fewer than 5,000 members. These proved not to be viable. Bankruptcies and mergers had reduced the number of health insurers to ten by 1998 and raised the average number of members to 301,000, discounting the successor to the old monopoly, the General Health Insurance Institute.

Slovakia introduced form B in 1995. Learning from the Czech experiences, the Slovak legislation stipulated that an insurer should have at least 30,000 members, rising to 300,000 within two years if it was to continue operating (Lawson and Nemec 1998: 245).

designed and rigorously implemented, can greatly reduce the chances of selection problems becoming so severe that they overshadow the innovation-spurring advantages of competition.

All these points could reduce the disadvantageous characteristics of form B, but they could not guarantee that they would cease entirely. There is no perfect solution. Form B brings with it the dangers of market failure. Form A, on the other hand, carries the prospect of government failures and the drawbacks of a monopoly.

In the authors' view, it is not the reformers who should decide on this. Indeed, this is a dilemma that should not be resolved by the legislature, either. The only competent judges are the citizens themselves. Let the reform create the conditions in which individuals may choose, and not just by answering questionnaires, or in parliamentary elections, by voting for the health-care program of some party or politician. Let them vote with their feet, by exercising a right to real entry and exit.[32]

The starting point could be form A. The monopoly public insurer that has financed basic care so far should continue to operate, either as a centralized organization or broken down into regional insurers. Let private insurers appear beside it, offering various supplementary insurance policies to consumers. This form already exists in most Western European countries. Although the proportion of supplementary services may not be high, it is increasing in extent and scope of care.

The road towards form B will have to be cleared with careful and diligent oversight. The first step will be to gather data and begin to develop a system capable of accurately risk-

---

[32] Giving citizens the right to choose between A and B suggests that the public-insurance monopoly for basic care under the former would not be an enforced monopoly, but rather a single insurer in a contestable market. It would be impossible to have both an enforced-monopoly form A and free choice to move to form B.

adjusting payments from the monopoly fund to insurers, even if everyone remains covered by the same insurer at first. Some experience is needed, in comparing the risk-adjusted premiums for each individual with the costs actually incurred, so that the risk adjustment can later be calibrated accurately. The original public insurer should have an incentive to help refine risk adjustment and other strategies to prevent selection, since it would be the victim of adverse selection if the payment system could not prevent private insurers from "cream skimming" profitable individuals.

It then has to be made legally possible for private insurers (if possible, companies which have proved reliable in activities outside the health sector and already known for supplementary health insurance) to offer insurance for basic care as well. Citizens will then be free to leave the old monopoly insurer and join the private insurer of their choice.

A word of warning: although it will be possible to withdraw from the publicly owned medical insurer, individuals will not have the right to cease altogether to pay the compulsory contributions (health tax, social-insurance contributions, etc.). In other words, under all the proposals in this book, there will always remain society-wide risk pooling for public financing of basic care.

It will emerge whether the insurers seize their opportunities by entering into the insurance of basic care.[33] It will also emerge whether citizens are inclined to disenroll from the earlier monopoly and choose a new insurer in the decentralized insurance sector. Finally, it will emerge likewise whether employers are prepared to contribute towards health insurance beyond mandatory payments for basic care, which insurers they choose for the purpose, and whether they act as

---

[33] Of course, it would be advisable to have discussions in advance with the private insurers, before the risk-adjustment scheme for premium support payments was devised. There would be no point in going through all that organizational and administrative work if the private insurers showed little interest in offering combined basic and supplementary coverage.

responsible sponsors on behalf of their employees without compromising broader social solidarity for basic care.

Although health insurance reform differs in many important respects from pension reform, it is interesting to note that a rather similar choice has opened in Hungary through the pension reform. This has made it possible for certain age groups to "vote with their feet" by transferring their accumulated pension rights to a private pension fund. It emerged that a very large number of people were keen to do that – far more, in fact, than the devisers of the reform had expected (Economist Intelligence Unit 1998: 24).

Choosing a form of medical insurance is harder than choosing a pension scheme in some ways. It is harder because it is not just about money, like a pension. Health care involves matters of life and death. Moreover, pension schemes do not have to deal with unpredictable catastrophic expenses in the same way health-insurance schemes must. As noted above, there should be regular open enrollment periods for all participating insurers. Consumers (and employers if they are selectively contracting on behalf of consumers) can change insurance companies, even as often as once a year. That includes the case where consumers dissatisfied with a private insurer decide to return to the publicly owned insurer. Changing the insurer may mean changing the doctor as well, which renders decision-making even more difficult.

If private medical insurance gains ground, it will not happen from one year to the next. It will happen gradually, over several years, as the insurance industry develops and becomes more attractive, and as people get used to the idea. The private insurers will have to compete for customers with the public insurer(s). It would be very damaging to sacrifice this fruitful and healthy competition in favor of forced, *Blitzkrieg* privatization of the medical insurance system.

The reorganization may bring difficulties. If very large numbers of people switch from the old monopoly to new insurers, the exodus may very well endanger its financial stability, because those who stay are likely to be an adverse selection of risks, so its costs will fall less than its customer base.

The only way to prevent adverse selection and a possible premium death spiral of the original insurer would be through accurate risk adjustment and supporting payment incentives (e.g. effective *ex ante* high-risk pooling, as explained above). In addition, along with the decrease in the public insurer's total turnover may come a fall in its social and political importance. Those to whom the power associated with a monopoly had importance may put up resistance.

Difficulties can be expected with the providers as well. Previously, their ability to count on patients and payment from the monopoly insurer for all or most of their capacity gave them security. Now they are faced with several buyers, pressuring them to provide more services for less payment. This may be more troublesome and stressful for them, although it will also make them less defenseless. They will certainly need to adopt a more market-oriented stance if they are to sell their activities. This change of attitude promises to be one of the main advantages of form B.

In the light of what has been said, there must be encouragement to experiment. Even so, form B must not be forced upon society by administrative command or legislative fiat. An attempt to do that in a rapid, radical way was made in the Czech Republic in 1992, without proper preparation or an adequate transition period. It caused much confusion, and in some cases, some serious abuses. As described in n. 31 above, principle 5 did not apply and the new role of the state was not framed sufficiently. It was likewise mistaken not to apply principle 7: insufficient time was given for preparation. All participants, including the sponsors and regulators entrusted with overseeing a smooth transition, will need time to adapt to the new system.

On no account should citizens be left at the mercy of

unregulated private insurers. There has to be state supervision, and, if need be, intervention. In line with principle 5, the state has to stand behind people as a guarantor of last resort. Even if a private insurance company should become insolvent, its individual insureds remain entitled to basic care. In such a case, the state – or, more precisely, the central fund collecting the compulsory contributions – will have to foot the bill. A sufficient reserve has to be set aside as a guarantee fund for this purpose, and it has to be made compulsory for the private insurers to contribute to it.

It is time to sum up the proposals regarding organization of insurance. Let managed competition develop, at first for supplementary services only, and then for comprehensive packages of basic and supplementary care. Where the German model applies, it should be augmented with form A. In other words, there must be a chance to purchase voluntary, supplementary health insurance, over and above insurance for the basic care ensured by public financing. The organization and legislative conditions for the development of form B, managed competition among insurers covering both basic and supplementary care, must be created. Since the public is divided over whether to choose form A or form B (see tables 9.2–9.4, pp. 332–333), form B should not be forced on anyone, but the freedom to choose should not be blocked off either. Private insurance companies, employers, and above all the members of the public will decide by their real choices how far they want to go in decentralizing health insurance.

The scope and financing of supplementary care

One task postponed from the previous sections is to see what health-care services can be left out of the "basic package." Let us take some examples as illustrations, without trying to compile a complete list:

(a) Diagnostic tests and general medical examinations of a preventive nature, as often as the patient desires, beyond the point where these are provided as basic care.

(b)   Health care designed to keep people in good physical condition, such as gymnastics, massage, and bathing treatments, available as basic care only for patients requiring direct intervention or for convalescents. The problem is similar with surgery to improve the eyesight.

(c)   In acute cases, treatment that is more comfortable for patients than those available as basic care. Where hospitalization cannot be avoided, a higher degree of comfort than the basic care (private room, better furnishings, radio and television, better food, etc.). There could be several grades of extra comfort with different prices.

(d)   Confirmation of diagnoses received through the basic-care system, based on a second or third medical opinion, where these are not covered as basic care.

(e)   If it is medically unclear whether hospitalization is necessary, or if it is, how long it should last, account can be taken of patients' preferences – home treatment where there is no medical objection, if patients prefer it and are prepared to pay the extra.[34] Conversely, prolongation of hospital stay at patients' request, even if it is not absolutely necessary from the medical point of view, so long as the patients pay the extra costs.

(f)   The part of post-acute care that is not financed as basic care (e.g. in a sanatorium or at home, with nursing in the latter case as well).

(g)   Doctors' visits at home, even in cases where the visit would be covered under basic care if the patient had gone to the doctor's office.

---

[34]   In some countries home nursing is provided as basic care under certain circumstances, against a relatively small co-payment from patients. This might be provided as privately financed supplementary care even in cases where it was not covered by basic care, or if patients sought a higher standard of home nursing than the basic care.

(h)   In the case of medically interchangeable drugs, choice of a more expensive drug in place of the cheaper one available as a basic care (assuming, of course, that its effects are not less favorable than those of the cheaper alternative).

(i)   Cosmetic surgery and plastic surgery for aesthetic purposes. Of course, in certain cases such as correcting scars or deformity resulting from an accident, they would be part of basic care, not supplementary care.

(j)   Many countries class dental care as a supplementary care, while in others only some costs of dental care are treated as supplementary.[35]

In none of the cases listed is there a hard and fast line between what counts as basic care, and what does not, so that it has to be financed privately. As GDP grows and the public becomes willing to devote more tax for the purpose, the sphere of expenditure covered as a basic care can increase. However, the line can be drawn at any given moment, and it would be expedient to ensure that such lines are actually drawn, to minimize unseemly disputes and corruption.

We would not expect strong objections to classifying as supplementary care the items of expenditure listed under points (a)–(j). However, mention must be made of two other, more controversial types:

(k)   As in every other profession, two doctors in the same position, with roughly the same training and the same length of professional experience, will not give the same performance. Individuals vary in their abilities, intellectual and manual skills, accumulated learning and expertise, knowledge of life, approach to patients, managerial abilities, and so on. There is no ethical or

---

[35] There is a lot of debate about this. Some consider that a radical removal of dental care from the basic care leads people to neglect their teeth, which ultimately causes social damage that outweighs the saving in public spending.

economic reason why they should all receive the same remuneration. It would not be right to set the same price for a routine operation if it was performed by a brilliant surgeon or by one of middling abilities, or for routine treatment by a brilliant dentist or a mediocre one. They will not perform the routine tasks to the same standard. This applies all the more strongly to treatment that is not routine.

Certainly, there should be a wider dispersion of doctors' earnings than there is in Eastern Europe at present. The differentiation allowed by the official pay scales is relatively little, although it is increased by income from gratuities and semi-legal private practice. It should be replaced by an openly acknowledged dispersion: let there be higher earnings for better doctors (or those thought to be better; discrepancies between perceived and actual performance appear in other professions as well). Higher earnings are the just reward for talent and industry, an indispensable incentive to sacrifice and continued training.

Who should provide the extra earnings for the better (or ostensibly better) doctors? The scales of pay for those employed by institutions in state ownership need to be spread much more widely. Some of the differentiation should be ceded to the sphere of activity covered by private financing. It falls outside the scope of this book to devise detailed strategies for implementation. Rather, this section simply outlines an approach. For doctors providing services covered by the basic benefit package, base remuneration, through salary, capitation, or otherwise, would come from public financing for basic care. Patients, exercising their freedom to choose their own doctor, could apply for treatment from a doctor who charges more, provided they were prepared to pay the difference (directly as a larger co-payment than would otherwise be required, or through private supplementary medical insurance). In other words, doctors would be allowed to "balance-bill" patients.

There is a danger that "star" doctors may end up dealing only with wealthier patients who pay more for their treatment. Bureaucratic regulation is ill suited to preventing this. It should be enough to appeal to doctors' healthy moral sense; the profession could provide for this in its ethical code. All doctors, however outstanding, would be expected to spend much of their time doing work in which there is no distinction between rich or poor, privately paying or only publicly financed patients. Organizational conditions have to be established so that doctors can fulfill these nondiscriminatory tasks, for the benefit of needier patients.

The problem of (k) connects closely with the next item.

(l)   There are some bottlenecks in health care, for instance some diagnostic or treatment facilities available only in a few places. Is it permissible for these to be offered to some patients out of turn, for a requisite fee, while others go on a long waiting list?

Most people's initial reaction is negative. This likewise clashes sharply with the specific egalitarianism that applies in health care.

The next reaction may be a cynical dismissal: that is what will happen whether we like it or not. Financial inducements and personal connections count for a lot when it comes to deciding who gets priority.

Better than cynical toleration would be to find an ethical, and at the same time effective, answer to this painful allocation dilemma. Again, the administrative side is ignored in favor of the general idea behind the procedure, which will be presented first of all through an example. The example may be contrived, but that allows it to express the ethical and economic problem more clearly.

Let us assume that a new, effective, but very expensive technical advance has not yet been introduced into a certain Eastern European country. A wealthy patient offers to buy the equipment and import it, so that it can be used for that patient's treatment, but offers it as a gift to the hospital, which means others can be treated with it as well. The patient has certainly obtained a privilege, as no one in the country has been treated with such equipment before. However, the privilege is accompanied by the salutary circumstance that others can benefit from the good deed as well.[36]

The first level of generalization from the example is that investment out of private donations must be permitted, even if the donor attaches certain detailed conditions of utilization. Such donations could be extremely useful because the system of basic health care can always make productive use of more capital.

Moving to a higher level of generalization, the possibility of cross-subsidies within an organization has been referred to earlier. This is widespread in many American and Western European private hospitals. Treatment of nonpaying or low-paying patients is financed out of revenue collected from wealthy patients. This would be permissible and desirable in the post-socialist region as well. The prices of some services financed from private sources should be set so that they incorporate a cross-subsidy.

Here it becomes possible to leave the example and formulate some general principles. The situation described

---

[36] The first author was told a story by a hospital doctor who was examining him with an expensive, modern piece of imported equipment. When examining one of the leading figures in the socialist party-state, he had told him it would be an advantage to examine him with a piece of equipment the hospital did not yet have. The leader concerned acted immediately. The apparatus was imported and presented to the hospital.

The story is analogous to the example given in the text above, except that the patron financed the extra import out of public funds, not his own pocket.

can be classified from the economic point of view as a special kind of secondary, redistributive tax. The first redistribution of health care occurs when people pay mandatory contributions proportionate to their income (not the care received). That is an income tax-type of redistribution. What is now proposed is an additional, secondary type of redistributive tax resembling a consumption tax. If some patients are prepared to pay for a service for which there is tight capacity, let them pay a *high* fee. Let this cover not only the cost of their own treatment, but a surcharge to meet the costs of others, unable to pay for themselves, and/or of acquiring further capacity or expanding the existing capacity. The scarcer the existing capacity, the higher the surcharge should be. Of course the capacity set aside for patients acquiring priority in this way should not equal the total capacity of the equipment. Some of it should be reserved for basic care.[37]

There may be relatively few instances of problem (1) in Eastern Europe these days. It has been discussed in detail because it presents in sharp relief the acute dilemma of principle 1 versus principle 2, sovereignty versus solidarity, and efficiency versus specific egalitarianism. The possible solutions to this dilemma need be opaque or cynical. Efforts must be made to find transparent, ethical, legally defensible, and efficient compromises between them.

The account so far has described the scope of services that might be deemed "supplementary," but only passing references have been made to ways of paying for them.

The most obvious way is for the patient to pay directly, out of his or her own pocket, as the expenditure occurs. This is

---

[37] The cross-subsidies would apply to the co-payment, not necessarily the fee that the provider receives for each service, since a distorted price structure with high profit margins on high cost procedures could lead to significant supply-side distortions.

quite common in Eastern Europe, even today. In some cases, it occurs legally, mainly in the private sector. A large part of the supplementary services listed are available in the private offices and clinics of doctors in private practice. There are sporadic cases where public hospitals and other health-care organizations are also prepared to offer extra services legally, for extra payment (e.g. a private room, better food, etc.). However, a considerable part of supplementary care is bought by patients semi-legally, by making "gratitude payments" to doctors. That was discussed in chapter 5 (p. 164) and it will be referred to again later.

The other possibility is to purchase insurance for certain supplementary services. Consumers each pay a set premium, in return for which the insurer covers certain costs as laid down in the policy. Unfortunately, the range of policies offered by the insurance industry remains narrow.

The country in the post-socialist region where voluntary private medical insurance is most common is Slovenia. There the National Health Insurance Institute and the Adriatic Insurance Company (AIC) administer voluntary supplementary health-insurance plans. In 1998, almost 70 percent of the population held a voluntary health-insurance plan with the Institute, either as an individual, or through trade union or special pensioner contracts. The policies taken out provided for 12 percent of the funds for health care in 1998. Most of these funds, however, cover co-payments, and only a fraction of them are purchased to cover extra services outside the scope of the compulsory health insurance (Health Insurance Institute of Slovenia 1999).

Private medical insurance in Hungary, Poland, and other countries is increasing but remains very small in extent so far. The obstacle to the spread of private insurance is phenomenon 'c', described in chapter 5 (p. 169). While access to the previously mentioned provisions, potentially coverable by supplementary insurance, can still be gained by paying out of one's own pocket for a couple of private visits to a doctor, there is no real risk to insure against, so that there will not be mass demand for supplementary insurance cover (Tymowska 1997). Probably this is the reason why the large private companies with experience in other branches of insurance have a much more restricted and narrower approach to medical insurance. [38]

With one unusual type of policy, widespread in Hungary, the insurer, instead of reimbursing the medical bills of an insured patient, pays the patient a specified sum proportionate to the length of the illness or hospitalization. On top of that, some policies also pay the insured a specified sum for certain types of surgical operation or treatment. Although the wording of the policy makes no mention of this, the tacit intention is clearly that the patient should pay the gratitude money out of the payment received from the insurer. This is a rational act of risk-reduction by the insured if gratitude money is taken to be ubiquitous and almost mandatory under the present circumstances. The large expenses associated with illness are covered by paying a monthly premium. At the same time, this insurance practice helps to conserve the gratitude-payment system, with its many detrimental effects. In any case, the incentive effect of the transaction is doubtful, because it encourages the insured and the collaborating doctor to lengthen the declared, justified or unjustified period of illness and the duration of the hospital stay. Moreover, such payments can be used to offset official co-payment requirements, which, as mentioned earlier, should not be generally allowed lest the disciplinary effect on demand be lost.

There is a vicious circle between demand for supplementary private insurance and the payment of gratitude money. While the latter continues, the demand for the former will remain small (and so will the supply). On the other hand, it

---

[38] At present, the insurance companies in Hungary, for instance, link life insurance policies with medical insurance cover, because the demand for pure medical insurance is not sufficient.

will be hard to eliminate gratitude payments before the chance of supplementary insurance is provided.

At the beginning of this section, twelve types of supplementary services were listed, from (a) to (l). Each of them entails insurable costs. Let us hope that eventually the private insurers in the post-socialist countries will produce insurance products that contribute to covering the costs of one or perhaps several groups of supplementary services. The supply will generate the demand for supplementary insurance (and vice versa), so that the more differentiated and varied the range offered becomes, the larger will be the number of buyers found. It would be a shame to wait until the private insurers can offer both basic and supplementary care together (in other words, for the form B discussed on p. 231 to win acceptance). It would be strongly in the interest of the private insurers to get to know the characteristics of medical insurance as soon as possible, gain experience in it, and win consumers' confidence. A good means of doing that is to establish a market in supplementary medical insurance. It is to be hoped that the availability of such insurance will also give more people access to supplementary services, since initially only the more affluent will have the cash on hand to pay for supplementary services when misfortunate strikes. By spreading the risk through smaller premium payments over a longer period, insurance can enable more consumers to have reliable access to these services when desired.

The role of employers

To discuss the role of employers in financing and organizing health insurance for their employees, basic and supplementary care need to be distinguished. First, let us confine the discussion to the insurance form A (see p. 230), i.e. to the case in which there is a public monopoly insurer for basic care.

With one exception, the regulations everywhere in Eastern

Europe prescribe separately the compulsory contributions to be paid by the employer and the employee.[39] However, the distinction is nominal (see Musgrave and Musgrave 1980: 494–6). Since the contribution is compulsory, it really forms part of wage costs in terms of its economic content.

Where the social-insurance contribution for health care is partly or wholly replaced by a health tax, it is worth considering the possibility of abolishing the distinction between the employer's and the employee's contributions. The employee's pay should be "grossed up" by a nominal increase, to a level where it includes the previous employer's contribution. The health tax can then be deducted from the increased wage, without affecting the net wage. This would dispel the fiscal illusion that employers were financing part of their employees' basic health care.[40] In fact, the actual financing burden falls on employees (or rather all health-taxpaying citizens). Since the macro-budget is decided in the political sphere, it would be extremely useful if the employees' tax awareness were clearer. They could then take a more considered position on whether they want a more generous basic benefits package, for which they, not their employers, would have to pay more tax, or whether they would rather pay less tax and be content with a relatively narrow scope of basic benefits.

Let us return to the present situation. The regulations in general stipulate that the employees' contributions are to be deducted from wages by employers. Then the employer's and employees' contributions are paid together into the requisite fund. The employers play only an administrative function in this, similar to the one that they perform by withholding personal income tax and paying it into the tax office. Presumably, they will continue to have to do so.

The situation with the financing of supplementary care is

[39] The exception is Poland, where contributions are entirely paid by the employee.
[40] This was the argument put forward by Count Otto Lambsdorff, the leading Free Democrat politician, during the debates on health-care reform in Germany (*Die Welt*, September 25, 1995).

radically different. Here employers have a free choice. They can decide to do nothing, or they can decide to contribute *voluntarily*. The degree of contribution may be widely dispersed. The employer's contribution to supplementary care constitutes an important fringe benefit. Employers may be induced to make such extra contributions by various circumstances. According to the efficiency-wage theory, employers are intent on attracting and retaining employees, for which they have a big need under market competition. Some employed groups may have won themselves privileges through wage bargaining. These two factors may act in conjunction. In some places, it may be an advantage for the employer or the employee, or both, that some of the costs related to labor are recorded as nontaxable fringe benefits, and not as taxable income.[41]

So far, there have only been traces of employer involvement in Eastern Europe, but it could play an important part in the future reforms.[42] So it is worth thinking out the implications in detail.

Employers not only contribute money for supplementary insurance; they also influence the choice of the insurer. A larger company or other organization may bring several thousand consumers to an insurance company, allowing it to spread its risk to a greater extent. This is an important function even if in form A it is confined to supplementary insurance. Its importance increases further under form B, when each insurer, in competition with the others, may cover both basic and supplementary care.

The insurers can be expected to compete vigorously for big

[41] Those devising the tax laws are aware of this effort and strive so to word the regulations that this cannot be used as a way of escaping tax.

[42] An American-type managed health-care company has been operating in the region since 1995 trying to introduce comprehensive pre-paid private healthcare. In four years it has created 15 medical centers in Poland. Some 35,000 people in about 1,000 companies are covered, of which many are well known Western corporations. The same company opened centers in Hungary and Romania as well (Medicover 2000).

employers bringing large communities of potential consumers, rather than for individual consumers. They will make more favorable offers (lower premiums and/or better benefits) to those who bring several thousand customers at once. Group insurance is cheaper than individual insurance for the same services, and the larger the group, the bigger the saving. This saving is shared in some proportion between the employer and employees.

In other words, employers can effectively play the role of a sponsor (chapter 3, p. 53), bargaining with insurers and providers on behalf of their employees. Through this bargaining, employers can obtain lower premium prices for insurance. Employers may also voluntarily take on a second role of a sponsor, namely contributing to private financing of supplementary care. Both functions presumably will benefit their employees.

Several problems could arise when employers take on this role. One would be that employers, through active bargaining, systematically receive lower prices (and/or better quality) for basic as well as supplementary care for their employees. This can compromise the requirement of specific egalitarianism regarding basic health care, since non-employees cannot buy the same package of high-quality care at a low price. Employees enjoy additional choices to which non-employees are denied access.

Another problem could be that employees become reluctant to change jobs, even for a more productive job elsewhere, for fear of losing the attractive health coverage provided by the current employer. Such "job lock" leads to inefficiency in the labor market. Regulations should be developed to avoid replicating this and other well known problems of an employment-based insurance system (see chapter 4, p. 124).

Opposite problems may also arise. Since the employer negotiates with the insurer and has an interest in saving costs, there is a danger that cost-cutting will come to the fore in a one-sided way, without the possible disadvantages for the quality of care being considered. In addition, individual choice may be reduced if the employer selects from the insurance companies available. The sovereignty of the individual would not be limited in this way if employees could choose freely from several insurance policies. In practice, however, employers exercise pre-selection. On one hand, this pre-selection may increase employee choice by making available an insurance option at a lower price than the same employee could obtain as an individual purchaser of that insurance. On the other hand, employer pre-selection may also reduce scope of choice in terms of number of options. Indeed, some employers are prepared to do business only with a single insurer, to cut down on their own expenses. They announce that they will give an employer's contribution only if the employees are prepared to go to the assigned insurer. So principle 3, competition among insurers, would work in practice, but it would seriously infringe principle 1, the sovereignty of the individual.

This problem cannot be avoided entirely, but it can be substantially alleviated through managed competition among several insurers, as the example of Harvard University given earlier illustrates.

Future legislation in Eastern Europe on employers' contributions could stipulate that a real choice of alternatives had to be given to employees, so that they were not forced into a certain course in this respect.

The relationship between insurer, employer, and employee just described applies most to large employers with several thousand employees. There is a different situation with small and medium-sized companies and other organizations employing smaller numbers of people. They do not bring a large number of new clients to the insurer and so they cannot extract such a favorable business deal. What can help is an association of small-scale employers. Such employer coalitions should also be allowed to develop as organized purchasers on behalf of their employees.

The role taken on by employers encourages a process that can lead to form B in the insurance market, where the competition between insurers widens. Indeed it seems justified to put it more strongly: this may be a prior condition for the form to work effectively.

Apart from the instruments mentioned so far (voluntary money contributions and group insurance), there is another way in which employers can cooperate in health care, and that is by providing facilities on the premises.[43] Some companies maintain company clinics, sometimes staffed not only by PCPs, but by dentists, pediatricians, or other specialists. Where work harmful to the health takes place, the medical personnel may organize special health protection and remedial holidays for workers. Companies under the socialist system provided occupational health care on a large scale. Many of these were closed after the system collapsed, in the first, overly enthusiastic wave of privatization and commercialization. As they get acquainted with Western European and Japanese experience, firms are realizing again that concern for employees' health is wholly compatible with capitalism. Even if it brings short-term costs, it may pay the company in the end by strengthening loyalty to the work place.

Whatever the form in which employers take part in financing the health care of their employees, their willingness to do so is influenced by the tax regulations. Most developed countries give tax concessions to encourage employers to take on such outlays. When the introduction of similar measures is considered in Eastern Europe, it has to be remembered that the tax concessions imply a redistributive transfer. Indirectly, the taxpayers as a whole are helping the employees of companies with health programs to gain access to supplementary provisions. This is not really in line with the guiding idea

---

[43] This is a second form of voluntary contribution to private financing of health care, through "making" provision in-house rather than "buying" services from separate providers.

behind the reform proposal advanced in this book, which would only finance basic care out of public money. Despite the inconsistency of this, it is worth considering a tax concession, because its advantages could outweigh its drawbacks. It is worth encouraging, at state level, employers to play a part in organizing and financing the insurance.

7

The supply side: delivery-system ownership, organization, and contracting

Encouraging private initiative

This book recommends a pluralistic delivery system, in line with the principle of competition (principle 3) and with international experience. This chapter deals primarily with ownership reform, but in relation to this, it also covers other problems concerning the economic issues of organization and contracting between producers (i.e. providers) and insurers.

Let us begin with what is not being recommended here. It is not that a great "blueprint" should be prepared, showing in advance which organizations should stay in public ownership and which should pass into private hands. The authors would advise firmly rejecting any privatization campaign that laid down beforehand when some critical threshold value for privatization had to be reached. Any decision that tried to organize the private health-care sector completely from above could only cause confusion.

On the other hand, much greater encouragement should be given to private initiative from below, in all its legally, ethically, and professionally correct forms. The book argues in several places for principle 1 to apply in the patients' interest. The principle also applies to providers, who have rights of individual sovereignty and initiative in their capacity as doctors, other health professionals, and entrepreneurs in the sector. Beyond basic prudential state regulation, there is no need for reformers to decide in advance what forms of private initiative are most desirable. Let them permit, and, indeed encourage, experimentation. It will emerge in due course what forms are most viable.

Of course, that does not mean that the government, the legislature, and the apparatus of state should watch the private initiatives in the health sector passively. They can develop to the full only if the state supports them. The existing regulations must be adjusted flexibly to changes in ownership. Rules to guide the lawful operation of private enterprise in the health sector have to be framed and a system of state supervision devised to oversee private providers. The actions of the state need not necessarily wait until private enterprise is in full operation. In many cases, they should precede events, creating the legal framework conducive to healthy development of the private sector. It is also worth considering whether the state should not support the expansion of the private sector by providing credit guarantees, especially initially, when the first, sporadic instances of private enterprise appear. This is in line with principle 5: a new role for the state.

Many reformers have a liking for uniformity, out of a pedantic sense of order and concern for transparency. Order is desirable, but it should be applied afterwards, when the situation is being reviewed. There is no reason at this stage to impose any strict, preordained uniformity on the forms permitted to exist, or to class them according to a few easily defined types. On the contrary, the healthy thing is to have various kinds of organizational innovations, followed, of course, by natural selection of those most effective. This is roughly what has happened in the other, commercial sectors of the economy.[1] If an organic, bottom-up approach was the

---

[1] There was much debate about this among economists in the early 1990s. The first author participated in these discussions and supported those advocating evolutionary development of the private sector and took issue with those (such as some Czechoslovak economists) who called for a rapid, forced campaign of privatization. On this debate see, for instance, Murrell (1995), Poznanski (1995), and Kornai (2000).

correct course of events there, the same is doubly true in the health sector, where special caution is needed.

Let us begin by looking at the expansion of the private sector as classified by the legal forms it takes:

(a)   One of the main lines of transformation will obviously be further expansion of the customary type of *individual private practice*. In an economic sense, these doctors are self-employed entrepreneurs.[2] (Alternatively, as will be seen shortly, several of them together may form a private partnership.)

Private practice can spread especially fast in primary care, with the privatization of family practice. Chapter 5 (p. 162) explained how this has been almost completed in the Czech Republic, Hungary, Romania, and Slovakia. It would be worthwhile for several other post-socialist countries to accelerate the process as well.

It is not easy to cut the umbilical cord binding PCPs to their previous employers (a local-government authority or other state body). Initially, hybrid forms may appear. For instance, doctors (individually or as partners) may operate as private entrepreneurs paying their assistants and other employees. However, the premises and equipment may remain in public ownership, but be made available to the doctors free of charge. A situation of that kind brings confusion regarding ownership, which will have to be clarified eventually. If the present owners want to retain the buildings and equipment in public ownership, they should insist that the doctors pay rent for them. Alternatively, they should privatize the fixed assets, by selling them, not handing them over free of charge.

Also widespread in the post-socialist countries is private dental practice.

---

[2] In this respect, the change resembles the process by which many lawyers who used to work mainly as state employees transformed themselves into self-employed attorneys in private practice (Mihályi 2000: 139–45).

Other specialists (such as gynecologists, oculists, ear, nose and throat specialists, or dermatologists) are able to deliver part of their services only in isolated private clinics. It is essential in these branches of medicine for patients to receive other components of specialist services in a hospital or another institution (such as a special diagnostic clinic). Certainly there is still plenty of scope for private medical practice in most post-socialist countries, not only in primary and dental care, but in other specialties as well.

(b)   Various kinds of cooperation among private PCPs and/or specialists in private practice emerge. The first such configurations have already appeared, and it would be worth encouraging them to appear more widely. There are several conceivable forms of cooperation:

(b1)   The doctor remains (in economic terms) a self-employed entrepreneur. However, several doctors can pool some of their resources into a *group practice*: they can share premises and support personnel, and buy and use jointly their medical and other equipment.

(b2)   Alternatively, physicians may take their cooperation a stage further by founding some kind of "*partnership*" of which they are co-owners. An organization of this kind may have employees as well, such as nurses, assistants, and secretaries.[3]

Form (a), the expansion of individual private practice, is likely to be followed, after some delay, by (b) forms, the various types of group practice and partnership. There is no reason to force the pace of such association, for which economic and professional considerations will provide incentives in any case.

---

[3] Private partnership, but also medical companies of type (d), to be discussed later, could well fit, in some countries, into the presently available legal frameworks. It is also possible that in certain other countries new legislation may be required, expressly to regulate the legal constraints and obligations on private partnerships and companies in the health sector.

(c) The previous points (a) and (b) refer to doctors who primarily treat patients outside the hospital, i.e. in an outpatient setting. Opportunities should also be presented
for medical partnerships in inpatient settings. Two lines
of development are possible:

(c1) One is for the hospital to enter into a contract with
a physician partnership that takes over a function
within the hospital building, bearing responsibility for this and keeping its own accounts. The contract might cover a specific diagnostic task, for
instance, running a laboratory, or providing specific types of medical procedures. Here the hospital is the "buyer" and the partnership the "seller."[4]
The hospital, instead of relying exclusively on the
services of its own employees, "contracts out" for
some services to be made available to patients on
its own premises by independent providers.

(c2) The other possibility is for a medical partnership
to rent premises, equipment, and perhaps support
staff in a hospital to provide services to its patients.
Here the association is the "buyer" and the hospital the "seller."

Of course, the roles are reversed regarding payment. In
case (c1), the hospital will receive payment for the
health service from the payer (patient and/or insurer).
In case (c2) the medical partnership will receive the
payment for the service. This means that (c2) represents
a higher "degree of privatization."

The effect of (c2), and other possible variants of (c),
is to divert into legal, regulated, transparent forms
transactions hitherto hidden in the mists of the gratuity
system and the health sector's "gray" economy. The
doctor is still receiving payment when the patient

---

[4] The arrangement somewhat resembles the "intra-enterprise economic
partnerships" (VGMK) found in Hungary within state-owned firms in the
final phase of the reform-socialist period.

makes use of the hospital's assets and staff, but it is happening in an open way.[5] There are legal contracts to decide in a straightforward way who gives and receives what.

Other health-sector personnel besides physicians should also be encouraged to work in the alternative forms (a), (b), and (c). This might occur separately from doctors, as self-employed individuals or through separate partnerships of masseurs, physiotherapists, or home nurses, or within a medical partnership covering the work of doctors and other health professionals alike.

The spread of such (c) forms – the development of contractual relations between hospitals and health-care partnerships – is likely to be more laborious than forms (a) and (b). The resistance may be to precisely the attributes cited as its main advantages: legality and transparency. The present, opaque state of relations between private activity and state-owned hospitals brings greater financial advantages to hospital-based physicians and other health providers than a straightforward contract relationship would. The "gray" economy provides a more fertile environment for gratitude money. The spread of contractual (c) forms should be encouraged by all who stand on the reform side, in the medical profession, in the state organizations dealing with health care, and in the political sphere.

(d)   Persons or corporate entities from outside the medical field must not be excluded from ownership of organizations, which take the legal form of private or public joint-stock companies engaged in health-sector activities.

Forms (b) and (c) differ from form (d) insofar as the

---

[5] Chapter 6, especially pp. 227 and 246, dealt with the organization of insurance and how financial flows between payers and providers might be structured. Chapter 8 will examine the incentives of the various payment methods in more detail.

owners of the former are insiders – physicians and other health-care providers – while all or most owners of form (d) firms are outsiders with no medical background. The owner of a private hospital or other private health-care organization may be a nonprofit institution (a foundation, a charity, a church, or a university). Alongside these, there may also appear profit-oriented owners (in most case joint-stock companies), for whom the sector is simply a place to invest.

There are great opportunities here. Private institutions each specializing in a specific health-care service are likely to be founded quite soon. Examples could be laboratories, diagnostic clinics operating special equipment of various kinds, dialysis units, clinics for eye operations, clinics for cosmetic and plastic surgery, and so on. Eventually, it will cease to be rare to find private hospitals conducting a range of medical activities as well.

At present the operation of private hospitals or outpatient clinics for profit is not prohibited by law in the post-socialist region. Among the obstacles are various limitations on financing, and the distortion of the principle of "sector-neutrality." (This will be considered in more detail later.) The prejudices against the private sector, found in the health-care bureaucracy and the political sphere, act as equally strong brakes on the development of private companies in the sector.

Prejudices have to be laid aside. Why should capitalist private enterprise not operate as efficiently in this field as it does elsewhere?[6] There is no need to designate its place beforehand, but it must be allowed to compete. If people want to found a new, "greenfield" institution and have the necessary capital, let them do so. If they offer favorable terms

---

[6] It is worth noting that a rather large body of literature comparing performance (quality, cost, uncompensated care, etc.) of forprofit and nonprofit hospitals, primarily in the United States but also elsewhere, finds generally few differences across ownership types (Sloan 2000).

for taking over ownership of an existing organization (such as a public hospital or outpatient clinic), then again, there can be no objection in principle. What has to be weighed is what commitments they are undertaking in health care, what developments they plan, what professional standard they guarantee, and what purchase price they propose. Do all these undertakings make for a more favorable situation than continuing to run the organization under the existing ownership conditions, possibly at a loss? These are the considerations on which the sale must depend. There is no need to wage a campaign to privatize organizations in public ownership, but there must be an approving attitude towards privatization transactions that are not just reassuring, but expressly advantageous.

It is worth drawing conclusions from the experiences with the privatization process in the business sector. At the beginning of the 1990s, there were still many supporters for the idea that ownership rights should be distributed free of charge, as a way of speeding up privatization. These days there are few advocates of this. There were unfortunate experiences in the Czech Republic, and above all in Russia, with the strategy of forced, hastily executed "mass privatization," the main instrument of which was give-away distribution of state assets. Yet this failed plan is recurring, now that the idea of privatizing public hospitals, clinics, and other larger care-providing institutions is cropping up in many Eastern European countries. Influential groups of doctors would gladly get their hands on valuable buildings and equipment obtained free or at nominal prices. There is a danger that the process may be contaminated by political or personal connections, and even bribery.

Instead of free distribution, there should be privatization by sale, at a respectable price, of the hospitals, polyclinics, and other organizations, along with their physical and human capital. If possible, this should be done on some kind of competitive basis, whereby rival offers can be compared under legally stable and impeccable conditions. Perhaps buyers should be allowed to pay the purchase price in several installments, or bank credit can be brought into the financing. Although detailed procedures that try to eliminate dishonest transactions slow the privatization process, why should there be a great hurry? The essential aspect is not the speed, but the improvement in the quality and efficiency of health care that results from the transformation of ownership. Some of the buyers may be insurers who wish to integrate insurance and provision (vertical integration), along the lines of HMOs. Others will be nonstate owners of similar organizations, looking to expand the scale of their operations (horizontal integration). Both forms should be allowed, along with other organizational innovations. Quite a long time is required for the transformation of ownership to run its course and translate into improvement in the delivery of health services. A forced acceleration of the natural growth would not have a happy outcome.

Decentralization of the insurance system began in the Czech Republic in 1992 (see chapter 6, p. 241, n. 31), in parallel with a privatization campaign on the supply side. Progress in the latter was especially rapid in primary care, dental, and outpatient specialist practices. Health-care institutions were placed in various categories, which received deadlines for privatization. However, the process came to a halt when it reached the hospitals, where the legal framework required was lacking (Vyborna 1995; Kokko *et al.* 1998).

The other Eastern European countries have not launched accelerated privatization campaigns imposed from above, as the Czechs did. Privatization and development of the private sector have begun sporadically (see p. 160), but most countries in the region face the opposite problem. Opportune measures of ownership reform for which the legal frames already exist are still being postponed.

There has to be strict professional supervision of the activity of private hospitals and other private enterprise in the health sector. Establishing the supervisory institutions and defining their legal status is one of the important elements of the reform. However, it should be added that organizations in the private sector do not need either looser or closer supervision than organizations in public ownership. Instances of negligence, neglectfulness, and malpractice may occur in either.

The change in the distribution of ownership forms brings with it a change in the scale of enterprise as well. Form (a) firms, by definition, are "mini-businesses." Forms (b) and (c) involve the development of small and medium-sized businesses. Form (d) firms may be of many different sizes, small, medium, and large, or even vast chains of hospitals. Whatever happens, the expansion of the private sector will reduce the concentration of large organizations characteristic of the socialist health sector. The change will resemble what has happened in industry and transport and in other service industries. Large concerns will remain significant, but the proportion of small and medium-sized units will rise dramatically, on both the input and output sides, in other words, in aggregate health-sector employment and in total supply of health care.

Strengthening the quasi-market elements in the public sector

The last section recommended strengthening the private sector in health care. Even if this objective should succeed, a very sizable public sector will remain. That is the experience internationally as well, as chapter 4 showed in some detail. Profound changes are needed in all the health-care providers where no radical change of ownership occurs, to improve the efficiency of care. The tasks here are similar to the ones that reformers seeking to introduce "market socialism" faced. The similarity is obvious: the organizations remain in public ownership, but the intention is to expose them, to a much greater extent, to market forces, for example through the pressure of competition with each other and with the private sector. The competition will not be perfect, since many hospitals and other health-care institutions will retain a national, or at least regional, monopoly of supply. The provider is faced with a monopsonistic single-payer, rather than an atomized mass of buyers, or, if there is a multi-payer situation, the insurance industry is likely to be heavily concentrated.

Above all, the spheres of ownership rights and associated responsibilities have to be divided more clearly between central government, local government, public hospitals, and other health-sector organizations. For the tasks that fall on the state, there is a justification for a higher degree of regional decentralization and an increase in the responsibilities and authority of the local government. As with the market-socialist reforms, it is especially important for the chief executive officer (CEO) of the hospital or other health-care institution to have much more independence and a broader decision-making authority than before.[7]

The CEO should not be expected to be the best doctor in the profession. The requirement is excellent managerial qualifications (Mihályi 2000: 146–8). He or she may have medical qualifications and experience, but it is not right to make that compulsory. The real yardstick is the ability, talent, and experience regarding health-care management.[8]

In many respects, the distinction between forprofit and nonprofit is a misleading one. A public hospital or other health-care institution needs enough income to cover its

[7] Hospital managers under the socialist system, like other high officials and enterprise managers, were selected mainly for their political loyalty. This habit persists in the post-socialist period. According to one source, for instance, fifteen hospital managers in Slovakia were dismissed in March 1995, but only in one case was the dismissal justifiable on strictly professional grounds (Lawson and Nemec 1998: 248).

[8] Extension training for this has begun in some post-socialist countries. The students have been drawn partly from the medical profession and partly from business professionals.

running expenses, and, beyond that, to equip, modernize, and maintain its premises and equipment. If the costs and revenues are calculated at reasonable prices (see chapter 8, p. 275) and the organization still makes a loss, that points to economic trouble that the management cannot ignore. To that extent, a public provider in the health sector cannot be an exception to the elementary rules of economics. The attribute "nonprofit" can refer to the presence of an owner that does *not* operate the institution for monetary profit, as opposed to a "forprofit" business, in which money has been invested by the owner with the express purpose of making one.

There should be more thorough, intensive bargaining by payers (mainly the insurers) over the prices for health-care services. Insurers should not be content to accept that it "costs what it costs." This is an unpopular task, which it should not take to extremes – the patients' interests should not be infringed – but it must combat waste of resources more effectively. Managed competition among insurers, outlined in chapter 6, will give insurance organizations an incentive to contract selectively with providers that can demonstrate cost-effective delivery of quality services. On the other side of the equation, the seller (provider) should be prepared to demonstrate how much the various procedures cost. They, too, will feel the effects of competition, particularly pressure to win contracts with insurers in order to gain a steady flow of patients. Providers will need to become more adept at issues of contracting and management, either through developing their own skills or hiring skilled contracting personnel to support their clinical practice.

The centralized system of wage regulation inherited from the socialist system has survived in the publicly owned hospitals of most post-socialist countries. This is another area where the aim must be to give to CEOs at least the powers that company managers gained under the market-socialist reforms: a high degree of autonomy in deciding the compensation packages for their workforce (see chapter 5, p. 157, chapter 8, p. 301).

It is worth considering whether the present legal constraints on procurement are not too cumbersome. A less constricting system might still provide a defense against the temptations of corruption.

There needs to be a re-examination of the present system of depreciation, and of the decision-making rights to do with investments. This ties in closely with the initial point: re-examining the allocation of ownership rights. There should be appreciable decentralization away from the present extreme centralization. Otherwise it will be impossible to apply principle 4, which calls for efficiency to be encouraged. The management of a public hospital or other publicly owned health-sector organization is responsible for the maintenance, modernization, and expansion of its physical equipment and infrastructure. Before this responsibility can be enforced, a large part of the decision-making powers and financing resources needs to be delegated.

8

The interaction of supply and demand: pricing, payment, hard budget constraints, and overall health-sector development

After exploring separately in chapters 6 and 7 the demand and supply sides in terms of financing, benefits, ownership and structure of insurance, and delivery of care, it is time to examine the interaction between them. Let us begin by thinking over the problem of prices, because they play an exceptionally important role as incentives on both the demand and supply sides and affect the allocation decisions in the political sphere. What costs should be included in prices? Where markets do not determine prices, how should administered prices be set? Discussion will then turn to broader issues of hard budget constraints and payment-system design (i.e. financial discipline, who bears risk, and to what extent prices are bundled together) and compensation for medical professionals (i.e. the level and dispersion of doctors' pay). After discussing the idea of sector neutrality (initially raised in chapter 6), the chapter concludes by describing how the proposed reforms answer the question of who decides about development of a nation's health sector.

Reasonable prices

In considering how reasonable prices should mediate between supply and demand in the health sector, particularly the issues of administrative versus market-based prices, the policy discussion has reached a point that is reminiscent of the debates about economic reform under socialism. The classic study by Hayek (1935) took the following line of thought. There can be no rational calculation conducive to efficiency unless there are prices that express relative scarcities. Such prices can be developed only by the market. Socialism eliminates the market when it abolishes private ownership and therefore becomes incapable of setting rational prices. The conclusion must be that socialism cannot operate efficiently.

Advocates of market socialism do not deny that rational prices are essential. Scholars from Oscar Lange to the present day have advanced various proposals for arriving at more or less rational prices without a true market, by simulating a market in some way.[1]

The difficulty of setting prices for health-care services is reminiscent of the problem under socialism, because it cannot build on a market mechanism in a comprehensive way. This arises partly out of recognition that there are significant "market failures" in the health sector (see the discussion of asymmetric information, moral hazard, and selection in chapter 3, pp. 54–62), partly from redistributive goals, and partly for less benign reasons of historical and political origin. The smaller the weight of the private sector on the supply and demand sides and the more the state interferes in the operation of the market mechanism, for any of the above reasons, the more inevitable it becomes that nonmarket factors will play an important role in determining prices. This also applies to most Western European economies, but it is true to a heightened extent in the post-socialist countries, which inherited from the socialist system a mechanism that all but eliminated private ownership and the market.

More or less real, market-clearing prices develop only in the narrow segment of the health sector where transactions take place legally between private sellers and private buyers.

---

[1] A good account of the voluminous literature on market socialism and the state of the debate is provided in a book edited by Bardhan and Roemer (1993).

That happens in private dental practice, for instance, where consumers can shop around for services, gain experience, judge quality, and become informed buyers. Many of the other transactions in the health sectors of Eastern Europe either take place without a price, on a basis of physical rationing, or at seriously distorted prices.

Before discussing this situation and proposals for improvement, it should be clarified that "price" refers to any payment for a good, service, or bundle of such goods and services. Several examples focus on disaggregated, *ex post* prices for specific health services, such as would be used for FFS reimbursement; but the same principles apply to aggregated *ex ante* prices such as case-based and capitation payments. The next section focuses on the incentive issues associated with the choice between different levels of "bundling" in payment for health services.

Let us take one by one some of the characteristic distortions of the health-care pricing system in Eastern Europe and outline the tasks of reform that they present:

1. The publicly owned hospitals and clinics in Eastern Europe generally do not know precisely what the typical average costs of their services are. They are unable to gauge what a normal childbirth or a routine surgical procedure costs. They do not know what it costs them to keep a patient in intensive care until the acute danger has passed after a heart attack, and so on. Yet knowledge of such costs would be the starting point on the supply side for setting reasonable prices.

    The task is obvious: calculate costs carefully and break them down accurately to reflect the actual costs of providing at least the major categories of services. That is more easily said than done. It calls for measures of various kinds: from compilation and application of accounting standards that suit the features of the health sector to organizing up-to-date bookkeeping and

introducing regular audits. Health-care providers will
have an incentive to undertake these changes if they are
faced with harder budget constraints and pressure for
improvement, so that lack of accurate cost information
leaves them at a competitive disadvantage.

This is another field in which Eastern Europe has
much to learn from the developed countries. Let us look
first at *cost accounting*. Modern sophisticated methods
of cost accounting are necessary for accurate pricing of
medical services and efficient management of hospitals
and other health-care providers. One difficult problem
is to define clearly the output, product, or service
(Berman, Kukla and Weeks 1994: 637). The relative
sophistication of the accounting system can generally
be measured by the level of detail of cost information,
the ability to classify costs according to different useful
categories, the timeliness and accuracy of information,
and so on. Classification of cost into fixed and variable
components and allocating them rationally to given services is particularly important for hospitals, where a
large part of total cost is fixed.[2] Sophisticated costing
systems can allocate costs by procedure or case (e.g. all
costs associated with treatment of cases in a given
diagnostic-related group).

2.   Although it was mentioned earlier, it must be reiterated
here that depreciation does not feature in the accounts
of the public sector in the post-socialist countries. Also,
the sector omits to build into its output accounting costs

---

[2] A common form of cost accounting, standard costing, first allocates costs
to components (materials, labor, and indirect fixed costs) and then incor-
porates relative value units and variance analysis to measure performance
against normative cost standards (developed through industrial engineer-
ing studies). There are several basic cost-accounting methods for handling indirect costs, such as the "direct method" or "multiple
apportionment" (Eastaugh 1992: 40–1). In the United States, hospitals
and integrated care organizations have adopted increasingly sophisticated cost-accounting systems similar to enterprises in other business
sectors in conjunction with the spread of case-based hospital payment.

a net income above the current operating costs (calculated without depreciation). The omission robs public hospitals and other publicly owned institutions of the opportunity to decide for themselves about renewal, modernization, and expansion of fixed assets, because there is no way they could finance this themselves. Moreover, this grave distortion runs through all the accounting calculations made in the health sector.

International experience is not uniform in this respect. Under German-type social-insurance systems, hospital operating budgets generally include funds for capital depreciation (Saltman and Figueras 1997: 199). The allocation of new investment is centralized in many countries, such as Britain, where basic provision is financed out of central taxes. Investment decisions in Australia are not wholly centralized, but tied to a central permit.

The minimum essential change seems to be to build the depreciation into the costs and to provide the cover for this in the price for services.[3] That leaves open the debatable question of whether net income devoted to *expansion* needs to be fully included in the costs calculated into the price, or only partly included.[4]

Let us assume that a decision has been reached on calculating depreciation and net income. The first task

[3] In Poland depreciation allowance was introduced in 1999 (OECD 2000: 151).

[4] It is theoretically conceivable to have a mechanism in which the net income flows primarily to the providers, where part of it can remain as a source for self-financed investment, and part can be paid into a central (or regional) fund and reallocated. This solution is the one that best ensures transparency through costs and prices, because it makes a clear distinction between two aspects: costing and pricing on the one hand, and the degree of investment centralization on the other. There is a danger that advocates of centralized investment decision-making will be ready to sacrifice transparency and want the investment funds to reach them directly, not by a roundabout route.

It has to be said that considerations of power are not the only criteria that speak for some partial centralization. It also helps to ensure that capacity is not duplicated unnecessarily.

is obviously to draw up and apply the requisite legal regulations. This is not easy, because the change is likely to raise the price charged for services.

The balance of the change in the financing burden that fall ultimately on households will be zero in macro-economic terms. There will simply be a regrouping of costs, with the cost of renewing and modernizing plant and equipment falling on the providers instead of the central financing institutions. The revenues intended for central utilization and the taxes that yield them can be reduced proportionately. It is another matter to say whether the government proves capable of applying this balanced budget solution consistently. Further-more, a zero balance on the macro-level does not pre-clude the possibility that some households will find their expenditures (the total of general taxation and ear-marked health contributions) have increased while others find expenditures have fallen.

3.   Calculating and reviewing costs is complicated by the whimsical and irrational distribution of subsidies to the health sector. Sometimes the cost of inputs is subsi-dized and sometimes the actual price set for the good (e.g. medication) or service (e.g. diagnostic procedure).

Changing this promises to be very difficult, among other reasons because the requirement of transparent cost accounting could conflict with the practical requirements of having the subsidy allocation that is politically most acceptable and easiest to organize. Transparency calls for all output to be sold at a rational price that covers costs, and for the subsidy to be given in money to those who pay full price for the service. In practice, it could be simpler to assist the needy by sub-sidizing just some inputs (such as certain medications), but that would immediately distort the costs. Many other, similar examples could be given.

The only hope is to overcome such distorting effects

gradually, one by one, in small stages, and to use direct rather than indirect subsidies to assist the needy.

4. The value of the work spent on providing health care is only partially reflected in the formal price. Apart from the official pay that features in the accounts, there is the hidden income of gratitude money that patients give to medical care providers. On the supply side, the official accounts show the provision to have cost less than the buyers (the official buyer, such as the single-payer insurance fund, plus the unofficial buyer, the patient) have actually paid for it.

Means of phasing out the gratitude-payment system will be discussed shortly.

The conclusion is hardly reassuring. No economist can be content to see prices that reflect relative scarcities being determined by such semi-bureaucratic, semi-market influences instead of the market. Simulation of the market is not the real thing, but there is no procedure to recommend that is any less disquieting. It has to be accepted that price formation in the health sector is one of the big problems to which there is no good solution. When reference is made in this book to *reasonable* prices, these qualifications should all be understood. Reasonable prices are ones that help in selecting efficient combinations of inputs and outputs.

It would be illusory to expect a new, more or less acceptable health-care price structure, approximating reasonable relative values, to emerge all at once in post-socialist countries. However, a start has to be made somewhere. If all actors in the health sector start to have a stake in reducing costs (which is the subject of later sections), there will be someone to protest at distortions in prevailing prices. Once the actors develop price and cost sensitivity, disputes and bargaining over prices will lead (by way of groping and multiple corrections) to reasonable prices. This can be expected to be a protracted process, in which market-based prices gradually, but never entirely, supplant administered prices, and the remaining administered prices give better signals regarding real relative scarcities.

Here the experience of other countries with setting reasonable administered prices may be of particular relevance, regarding both decision-making processes and institutions. Let us consider procedures in two countries with quite different systems, Japan and the United States. Japan has used its fee-revision process effectively to control costs in its FFS system. The Minister of Health and Welfare revises fees based on recommendations from the twenty-member Central Social Insurance Medical Care Council, with heavy influence from the Japan Medical Association (Ikegami and Campbell 1999: 63). To update drug prices annually, the government surveys wholesale market prices and sets the fee schedule price a certain percentage above the average competitive market price to allow a small profit (Ikegami and Campbell 1999: 64). To update the fee schedule for medical procedures (for both physicians and hospitals), the government examines data on providers' financial conditions and health-insurance claims to determine the volume-weighted average increase for all services, and then apportions a chosen net increase across the 3,000-plus fee schedule items. Increases and decreases of different categories of fees are used to try to control overall cost increases and to compensate providers for differential technological changes.

In the United States, an expert commission conducts analysis and develops recommendations for Congress on policies affecting the publicly financed Medicare program, including methodologies for determining and updating payments. Private health insurers and providers frequently adopt these payment methods as well. Originally there were two separate commissions; in 1997 these were consolidated into the Medicare Payment Advisory Commission. This system of expert advice has overseen such policy changes as adoption of a Medicare Fee Schedule, founded upon on the Resource-

Based Relative Value Scale (Hsiao *et al.* 1988); the Prospective Payment System for hospitals; and, more recently, risk adjustment, prospective payment for hospital outpatient services, etc. [5]

One more comment has to be made to conclude the discussion of prices. Most Eastern European countries suffer from inflation to a greater or lesser extent. One of the fundamental causes is the effort to adjust the distorted relative prices inherited from the socialist system. Although in theory it is possible for some prices to fall while others rise, in practice there is downward price rigidity. So the adjustment of the relative price system during the post-socialist transition has meant in the business sector that some prices stay the same, or rise more slowly, while others go up faster and more persistently. This is the context in which the adjustment of health-sector prices comes onto the agenda. Every change whose necessity has been mentioned so far has the effect of increasing the accounting costs and prices paid by direct purchasers. That includes adjusting prices to reflect depreciation and net income, turning gratitude money into legal, recorded wage costs, ending the subsidies on certain inputs in favor of open transfers of income, and so on. These price-increasing factors may be offset to some extent by the cost-reducing influences of greater competition and incentive to efficiency, but probably not entirely, and not immediately. This means that one of the greatest challenges confronting the price reform in the health sector will be its running up against macroeconomic efforts to slow down and eventually eliminate inflation. This reduces the hopes of success in the short run, and suggests a need for gradual rather than rapid change.

---

[5] Mention was made at the end of chapter 6 (pp. 226–227) of the procedure for compiling the basic package adopted in Slovenia. This includes among its features the determination of reasonable administrative prices, at least for the treatments contained in the basic package.

The hard budget constraint and other incentives

It has already been pointed out in chapter 3 and other parts of the book that altering the ownership and the organization of the delivery side is not enough to make the health sector perform its tasks well. Without adequate incentives, the actions of the participants will pull either one way – towards unstoppable demand and runaway costs – or the other – unbridled cost-cutting at the expense of quality, and efforts by providers (or, after decentralization, by insurers) to avoid treating or insuring higher-risk patients.

What can be done? Let us foster no illusions: there is no perfect solution. However thoughtfully designed the incentive system, there remains a danger that loopholes will be discovered and exploited by those acting selfishly in their own interest, at the expense of patients or the community of those bearing the financing burden. Nonetheless, if care is taken, it will be possible for a complex system of incentives to develop that minimizes the potential for abuse:

1   Financial discipline has to be imposed. Even in a traditional market economy, some public provider or non-profit insurer may feel it has a moral right to special treatment, for instance to tax concessions or to a bailout in the case of a deficit, by virtue of serving the noblest of aims, the cause of health. Such expectations are even more frequent in the post-socialist countries, where this behavior became customary in the past. The soft-budget-constraint syndrome spread not just in the health service, but in every area of the economy under the socialist system.

In the authors' view, it is unjustified to expect an automatic bailout. Many other areas could claim special importance in a similar way. Loosening financial discipline is not the best way for society to reveal its respect for the health sector. If the public wishes to express it in a financial form, its political representatives should vote the health sector a bigger *ex ante* macro-budget for basic provision. *Ex post*, it should not yield to pleas or blackmail to allow looser macro- and micro-budget constraints or a bailout.[6]

No publicly owned or nonprofit organization should be allowed to operate with consistent losses. If the reason for the deficit is that the prices of the inputs and outputs were distorted, they should be corrected. If the reason is a larger burden of high-cost cases than the payment reflects, then the payment should be refined to better reflect costs (through risk adjustment and other strategies, discussed below). However, if there are other, similar organizations operating with the same prices and a similar case-mix of sicker and healthier patients, but not making a loss, the fault must be low efficiency, to which the correct response is to augment or dismiss the management and restructure activities. A financial subsidy should be given at most temporarily, accompanied by a firm warning that it will be phased out gradually and cease on a specific date.

Hardening of the budget constraint also raises complex political, legal, and economic problems in the business sphere of the economy. The process has been uneven during the post-socialist transformation, with some countries making good progress while others hardly advancing at all. However, it is true of the whole region that softness of the budget constraint prevails much more in the health sector, among providers and insurance institutions, than it does in the business

---

[6] A provincial hospital in Hungary overstepped its budget to an extraordinary extent in 1998. One of its senior physicians, a cardiologist with a national reputation, then began a hunger strike, and the deputy finance and health ministers were obliged to enter into negotiations *in situ*. Eventually, the doctor's campaign forced the government to cover the hospital's losses.

sphere. Hardening of the budget constraint is one strong indicator of the consistency with which efficiency-oriented reforms are being implemented.

If strict financial discipline is applied, a single rescue might be justified, as a way of improving the conditions for the reform process. However, if the health-sector institutions become indebted and the losses build up again, there will be no subsequent defense for another bailout.

2   Chapter 3 explained why it is essential to apply the principle of cost sharing on the supply side and the demand side. On the demand side, there is no need to repeat the recommendations already argued in detail in chapter 6 (p. 213), calling for the general introduction of co-payments. To some extent at least, this gives patients an interest in exercising self-restraint in their consumption of health care, even if the public purse is still paying most of the costs.

3   Let us continue exploring the cost-sharing principle on the providers' side, starting with relatively larger organizations, hospitals, and outpatient clinics. Tables 8.1 and 8.2 show the situation in 1997. The former groups the information according to payment systems and the latter according to categories of care.

A hospital or clinic under the socialist system was granted a global budget. With this system of payment, the payer allocates a comprehensive budget to the provider, rather than paying for the specific services for each patient. Under socialism, the starting points for drawing up the *ex ante* budget were the historical capacity and historical costs, corrected at most for the easily identified changes of capacity (for instance, the addition of new beds) or the rate of inflation. Combined with a soft budget constraint, little to no performance requirements, and no competition, this global-budget system was similar to unquestioned reimbursement of

Table 8.1 *Payment systems, Eastern Europe: survey according to payment alternatives, 1997*

Country	Global budget (1)	Full-cost reimbursement (2)	Fee-for-service (3)	Case-based payment (4)	Capitation (5)	Payment per bed day (per diem) (6)
Albania	OPC and IPC	–	–	–	PC	–
Bulgaria	PC, OPC, and IPC	–	–	–	–	–
Czech Rep.	IPC[1]	OPC and IPC	PC, OPC, and IPC	Some IPC	–	–
Croatia	–	–	OPC and IPC	–	PC	–
Hungary	–	–	OPC and IPC	IPC	PC	–
Macedonia	OPC and IPC	–	–	–	PC	–
Poland	PC, OPC, and IPC	–	–	Some IPC	–	–
Romania[2]	PC, OPC, and IPC	–	–	–	–	–
Slovakia	–	OPC and IPC	OPC	Some IPC	PC	IPC
Slovenia	–	–	PC, OPC, and IPC	–	PC	IPC

Notes:

PC = primary care; IPC = inpatient care; OPC = outpatient care.

[1] The global budget was reintroduced in June 1997.

[2] Hospitals held territorial funds for primary care and secondary care and were responsible for financing of dispensaries and polyclinics.

Sources: NERA (1998b, 1999); PHARE (1998: Annex); WHO (1999b).

Table 8.2 *Payment systems, Eastern Europe: survey according to three levels of health care, 1997*

Country	Primary care	Outpatient care	Inpatient care
Albania	Capitation	Global budget and salary Planned: FFS	Global budget and salary
Bulgaria	Global budget and salary	Global budget and salary	Global budget and salary
Czech Rep.	FFS Planned: capitation	FFS with national cap and full-cost reimbursement for certain inputs	FFS with national cap, full-cost reimbursement for certain inputs and *per diem* fee Since june 1997, global budget
Croatia	Capitation and FFS	FFS and salary	FFS
Hungary	Capitation	FFS with national cap	Case-based payment (DRG)
Macedonia	Capitation	Global budget and salary Planned: FFS	Global budget and salary Planned: case-based payment
Poland	Global budget and salary Since 1999, capitation and FFS	Global budget and salary Since 1999, capitation and FFS (according to the choice by the territorial fund)	Global budget and salary Since 1999, case-based payment (according to the choice by the territorial fund)
Romania	Global budget and salary Since 1999, capitation and FFS	Global budget and salary Since 1999, capitation and FFS	Global budget and salary Since 1999, case-based payment
Slovakia	FFS Experimentally: combined with capitation	FFS	*Per diem* fee paid prospectively Experimentally: case-based payment
Slovenia	Capitation and FFS with a national cap	FFS	*Per diem* fee and FFS with a national cap

Sources: PHARE (1998: Annex); WHO (1999b).

costs. Earlier, low-efficiency combinations of inputs and outputs were approved repeatedly, and there was no incentive to operate efficiently.

This payment system was retained initially during the post-socialist transformation, as column (1) of table 8.1 makes clear. Later, several countries began to augment or replace this with other systems.[7] It also emerges from table 8.2 that, by the end of the 1990s, most countries had moved more or less comprehensively towards a performance-based payment system.

Many post-socialist countries in the late 1990s adopted for hospitals and outpatient clinics some variation of FFS payment based on a relative point system. By paying providers according to the number and type of services they provide, FFS links payment to performance as measured by volume of services. The more services provided, the more revenue received.

Chapter 3 (pp. 84–99) has already provided analysis and some empirical examples of how payment systems influence the performance of providers. Although the effects of changes in payment have not been analyzed thoroughly in any Eastern European country so far, it can be said that in some cases, the effects of these new supply-side incentives have been quite dramatic. The Czech Republic is a particularly instructive case. Theory and other countries' experience would suggest that introduction of FFS payment combined with a full reimbursement for certain material costs would lead to increased expenditures, perhaps jeopardizing the financial sustainability of reforms. Indeed, after introducing open-ended payment under a social insurance system, Czech real health-care spending increased by almost 40 percent in two years (Marree and Groenewegen 1997: 64). Private practice physicians paid on a FFS basis

---

[7] For a description of the payment systems, see chapter 3 (pp. 84–93).

billed significantly more in every category of service than state (primarily salaried) providers did (Massaro, Nemec and Kalman 1994). The early Czech experience serves as a graphic illustration of the cost-increasing effects of open-ended FFS payment and the lack of supply-side cost sharing. Finally, there was a return in mid-1997 to the global-budget method, after no amount of fine-tuning had proved capable of cutting back the costs. Each institution receives as its quarterly budget 100 percent of its previous quarterly budget, so long as the performance of the hospital as measured primarily by volume is not less than 70 percent of the performance in the previous period. According to Czech doctors, the effect of the change was immediate, with a 30 percent fall in those measures of hospital performance upon which payment was based (Benedict 2000). This once again illustrates how rapid and thorough the reaction to payment incentives can be.

Another and in many ways more sophisticated incentive system than FFS is case-based payment. In this case the payment "bundles" prices for all services used in treating a given case. However, this payment method is not unimpeachable either, as chapter 3 (p. 88) pointed out. One example of its problems comes from Hungary, where the system was introduced quite early on, in 1993. Almost at the same time, hospitals widely adopted a software system known as Sámán, which sought to provide "optimum" coding for maximizing hospital profits. For instance, where combinations of illness were present, it stated which of the illnesses should be treated as "primary" in the diagnosis and what complications it was worth reporting to raise the sum of money paid for the treatment concerned. This is an understandable response to payment incentives that is also prevalent in other countries using case-based payment.

Another problem in Hungary was the lack of coordination between hospital and outpatient payment. Every department of every hospital or outpatient clinic sought to wangle as many points for itself as possible and to see whether inpatient or outpatient treatment yielded more income from treating a patient. This activity became known as "point hunting" (Féderer and Nemes 1999). For instance, if a patient is treated for persistent nose-bleeding as an outpatient in a children's hospital, this is a loss-making transaction for the hospital. However, if the same patient is hospitalized for a few days, a profit is made. To take another example, if tests are done on a patient in hospital and it turns out that the patient is healthy, the social insurance does not pay. So the hospital has a financial interest in classing all the patients who have spent time in the hospital as ill. These examples illustrate the importance of coordinating payment systems so that payment for a given set of services (such as treatment of persistent nose-bleeding) is "site-neutral," not overly rewarding inpatient rather than outpatient care.

The adverse effects of the hospital payment system in Slovakia have led to several alterations since 1993. For more than a year, payment was made according to a point system combined with a per-bed-day (*per diem*) rate. Then, for 13 months, came a system that combined a lump sum with the *per diem* rate. Finally, since 1995, all the current costs of the hospital are paid in the form of *per diem* payment, which is reviewed from time to time (Lawson and Nemec 1998: 247). It can be predicted that *per diem* payment will lead to longer hospitalizations in Slovakia than for similar patients in countries with different incentives, such as those with case-based payment.

All of these examples illustrate that the incentive system for hospitals and outpatient clinics needs

further refinement in most countries. Where FFS is
used, the relative "prices" (the relative point values of
the transactions) need to be improved. In some cases it
might be advisable to break down the budget constraints (the "caps") on which the distribution of
payment proportionately to the points obtained is
based, into smaller units, not just applied to the organization as a whole. Probably more effective would be to
move away from pure FFS payment and introduce more
supply-side cost sharing, such as adopting case-based
payment with some additional fees for specific services.

In line with the recommendations so far, it is worth
considering whether to apply the cost-sharing principle, to each hospital or clinic as a whole and to the
various divisions of them keeping separate accounts.
This would mean, for instance, that each unit receiving
an *ex ante* budget would be entitled (wholly or to a previously determined extent) to retain its *ex post* savings.
On the other hand, it would be obliged to cover out of
its reserves any *ex post* deficit. As already mentioned,
this practice has applied to hospitals in Slovenia for
several years (Health Insurance Institute of Slovenia
1999: 28), and helped to make it rare for a hospital there
to run up a deficit. This illustrates how global budgets,
combined with a hard budget constraint (and perhaps
also performance monitoring and/or competition), can
give far greater incentive to efficiency than under the
socialist global budget system. Yet this practice should
not be taken too far. Imposing a hard budget constraint
and supply-side cost sharing on smaller and smaller
units increases the risk those units bear, and the pressure to control costs through quality-cutting and discrimination against expensive patients.

4.   The capitation form of payment, or some variant of it,
     has already become the most common for primary care
     in Eastern Europe (see table 8.2). Patients register with

a chosen PCP on a long-term basis. The doctor then receives a capitation payment for each patient, so that his/her pay is proportionate to the number of patients on the list.[8]

The drawback of the capitation system, like any form of full supply-side cost sharing, is the one-sided emphasis it places on cost reduction in the PCP's own clinic, including savings of the doctor's time. It serves the doctor's best interest to register as many patients as possible and to spend as little time as possible treating them.[9] This can lead to superficial examinations. However, the harmful tendencies can be mitigated and greater attention encouraged if the privatization of primary care and guaranteed choice of PCP is followed by real competition among doctors for patients (principle 3). This means issuing an adequate number of licenses to practice as a PCP, so that the total capacity (the supply) somewhat exceeds the patients' usual demand for PCP services. Capitation gives financial incentive for doctors to compete for patients. If too few permits are issued (perhaps in response to pressure from the lobby of PCPs already practicing), professional exclusiveness will create a chronic shortage. The effects of such a constant excess of demand over supply are familiar to all Eastern Europeans from the socialist period. It is not enough to declare legally that citizens have a right to choose their doctor freely. Where there is a shortage, some patients will be obliged to choose less popular doctors with shorter queues at their offices. To avoid this, ownership, competition, and payment reforms need to work together to guarantee patients genuine choice.

[8] Capitation resembles small-unit global budgets, as just discussed.
[9] PCPs in Eastern Europe are allowed to register a limited number of patients only, usually around 2,000. In Hungary, there is also a threshold on capitation payment, beyond which a regressive adjustment factor applies in order to prevent overregistration (OECD 1999a).

PCPs play an important role under the reforms, as the initial "gatekeeper," who refers or declines to refer the patient to a specialist. They are expected to decide such matters according to their best professional judgment, but their decisions will obviously be influenced by self-interest. If the capitation payment covers only their income and the expenses of their office, they have an interest in referring patients to a specialist or a hospital as rapidly as possible. This will save time for them and their assistants, and yield greater revenue by reducing office expenses. It may also impress patients, so that the doctors improve their competitive position by pursuing this policy. Frequent – indeed, excessive – referrals also reduce the doctors' decision-making risk, by "covering" them against complaints of misjudgment. However, PCPs following such a strategy are not doing their job as gatekeepers: they are leaving the gate wide open. Since this is very costly for the health-care system as a whole, tending to overburden expensive specialists and hospitals, various measures have to be employed to discourage PCPs from excessive referrals.

One approach is informational and administrative. PCPs should receive operational guidelines, advising them about when they should send patients for tests, for consultations with a specialist, or for hospital treatment. Of course, they have to decide each case according to their professional knowledge and judgment, but the more help with clarifying the valid decision-making criteria and even specific instructions they can be given, the more reliable their decisions will become.[10]

---

[10] The problem resembles the one discussed in chapter 6 (p. 216) with compiling the basic package. There also the recommendation was to have guidelines and specific directives, but without taking out of doctors' hands the specific, individual right of deciding or relieving them of the responsibility for their decisions.

Apart from resembling the question discussed in chapter 6 (p. 216), the problem overlaps with it. The arguments here focus on family doctors

Another approach involves financial incentives. Under the British "GP fundholding" and "Primary Care Group" system (mentioned in chapter 3, p. 90, n. 26 and table 4.7, p. 118), GPs receive a spending quota (budget or fund) proportionate to the number of patients registered with them, to cover the health expenditures of their patients. The regulations stipulate what types of expenditures must or may be paid out of the quota. The general practitioners have to decide what to cover out of this quota and for which patient, within the framework of the regulations, of course. This system in effect makes the general practitioners insurers as well as providers, since they bear the financial risk of which patients need what services. It is worth considering a similar system for PCPs in Eastern Europe. [11] For instance, if doctors in this part of the world had to cover specialist treatment, tests, and hospital expenses out of a fixed budget, that would curb their propensity to "pass on" patients without hesitation. It would increase the PCPs' room for maneuver and incentive to reduce costs, but it would also increase their power over their patients and their incentive to avoid high-cost patients. There should be no rush to introduce this new mechanism. The time to take incentives further will arrive once the individual or group practices of the PCPs have consolidated and both providers and patients have gained experience with the new situation.

providing primary care. One of the criteria by which a PCP might decide not to refer a patient to a specialist or a hospital is that the consultation or treatment is not part of the basic package. Alternatively, the PCP might make the referral but coupled with the advice that the recommended consultation with a specialist would be at the patient's own expense.

[11] Several large Polish cities, including Krakow, have experimented since 1996 with a form similar to the system of British GP fundholding, known in Poland as "family practice" (Windak *et al.* 1997, NERA 1998b). The Krakow PCPs contract with the regional authority to take responsibility for a district in exchange for a capitation payment. This covers not only primary care, but specialist and diagnostic provisions as well. However, experiments of this kind remain sporadic in Eastern Europe.

5   The mechanism described under point 4 (PCPs as gatekeepers and the question of covering specialist and hospital expenditures out of an expenditure quota awarded
to PCPs) is only a few steps removed from the institution of the HMO. This, it was explained earlier, inte-
grates insurance and provision. On paper, it seems to be
capable of overcoming both the harmful tendencies: for
costs to run away and for quality to decline. The fact
that HMOs compete with each other for the favors of
employers and insured individuals acts as an induce-
ment to them to cut their costs and give the patients the
best care they can. However, it also gives incentive to
cut corners on aspects of quality that are difficult for
patients and employers to observe, and financially
rewards efforts to avoid unprofitable patients.

American experience suggests there is a danger that
cost-cutting at any price may become dominant. This
path should be followed with caution, therefore. It
would not be right in Eastern Europe to prevent HMOs
forming as a voluntary initiative. The legal framework
in which they can operate has to be erected. On the
other hand, the introduction of them should not be
forced or be the subject of an intensive campaign.[12]

6   Several of the payment methods already mentioned –
case-based payment, capitation, GP fundholding –
involve high levels of supply-side cost sharing and
therefore strong incentives to avoid costly patients. To
mitigate these undesirable incentives, payers should
adjust payments to insurers and providers to reflect the
expected cost of treatment (see chapter 3, p. 90).[13]

[12] This gradual and voluntary approach is essential if there is to be individual sovereignty in choice among competing insurance options. However,
it may also make the problem of risk selection worse, since those who voluntarily choose HMOs may very well be healthier than average. This
problem is best addressed by risk adjustment and mixed payment, as discussed under point 6.
[13] This would be useful already under form A, monopoly insurance for basic
care. It will become even more critical under form B, managed competi-

Risk adjustment is not unheard of in the region. The Czech Republic introduced a simple risk-adjustment mechanism, based on age, in 1993. This is a step in the right direction, since insurers are less likely to discriminate against the elderly if they are paid more for treating them. Moreover, information about age is easy to collect and use for adjustment of payments. Unfortunately, age (and other demographics such as gender) can explain only a small fraction of the differences in costs among patients. More sophisticated risk-adjustment systems require more extensive information about individuals.

Mixed payment, using intermediate levels of supply-side cost sharing, is a complementary, and in some ways easier, method of avoiding risk selection. It also mitigates incentives to cut quality. Mixed payment involves both an *ex ante* fixed payment and some *ex post* payment based on patients' actual use of health services. The *ex ante* payment should be risk-adjusted. Countries will need to experiment with the appropriate fraction of *ex ante* fixed payment relative to *ex post* reimbursement.

Finally, it would be advisable for countries to consider mandatory high-risk pooling (see chapter 3, p. 92). Under this system, insurers (and perhaps other providers at risk for care, such as capitated PCPs) would be required to contribute to a pool of funds to cover the costs of high-risk patients. In exchange, insurers are allowed to place, at the beginning of the period in question, a small fraction of their patients in the high-risk pool. The expenses of treating these high-risk patients are reimbursed from the pool of funds more generously than otherwise. With this mechanism insurers need not try to avoid high-cost patients. This will help to give such patients genuine choice.

tion among insurers of both basic and supplementary care (see chapter 6, p. 231).

7   Institutional forms of self-protection for patients need
     to be developed to offset the potentially damaging
     incentives associated with HMOs and all the forms of
     provider cost-sharing described earlier.

     Within the framework of the basic benefit package,
     there should be ways in which patients can appeal
     against a medical decision or make a complaint. In hos-
     pitals and other large institutions, chances of doing so
     are provided within the internal hierarchy. A patient
     may complain about a doctor to a senior, departmental
     physician, or against the senior physician's decision to
     the head of the hospital. The decentralized PCP system
     will have developed similar forms for appeals and com-
     plaints. It is most important that the subsequent inter-
     vention – or, where justified, the alteration of a decision
     taken at a lower level – should occur swiftly.

Apart from that, patients' ability to choose has to be broadened through the availability of supplementary care. Those
who do not trust in the medical decision reached as part of
the basic benefit package should be able to consult a doctor
of their choice, provided they can pay the cost out of their
own pocket or through private insurance. The same applies
to patients who do not want to go to the hospital to which
they are referred, who want extra tests that have not been prescribed, and so on.[14] The simple knowledge that patients can
check on medical decisions by consulting with other specialists and having other tests encourages greater attention and
deliberation in clinical decisions in the sphere of basic care.

[14] There is a danger that patients may fall victim to "supplier-induced
demand" (see chapter 3, p. 85) through the system of supplementary care,
spurred by the financial interest of those providers (especially if under
FFS payment) and by attempts to control costs through restricting the
basic benefit package. Some brake on such tendencies within supplementary care is provided by the buyers' ability and willingness to pay.
Additional constraints come from managed competition between insurers of integrated basic and supplementary care, especially where provider
payment involves supply-side cost sharing rather than FFS.

It is time to sum up what has been said about the extent to which various incentives can act as a brake on an unbridled increase and "running away" of demand and costs.

The need for a specific item of medical treatment can obviously be satisfied. The number of people suffering from heart disease sets an upper limit on the number of heart operations to be performed. However, society's aggregate need for resources for preserving health and preventing and treating illness is infinite, especially when one considers that scientific and technical developments are constantly offering new, more advanced means of treatment. So the difficult problem is not what the sector should provide but what it should not provide: how can an effective constraint be placed on demand? Who is capable of saying "no," and enforcing it?

There are two pure cases here.

One is the case of political dictatorship and the related centralized command economy. The person or group exercising political power decides how much to spend on health care, and that is that. Rejection of all extra claims for health care is possible. Stalinism, the classical socialist system, stood close to this theoretical type. The result was a low place for health care on the scale of priorities. This and some other factors led to a deterioration in the health indicators for the population, shortages, queuing, backwardness in standards of care, favoritism, corruption, and so on.

The other pure case is to leave health care entirely up to the market mechanism. Theoretically, services would be restricted to those who could pay the market price for them. This would often be higher than the price under perfect competition, because competition is imperfect on the supply side. The "no" comes from the patients seeking treatment, "voluntarily" from a legalistic point of view. If they cannot afford health care, they do not seek it. A pure market mechanism of this kind deprives much of the population of the benefits of health care.

Capitalism stood close to that theoretical pure type in the

early stages of its development. It has persisted in many developing countries.

Developed capitalist economies and developed political democracies reject both extreme pure cases. They develop "mixed," composite solutions that try to avoid the unacceptable aspects of both pure cases. However, this *inevitably* means there is no one to say unambiguously "no": the demand constraint softens.

A complete hardening of the demand constraint is ruled out for ethical reasons. Most right-minded people would reject the first pure case as political tyranny and the second for excluding poorer people from health care.

The political forces in a democratic system know they would lose their electoral support if they advocated either of the pure cases. Neither has any political chance at all.

Although some people tend to think that every problem has a solution, in actual fact there is no perfect solution to the hardening of the constraint on demand for health care in a democratic, capitalist society, and there never could be. The recommendations put forward in this section have a more modest purpose. They are designed to ensure that the demand constraint becomes *appreciably harder* than without these new measures. The main ideas can be summarized as follows.

Encourage as many actors as possible in the sphere of basic care to say "no." This function should not be confined to one or two actors: to just the government, Parliament or local government, or just the providing organizations, the hospitals, clinics, and PCPs, or just the insurers, or just the patients. Each of them separately and all of them together should feel the constraints of the ability to pay.

Allow the private sector to develop healthily on the provision and the financing sides. The nature of this property form is more conducive to the hardening of the demand constraint; private hospitals, private doctors, and private insurers are more resistant to the temptation of uncovered demand.[15] Additional instruments for hardening the demand constraint include payment incentives, managed competition, and institutions for assessing technology and determining the basic benefit package.

The division of labor among the several players should not consist of some pushing up expenditure while others try to keep it down. Where possible, every player should display ambivalent behavior, sensing the concomitant advantages and disadvantages of both raising and reducing costs. The word "ambivalent" is used in an approving, not a disparaging sense, to mean that the choice is preceded by hesitation and consideration. This behavioral requirement applies equally to politicians, insurers, doctors, and citizens in their role as patients and voters.

The web of specific interests outlined above does not impose a hard constraint on the aggregate demand for health care. Even with these reforms fully put into practice, each society will still have to make its own decisions regarding a balance between demand for health care and limited resources. Nonetheless, the proposed reforms offer some kind of barrier to unsustainable increases in demand (and therefore expenditure).

Doctors' pay: the medical profession and the reform

This book has already dealt in several parts with incomes of physicians and other medical-care providers and the effect that reform would have on the medical profession. It is now time to sum up these remarks in a single framework. Let us begin with the material circumstances.

[15] Of course, private insurance does not guarantee complete defense against a soft-demand constraint. Insurance as an institution carries the risk of moral hazard (see chapter 3, p. 59). Both the insured and the doctors treating them may feel there is no need to be thrifty with expenditure because the insurer will pay.

Table 8.3 *Status of physicians, Eastern Europe, 1998*

Country	Public sector	Private sector
Albania	Most physicians	
Bulgaria	Most physicians	
Czech Rep.	Physicians in public hospitals	Physicians in primary and outpatient care
Croatia	Most physicians	
Hungary	Physicians in outpatient and inpatient care	Physicians in primary care
Macedonia	Most physicians	
Poland	Most physicians	
Romania	Most physicians	
Slovakia	Physicians in public hospitals	Physicians in primary and outpatient care
Slovenia	Most physicians	

Note:
Dentists are not included.
Sources: PHARE (1998: Annex); WHO (1999b).

The pay of doctors in Eastern Europe, after a decade of post-socialist transformation, comes from three main sources. (The discussion here focuses on physicians; similar principles apply to other health-care providers. It is confined to doctors offering medical services – that is, active clinicians – employed by or contracting with health-care providers and insurers. It disregards those with medical qualifications who work in the state bureaucracy or other fields as administrators and policy-makers rather than clinicians. The former account for the vast majority of the profession, and they are meant whenever reference is made to "doctors.")

1 Most doctors in Eastern Europe are public servants (see table 8.3). Their pay is strictly regulated, within narrow bands at each level in the hierarchy. The pay difference between the highest and lowest bands is also quite small. A career in the public sector offers benefits in

terms of influence and job security, but not in official pay, where the wide quality dispersion in medical work – in expertise, experience, care, and decency of behavior towards patients – is not reflected in the differentiation of official pay.

Tables 5.12 and 5.13 (pp. 167 and 169) present numerical comparisons of medical earnings in Eastern Europe and in the developed, traditional market economies. The Eastern European data consider only the income received from source 1, the official pay from the public sector. The difference revealed is striking. Doctors in the developed market economies are among the best-paid professions. This is true not only in the United States, where most doctors work in the private sector, but also, for instance, in Germany and Austria, where a very high proportion of doctors are employed in the public sector. In contrast, official compensation for physicians in Eastern Europe is falling steadily behind, to a level near the average for all professions.

2   These days, many doctors in Eastern Europe engage in legal private practice. If the pay of two doctors of the same seniority is compared, one of whom works exclusively in the public sector and the other exclusively in the private sector, the latter will almost always earn substantially more than the average for his or her group. Unfortunately, however, we have no systematic data to support this observation.[16]

Unlike official earnings in the public sector, individual incomes from private medical practice are widely dispersed. They depend on whether the private practice represents a small, occasional side-income, or the main source of income (as with private full-time PCPs).

---

[16] In Poland, employees of emergency units in private health-care firms earn an average of 3,000 złoty a month, while a surgeon in the public sector with 30 years' experience takes home only 1,500 złoty in official pay (Kocinska 2000).

Earnings also depend, of course, on the state of the market for the service concerned, and on any administrative rules or other noneconomic factors (such as a recommended schedule of doctors' fees), which force fees to diverge from market prices. The intention is not to idealize the relative prices that develop in this way, in other words the income earned from providing some services relative to other services. However, these prices can be said to reflect, well or badly, relative scarcities on the market for medical care and the value judgments of the buyers (the patients), unlike the official scales of pay, which mainly reflect a value judgment by the bureaucracy.

3   Further, large medical incomes occur alongside legal private practice, in the "twilight zone" between legality and illegality. The main item of income concerned is the gratitude money described in detail in chapter 5 (pp. 164–175).

Income from gratitude payments is widely dispersed. Gratitude money reflects the image, true or distorted, that patients have of the medical care they receive and of the extra attention they hope to obtain by their payments. Also reflected is the recipient's reputation, based on real performance and professional expertise. In addition, patients are compensating doctors for their position of power, or, more precisely, how far a doctor is willing to exercise that power in the interest of a patient making a gratitude payment: whether he or she obtains the patient extra concessions, prompter treatment, and so on. The buyers' value judgments are seriously distorted by the absence of transparency in these transactions.

The picture of these three sources together is extremely unfavorable. Even with the addition of sources 2 and 3, the average earnings of the medical profession are unacceptably low in the Eastern European region. They do not reward the great professional knowledge, the outstanding responsibility, and the stressful intensity of this work. Within the profession, there are inequitable distortions in the spread of individual earnings.

The changes that this book recommends could shift medical earnings in a favorable direction. The real motive force here will be the growth of the legal private sector. A higher proportion of doctors than previously will switch fulltime to this sector in some form, in individual or group practice, as a member of a partnership, or as the employee of a private organization.

Continuing an existing trend, many doctors who do not join the private sector full-time will put one foot in the private sector while keeping the other in the public sector. The recommended reforms offer various legal frameworks for such a division of working activity (for instance, partnerships or medical firms cooperating with a hospital or outpatients' clinic, or doctors spending some of their time in a public organization and the rest in private practice). These "half-in, half-out" forms can be expected to spread after the reforms, so long as all the authorities and bodies concerned are prepared to sanction their application with sufficient flexibility while attempting to enforce that it does not take on undesirable and illegal forms.

The expansion of the private sector has a dual effect. The average earnings of the medical profession will increase relative to other professions, and there will be an increase in the dispersion of individual medical incomes, but one that correlates better with quality and the value judgments of patients. This change will not come from centrally controlled adjustments to medical pay scales. It will be a spontaneous result of the change in ownership relations. This is precisely what gives it its impetus. In this context, there is no need to lobby for higher medical earnings. Instead, the allocation of ownership has to be reformed.

Furthermore, the process described may react indirectly on

source 1, the pay in the public sector, as well.[17] Only very obstinate or stupid political leaders and bureaucrats would watch with arms folded as the best doctors moved over to the private sector. Where society wants to maintain the integrity of its public health-care institutions, it will have to pay its doctors better, eventually, to prevent them being enticed away by private-sector earnings opportunities. Of course, that will also mean ending the rigid and compressed mandatory pay-scale of doctors and allow more room for the medical labor market to influence their salaries. And it will make it even more critical to apply the recommendations of the previous section regarding hardening the demand constraint for the health sector, lest the increased dispersion and average level of doctors' incomes contribute to unsustainable growth in costs.

It can also be expected that these changes, taken together, will make it possible to abolish gradually the system of gratitude payments. The recommendation is not that there should be drastic legal regulations banning this objectionable institution, if for no other reason, because ways would be found to evade them. Wherever transparent, legal purchase and sale is lacking and there is a chronic shortage, there will appear the "shadow" economy and the kind of corruption in which the buyer bribes the seller. Gratitude money should be redeemed, converted into legal and transparent payments, not banned.

There will be various changes to induce patients to abandon making gratitude payments as well:

- Many supplementary services will become purchasable legally, from public hospitals and clinics or from the private sector. The payment will be covered by the patient directly or through supplementary medical insurance.

---

[17] It is worth noting how high doctors' earnings compare with average earnings in Germany, the birthplace of social insurance (see table 5.12, p. 167). The presence of an opportunity for doctors to leave the public sector pushes up the earnings obtainable in the public sector as well.

- Partnerships or medical companies contracting with a hospital may provide a legal framework for the often unclear relations that arise between patients, doctors treating them, and public hospitals. For instance, patients often tuck payments into their doctor's pocket to secure extra tests performed on a public hospital's equipment. Under the new framework, patients could make a legal payment to the private group treating them, which would in turn pay a rent to the hospital for the equipment used. As for the fee for a private room, it would be paid to the hospital cashier, not to the chief physician.

- Compulsory co-payments will also help to wean people of the bad habit of making gratitude payments.[18] This is not just because they mop up some of the patients' money and leave less for other health-care expenditure. It is also because many patients have insufficient confidence in something they receive free of charge. Having made a co-payment for it, they may not feel like paying again, in the form of gratitude money.

All these changes act together and interact with each other. Rapid success should not be expected. However, there is a remarkable yardstick available here. The aforementioned health-care reform can be said to be put into practice successfully once the inveterate bad habit of giving and taking gratitude money has disappeared.

The reforms certainly alter the situation of doctors, for whom there will be both gains and losses. Just what particular doctors gain and lose depends on their precise specialty, their status in the hierarchy, their personal talents, and to some extent on luck. So let us look at the main types of gain and loss.

[18] The deep imprinting of habit is apparent in the way some patients in Poland and Hungary even make gratitude payments when they are paying the total cost of a health provision out of their own pocket (Poland: Chawla et al. 1999; Hungary: personal interviews with doctors).

To put it somewhat ironically, the present health-care mechanism has given rise to some curiously feudal, oligarchical privileges. For instance, hospital-based physicians who are in control of a certain number of beds have obtained an almost guaranteed source of power and gratuity income. Through a chain of reciprocal favors, they have been able to place their patients, and those of friends and colleagues, in the places of treatment they consider the most advantageous. Those who have built up a good position in this network of connections may well have fears that the reform will break up the network and undermine their little empire.

These anxieties are not unfounded, but there are some reassuring arguments to place against them. Doctors who excel professionally over their fellows will still gain an advantageous position in a world of more open, upright, legally justified transactions. Furthermore, doctors who combine the requisite professional expertise with other capabilities will also find their feet. This applies to those who make clever, inventive entrepreneurs, who are good at relating to people, and who understand finances, administration, and management. The second group of characteristics should not be underestimated. They are as important in the health sector as in any other sphere of society.

There is another criterion besides the financial one that the medical profession should consider. The health system in the Stalinist period, the classical socialist mechanism, turned doctors into cogs in a huge centralized, bureaucratic, hierarchical machine. The first ethical postulate, principle 1, the principle of individual sovereignty, applies to doctors and other medical-care providers as well as patients. Decentralization, parallel operation of several ownership forms, a wider choice of jobs, and competition among organizations will bolster the individual autonomy of physicians and others working in the health sector.

Neutrality between sectors

The development of the private sector in the delivery and financing of health care was made possible by the post-socialist transformation. This book argues that this transformation should be encouraged. However, there is a danger of the health sector being split into two parts by an inconsistent, distorted process of reform. Private hospitals and individual private medical practices will serve the richer sections of society, who can afford to pay directly or to purchase private medical insurance. Many services that are in the basic package will also be paid for privately. Meanwhile the public hospitals and outpatient clinics, along with their associated PCPs, will serve the less wealthy, paying for their care out of public funds.

There are already some signs of such a split, which could cause serious damage. It could become a vicious circle. Suppose that the narrow scope for sales holds back the development of the legal private sector, which does not appear to be lucrative enough to make it worthwhile for medical companies to form. The only source of finance for modernizing and developing public hospitals is the public purse, but this distributes its funding very meagerly. The outcome is that neither the private nor the public sector develops adequately. The private insurers, if they are excluded from participating in basic care, have little interest in entering the market for medical insurance. More prosperous people, having abandoned many of the almost-free services offered by the public sector, in favor of what they hope will be better service from private providers, feel it is unjustified that they should still be contributing large sums to the social-insurance system. This eventually induces them, through their political representatives, to shake off that burden as far as possible.

If such a vicious circle develops, it will be difficult to break. It is much better to prevent it developing or becoming entrenched. That is what a consistent application of the principle of sector neutrality can help to achieve. The phrase "sector neutrality" became current in debates in Eastern Europe, for instance in Hungary, Poland, and the Soviet Union, during the experiments with market-socialist reform. That was when private enterprise began to reappear (in the commercial sector, not the health sector, of course). The legal regulations of the time enforced discrimination in favor of the state sector: state-owned enterprises could buy only from state-owned enterprises. Private firms could do business only with other private firms or with households. This bureaucratic discrimination was augmented and strengthened by the official ideology, which stipulated that a state manager who was a believer in socialism should not support the development of capitalism by obtaining inputs from private firms. Arguing against this outlook and procedure, the advocates of reform recommended the principle of sector neutrality. There should be no discrimination according to form of ownership. State-owned enterprises should be free to obtain their inputs from the supplier who offers the best terms.

This nondiscriminatory behavior has to apply in the health sector of the post-socialist period, in both delivery and insurance. There have been mentions in separate places of how the principle applies in specific interactions. It is time now for a general summary:

1   Services in the basic benefit package have to be financed mainly out of public funds whether they are delivered by a public provider or a private one. The institution that allocates public money for the purpose should have no right to discriminate against providers according to their ownership form.[19] Let it respect the decisions of patients and doctors in cases where they can choose a provider directly. Where the financing institution is to

---

[19] This principle applies in the Canadian health system, for instance, where the main source of financing is public money, but much of it is spent on care delivered by private providers.

decide, let its choice be influenced not by prejudices against various forms of ownership, but by criteria of efficiency. The rules of fair competition have to apply to public and private providers alike. This can include competitive bidding and special forms of auction for bigger orders and comprehensive contracts.

The enforcement of sector neutrality will not be easy. The Polish reforms started in 1999 introduced sector-neutral financing. Nevertheless, regional social insurance funds tend to prefer public institutions, even if those provided more expensive and lower-quality care than private ones, and sign contracts with competing private companies only sporadically (Kocinska 2000).

There is public outcry from time to time at reports that the single-payer public insurance institution has entrusted some task to a private firm, using public money. This kind of prejudice, which obviously persists from the socialist period, has vanished altogether in the business sphere. It is highly desirable that the prejudice disappears from the health sector as well. One of the messages of the reform should be to handle money very carefully, because it comes from the taxpayers. If a private organization or individual can offer better terms than a public organization, then the former should obviously be chosen.[20]

2   The institution allocating public funds should be prepared to countenance shared financing of any activity. If its own system of fees prescribes that it can pay 100 units of currency for a certain purpose, but the patient chooses a provider who charges 150 units, let the public

---

[20] If a Hungarian private health-care company receives money from the Social Insurance Fund, it is not allowed to accept money directly from patients. On the other hand, many public organizations financed by the Social Insurance Fund demand a co-payment for an increasing number of provisions. This situation flouts the principle of sector neutrality and also withdraws the private providers from the influence of the co-payment incentive (Nagy 2000).

financing pay its 100 and agree to the patient paying the 50 difference.[21]

Let us look at this problem from the point of view of a patient – not a rich one, but a middle-income patient, let us say. If the principle of sector neutrality is not applied, he can choose between two extremes: paying 0 (for instance, in a public hospital) or paying 150 units (for instance, in a private hospital). The fair choice would be between paying 0 or paying 50, the second being the *extra* cost. This would produce a situation of fair competition between the various forms of ownership.

Application of the sector-neutrality principle, as just described, could cause a substantial shift in the allocation of expenditures, reducing the load on households and increasing the public financing of expenditure. This is the macroeconomic fiscal price to pay so that all the taxpayers contributing to basic care can feel they are receiving fair treatment from the system. They will participate equitably in the benefits, regardless of which provider they choose. This sense of the system's fairness should increase the political support for payment of health-care contributions.

3   Public providers should not be content to leave all supplementary services to private providers. They should try to win the competition with the private sector not by fortifying themselves with regulations granting them privileges, but by broadening the choices that they offer. For instance, hospital patients may want to have the comfort of a single room. That should not leave them obliged to seek a private hospital, or to bribe the chief physician of a public one. The desirable thing is for as many public hospitals as possible to offer such a choice, legally.

[21] In the literature this is often referred to as allowing providers to "balance-bill" their patients (that is, bill the patient directly for the extra 50 above the official fee schedule).

Apart from this illustration, chapter 6 (p. 246) listed several kinds of services that might be deemed "supplementary." Public hospitals and other public providers should add these to their scope of delivery, setting reasonable prices for them and offering them legally to patients. This has already started but not yet become an important source of income for public providers.

4   The principle of sector neutrality is also important for managed competition among insurers. Chapter 6 (pp. 227–246) discussed the question of decentralizing the insurance industry in detail. To summarize that discussion, there is discrimination against private insurers in the arrangement labeled form A, in which insurance for basic care is the monopoly of a public institution. Form B, on the other hand, is sector neutral. Citizens' entitlement to basic care is manifested by the premium support or voucher that they each receive. Which insurer to take it to is their decision. Although the authors retain *reservations*, expressed in chapter 6 (p. 240), about introducing form B too rapidly, here two further arguments in its favor must be added, about sector neutrality. One is that form B will make the insurance industry more interested in entering into health insurance.[22] This is the only way to give real impetus to private insurance for supplementary care as well. The other, connected advantage is that it will increase the freedom of choice for individual patients (as long as steps are taken to prevent risk selection from compromising choice for high-cost patients).

The application of sector neutrality will broaden the opportunities for development in the health sector. Running down the summary, the market will be broadened for private providers by changes 1 and 2, for public providers by change 3,

---

[22] Extending the principle of sector neutrality to insurance is one necessary condition before any integrated private insurer–provider organization, such as an HMO, can operate.

and for private insurers by change 4. Changes 1–3 can be rapidly made. Change 4, as mentioned earlier, requires a longer period, even where decentralization of the insurance industry has been chosen after weighing the advantages and drawbacks of form B.

Who decides about health-sector development?

It was promised in the introduction to the book that the subject would be the political and economic mechanism by which allocation is decided in the health sector, not the allocation decisions as such. "Who is authorized to decide?" was the question raised. This section, concluding the recommendations, sets out to summarize the responses given to that question.

The starting point consists of the material and intellectual resources currently available to the health sector. No one is thinking of reducing these. The question of raising them can be phrased in a stronger form. Who is qualified to decide about bringing in extra resources, and what procedures will govern the process of allocating those resources to increase the size of the health sector?

The recommendation breaks the decision-making problem down into two ethically, legally, and economically distinct parts. Those who accept the recommendations as a foundation for reforms have made a crucial decision already, by accepting the basic ethical principles 1 and 2, of individual sovereignty and of solidarity:

(i)   Everyone must be guaranteed access to basic care, financed mainly with public money. This includes some redistributive elements, apart from the commercial-insurance aspect: the collection of compulsory contributions to guarantee adequate public financing for the basic benefit package. The size of these compulsory contributions and the macro-budget for basic care are decided within the institutional framework of the democratic political process.

(ii) It must be possible for everyone to buy health services supplementary to the basic package, under regulated market conditions, with their own money or through commercial insurance. The legal framework for such transactions will have to be created on both the delivery and the financing sides.

The proposals being made here set out to enhance the freedom of choice for all the actors. They extend the patients' right to choose a doctor freely. Patients who do not wish to accept their doctor's decision about further referrals may appeal against it, or they may pay for a second medical opinion out of their own pocket, without a referral, or they may change doctors. There will be several outpatient clinics and hospitals offering them similar standards of care. It will be up to patients or their PCPs, acting on their behalf, to choose between competing providers. Decentralization under managed competition will also increase the choice in insurance.

The choice for doctors will widen in terms of the ownership forms in which they may practice. They will be able to choose whether they want to remain part of a bigger organization or seek greater autonomy and opportunities for enterprise.

The choice for employers will widen in terms of the forms available for those who want to contribute towards effective organization and financing of health care for their employees.[23]

The choice for individuals will widen, but without sacri-

---

[23] Of course the separate increases in choice for the various actors may also lead to conflict and limit the choice of the individual. For instance, the decentralization of insurance increases the scope for individuals to choose among insurers and insurance policies, but an insurer may curtail the choice of doctors and hospitals available to its policyholders and an employer curb the choice of insurers available to its employees.

ficing the principle of solidarity. The reforms being recommended are designed to work together to guarantee universal equal access to the basic benefit package.

The proposals give unequivocal support to the guiding ideas just outlined. However, they intentionally leave open several, relatively subordinate decisions, and instead weigh the advantages and drawbacks of various alternative courses.

On the financing side, the authors' sympathies lie with the idea of a health tax, because of its transparency, but they do not reject the idea of compulsory contributions taking another form. Despite some drawbacks, decentralization and managed competition in medical insurance seems to offer great advantages, but only if there has been thorough preparation for the change and the idea has won public support. Several possible mechanisms have been outlined for guaranteeing the principle of equal access to basic care under a system of managed competition between insurers who may offer integrated packages of basic and supplementary services. It is felt to be important to allow and even encourage an active role for employers in managing competition among commercial insurance companies, which could take several forms.

No uniform scheme is presented on the delivery side either. The aim is for variety: various forms of ownership, various scales of provider organizations, and various systems of payment can exist side by side. With investment decision-making, the recommendation has been a greater degree of decentralization than hitherto. However, the question of how far to take decentralization and what decisions should still be made centrally has been left open.

Let us be optimistic enough to assume that some Eastern European country adopts these proposals. That in itself would not determine ultimately the extent to which the health sector developed. The essence of the approach taken in this book is that the guidelines are determined by the electorate as a whole, through the political process, and households as a whole, through the market mechanism. Nonetheless, it is worth risking a few predictions.

No sudden increase in public financing for health care can be expected. Most Eastern European countries are suffering from fiscal problems. There is a chronic budget deficit hanging over the economy. Periodic success in alleviating this for a time is followed repeatedly by a relapse. Most political forces would like to reduce the ratio of state spending to GDP, or at least prevent the proportion from increasing. In a situation such as this, there are no grounds for expecting a substantial rise in the proportion of GDP spent on basic health care. If calculations are based instead on a constant proportion, only GDP growth can bring an increase in the spending on basic care.

On the other hand, it seems likely that many households will be prepared to raise the proportion of their spending they devote to health care, as their total income (net of tax and other compulsory levies) increases. Summed up in macroeconomic terms, that means the proportion of GDP represented by *total* health-care spending could rise, concurrently with an increase in the proportion of total health-care spending financed out of private money.

This forecast does not aspire to universality. The historical starting point in the traditional market economies, a century and a half or two centuries ago, was that health-care spending was financed by households, with very little public spending. At a later stage of capitalist development, the proportion of total health spending paid from the public purse began to increase. This shift became more accentuated after the Second World War. (See Kornai and McHale 2000, using data from the 1990s onwards, and Schieber and Maeda 1999, using more recent data. See also n. 2, in chapter 4, p. 107). In Eastern Europe, the initial state, following the collapse of the socialist system, has been the opposite. Financing out of public money was dominant, dwarfing the part played by private money. So the dismantling of the institutional barriers and prejudices are likely to release large and growing private resources for health-care development.

To clarify how this forecast about Eastern Europe relates to the trends that can be observed in the developed countries, it is possible to use the econometric analysis referred to in chapter 5 (p. 179) (Kornai and McHale in 2000). Let us call the "public share" the ratio of the part of health-care expenditure financed out of public money to the total expenditure. The analysis sought to arrive at a numerical estimate of the role played in determining the public share by economic and demographic explanatory variables on the one hand and political factors on the other. A time series for the OECD countries was used as a pattern. It emerged that the results of the calculation depend largely on whether the United States was included or omitted from the sample, since it was a clear outlier.

The economic and demographic indicators (GDP, age structure, etc.) explain about half the variance in public shares of health-care spending. The following observations emerged from the many types of calculation as a robust result:

- The public share rises as GDP increases (among these developed market economies and in recent times, controlling for other factors that change the share of public financing as a country develops).
- The public share rises as the proportion of the elderly in the population increases.
- Urbanization tends to raise the public share.

These observations apply whether or not the United States is included in the sample or controlled for separately with a dummy variable, although the numerical values of the regression equation are affected by this difference in specification.

A further level of analysis incorporated political explanatory variables. These included how long left-wing or Christian Democrat-type political parties had been in government. Introducing these variables substantially increased the explanatory power of the equation. The influence of left-wing parties increases the public share, while that of Christian Democrats tends to reduce it, although not very strongly.

These findings were used to see what the predicted public share would be in the Eastern European countries if the behavior pattern described in the regression equation were followed. (The logic behind such a mental experiment was described in chapter 5, p. 179.) The result of the calculation appears in table 8.4. The authors of the analysis refrained from comparing this with the actual public share, as the Eastern European data were thought too unreliable for this (unlike the figures for actual total spending, quoted in chapter 5 p. 000, which are utilizable, despite some uncertainties). Only for Hungary did they dare to compare the predicted and the actual public shares, because in that case, it was possible to cross-check the data thoroughly. Figure 8.1 shows the results of this comparison.

Both table 8.4 and figure 8.1 show clearly that the result depends to a large extent whether or not the United States is included in the sample. If the United States is "omitted" (that is, controlled for separately with a dummy variable), Hungary's actual public share falls below the predicted public share ("predicted share with US dummy"). If the US data are included in the sample, it remains above the predicted share ("predicted share without US dummy").

It has to be recognized that this is not a problem of statistical sampling, but something of more fundamental importance. The regression equation from which the United States was "omitted" is dominated by the past institutional structure of the European countries, or nonEuropean countries similar to them. The question posed in chapter 4 (p. 112) remains open: will the situation in Western Europe, Canada, and other OECD countries stay unchanged? There are several signs that the trend is altering somewhat in these countries, in favor of increased scope for private financing. So, if such calculations are repeated in a decade or two, the regression

Table 8.4 *Predicted values for public share of total health spending, Eastern Europe, 1990–1994*

Country	Predictions based on regression without dummy for the United States				
	1990	1991	1992	1993	1994
Bulgaria	59.2	61.4	63.8	64.8	65.9
Czech Rep.	54.5	56.2	57.0	57.7	57.9
Hungary	59.9	60.8	61.4	61.4	61.8
Poland	49.0	49.9	50.6	50.9	51.5
Romania	54.4	55.6	57.6	58.1	59.1
Slovak Rep.	52.1	52.6	55.9	56.1	53.9
Slovenia	..	50.7	52.1	52.7	53.2
	Predictions based on regression with dummy for the United States				
Bulgaria	84.9	86.3	88.0	88.7	89.7
Czech Rep.	83.0	83.9	84.4	84.8	85.2
Hungary	86.5	86.7	87.2	87.1	87.5
Poland	76.8	77.4	78.0	78.1	78.8
Romania	82.1	82.7	84.2	84.5	85.4
Slovak Rep.	81.0	81.0	83.5	83.5	81.8
Slovenia	..	80.1	80.8	81.3	81.8
OECD average	*75.3*	*75.3*	*75.3*	*75.0*	*75.0*

Note:
Predictions are based only on development and demographic variables.
Source: Kornai and McHale (2000: 393).

equation "omitting" the United States may be closer to the present pattern for the sample including the United States.

It is especially worth noting how important a role political forces play in explaining the public share of total health-care spending.

What does all this mean for Eastern Europe? There is no

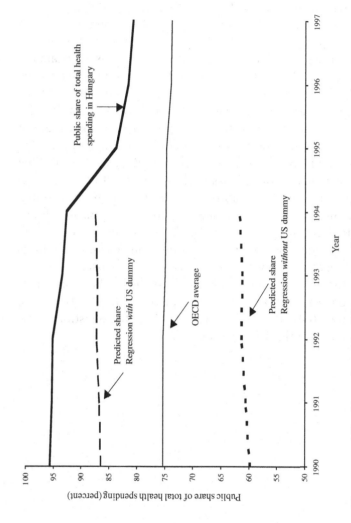

Figure 8.1 Hungary, public share of total health spending during the transition, 1990–1997

Source: Kornai and McHale (2000: 394).

country whose future political and economic mechanism for health care is predetermined. It is also clear from the regression equation that the future health-care mechanism is not written *ex ante* in the history book of fate. If international trends are analyzed with sufficient thoroughness, they could be compatible with an ultra-cautious or a radical reform. Even if the entire interdependent set of reforms advocated in this book is adopted, there will still be considerable freedom to decide – between smaller or larger basic benefits and their associated public shares; between alternative institutions for defining and updating the basic package; between more or less rapid development of supplementary financing and the associated amount of total health spending; and so on. What will actually come to pass will be the result of interaction among the political and social forces in each country. Although not all of the choices could be easily reversed if so desired, future citizens will also have a scope for voice in re-shaping their health sector. Present and future generations will bear the responsibility for what they choose.

The last few sections and especially the last few pages have turned from the kind of prescriptive guidelines typical of chapters 6–8 to a forecast. That leads to the questions to be discussed in the final chapter.

9

Concluding remarks

The role of factors beyond the economic mechanism

One idea running through this book has been that the health sector cannot be reliably regulated solely by purely bureaucratic, governmental coordination or by purely market coordination. What is needed is a combination of the two, and a far more favorable combination than the one so far. That is why several changes have been recommended in ownership, the structure of health-care financing and insurance, incentives, and prices, in other words, in the economic mechanism of health care. Having said that, not even the best of combinations is going to be sufficient to ensure that the sector operates well. Other factors are also needed.

Governmental supervision and regulation of the health system has to be reinforced, on the delivery and financing sides alike. The supervision has to cover not only the private sector, but public organizations as well. Suppose that a public hospital or outpatient clinic receives greater economic autonomy, in line with the proposals in this book, and that the various financial incentives exert a stronger effect on its management and on its employees. Those circumstances will introduce into their behavior features similar to the ones found in the private sector.

People in the post-socialist countries consider this proposal for state oversight self-evident. Aversion and opposition to the spread of private ownership and the market will be lessened if the development of state supervision and coordination are given emphasis in the reform proposals. The aversion to state intervention tends to come from some of the Western advisers, or, more precisely, from economists with libertarian inclinations. However, if every country in the world exercises state control over aviation, road transport, or environmental protection, the state obviously has to take a similar role in health care.

Here the starting point in Eastern Europe is the state health sector embedded in the centralized command economy, which the state health-care bureaucracy has learned to control. This function has to be exchanged for a new sphere of coordination and supervision. The accent has to shift from issuing directives to spreading information, inspecting, and coordinating. The earlier overcentralization should be countered by transferring more of the state tasks to local government.

Apart from the regulatory and supervisory role of the executive branch of the state, the *judicial branch* will also have an important role to perform. Patients under the socialist system were not able to sue their doctor or hospital for medical malpractice. The most that could happen to those who made mistakes was to undergo disciplinary proceedings within the health-sector apparatus, and this was quite rare. The absence of judicial remedies contributed to the defenselessness of patients. Now the situation in Eastern Europe has begun to change. Legislation has been introduced on patients' rights, with regulations on the procedures for dealing with patients' complaints. (For Poland's experiences with this, see Calnan, Halik and Sabbat 1998: 329–31.) Lawsuits are becoming more common. Some countries have already developed systems of insurance to spread the risk of damages awarded in medical malpractice suits.[1] Such suits

---

[1] The development of what is called "defensive medicine" coupled with the insurance costs, results in a substantial increase in health-care costs. Defending patients and reducing their defenselessness does not come free of charge.

may be too frequent, in the United States, for example, or the damages awarded by the courts too high. It would be worth guarding against excesses, but much the bigger danger at present is that victims will go to court too seldom.[2] Legal prosecution of malpractice by the courts is one of the most important incentives for doctors to respect the interests of patients.

There is an important role awaiting the *media*. Revealing irregularities in the health sector is not taboo for the press or the other media in countries with long-standing democratic traditions. For instance, after HMOs and other forms of managed care spread in the United States, it became more common for doctors to save money by omitting tests and interventions that were essential to the treatment of a patient. The fact that many such cases were documented in the press and the electronic media directed public and political attention to the problem. Notwithstanding the limitations of anecdotal evidence, this media attention played a useful role in prompting corrective measures from the managers and providers within managed-care organizations. Meanwhile, the legislators and the courts sought legislative and judicial means of preventing such distortions.

The health sector is entitled to expect the police, the prosecution service, the courts, and the press to respect its special circumstances, for instance the confidential nature of treatment and the doctor–patient relationship. However, in a constitutional state this cannot give anyone total immunity from observing the principle of transparency. Neither state ownership nor market competition can prevent abuses and negligence from occurring. It is justified for patients to be able to sue a doctor or a hospital for bad treatment. It is also necessary for such negligence to receive publicity in the press.

---

[2] Even in the litigious United States, a detailed study of the medical records of 30,000 patients in New York State found that only 1 malpractice claim was filed for every 7.5 patients who suffered a negligent injury (Weiler *et al.* 1993:139).

Whatever the economic mechanism, there is a need for the supervision and incentives that the judicial service and the press provide.

Also important, alongside the activity of state regulators, the courts, and the media, is control *within the medical community*. Voluntarily, without any external compulsion, the medical profession has to take measures against colleagues who behave improperly, who are insufficiently attentive to their work, who treat patients badly, who do not keep up to date with medical advances through ongoing training, and who are wasteful with resources. The medical profession all over the world is organized into associations resembling guilds. Professional pride is widespread, like the "honor of the regiment" in the armed forces. For example, in lawsuits involving medical decisions, it can be difficult to obtain an objective professional opinion; doctors find it hard to testify against fellow doctors.

The greater the extent to which doctors impose discipline on their own profession, the less the need for outside intervention. There already exist various professional councils and boards, nationally and locally, in hospitals and other organizations. There is a civil society developing among the professionals of the health sector (including nurses and health-sector managers, lawyers, and economists, as well as physicians). The nature of this organism is such that it has to develop of its own accord, by common thought and deed. It is to be hoped that this network of civil organizations will continue to broaden, and prove able to counteract (for instance, with statements of principle and specific interventions that carry weight of precedent) the harmful side-effects that derive from economic incentives.

Litigation and press publicity are important weapons in *patients'* hands. They can make enhanced use of them if they are not isolated from each other, if there exist civil associations representing their interests. These usually organize around specific types of illness, because the common problems shared by sufferers and their families engender a kind of comradeship among them. Such bodies can champion the patients' cause and arrange for legal representation.

The supporters and opponents of reform

An attempt was made in chapters 6–8 to back the recommendations with ethical and economic arguments. However, the authors have no illusions. They do not believe that if good enough arguments are presented to everyone, the cause is won. So far, there has not been a single country where comprehensive reforms of the health sector have been implemented quickly and easily.

One difficulty in gaining acceptance for the proposed set of reforms is that some of its probably beneficial effects only appear after a delay and are not "tangible" to the average citizen. Stronger market forces, the development of competition among providers, and a more rational system of financing and payment will certainly contribute to accelerating technical development and improving the quality of health care, but not immediately. Everyone will feel the advantages eventually, but only later and indirectly, while some groups experience the risks and drawbacks much sooner.

Another reason for the opposition is sincere and justified anxiety among experts of health care. The shift to private ownership and the market, with the decentralization of decision-making that it entails, certainly does induce some dangerous tendencies. The poor and high-cost patients may become discriminated against and have necessary treatments denied them, or alternatively, health-care expenditure may run away. This book has tried to address these problems, by showing how to ward them off or minimize their effects. The authors are convinced that the favorable effects of the recommended changes will outweigh their unfavorable side-effects if sufficient attention is given to those aspects of the proposed reforms designed to curtail these adverse side-effects.

Alongside the justified anxieties, there are some unfounded prejudices. There is a generally accepted program in Eastern Europe designed to turn to private ownership based on a market economy. Everyone agrees on this, apart from some extreme left-wingers and obstinate orthodox communists, as far as the overall *economy* is concerned. Nonetheless, there remains in many people, deep in their souls, the old prejudices against private ownership and the market. These burst out when it comes to the health sector.

Private health-care providers must not be allowed to profiteer at the expense of patients. However, such fears may be remnants of earlier indoctrination, in which every capitalist was represented as a bloodsucking parasite, preying on the buyer. In reality a capitalist firm competes for the buyer's patronage with other, private or publicly owned firms. Every industry has instances of sellers trying to obtain extra profit at the expense of quality. The only way to lasting success is for the firm to invest in better quality, customer service, and technical development, and if possible reduce costs at the same time. Hospitals are certainly a "hazardous industry," where a private firm seeking profits at the expense of quality could do serious damage. Its victims could hardly console themselves with the thought that competition would eventually eliminate the greedy, short-sighted capitalists who abuse their position. There is no denying the danger, but – as emphasized earlier – it remains even if the hospital is in public ownership; cost-cutting at any price and human negligence in general can cause problems there as well. Nor are hospitals the only hazardous industry. Consumers' lives can equally be threatened by faulty aircraft components, the careless driving of a bus, or negligent handling of food. Should private business be banned in favor of public ownership in all these fields as well?

Not everyone's aversion is ideologically inspired. Many people of a suspicious turn of mind oppose any innovation.

They prefer to the unknown even something obviously imperfect that they know.

However, the main cause of opposition to reform is a perception that the changes will damage personal interests. It would be good to be able to devise a Pareto-optimal reform in which no one was a loser and many were winners. This cannot be guaranteed, although the program recommended in this book comes close to this *in the long term*. In the short term, however, there will be losers, who have good reason to be averse to the reform. A sober assessment has to be made of whose interests are infringed, and of whether such groups can be partially compensated, neutralized or isolated:

- The leading groups in the health-care bureaucracy have fears for their undivided power, from decentralization and competition, and from the democratic process allocating public money. Their opposition will weaken if they think of what has happened during the post-socialist transformation in industry, commerce, or the financial sector. Talented, expert, adaptable people found themselves in a good position after the reforms. Indeed, they now earn more than they did when they held high posts in the socialist bureaucracy.

- Doctors who receive especially large sums of gratitude money fear they will lose their opaque source of income, on which they are able to evade tax. Those who have simply milked the patients by virtue of their high position have good reason to fear the reform, which will place doctor–patient relations on a cleaner, more transparent footing. Their opposition cannot be avoided. On the other hand, those who were able to earn gratitude from their patients by their expertise, conscientiousness, and humanity can be reassured. They have strong chances of being successful in the reformed health-care system as well. Their total income, after gratitude payments have been eliminated, could rise steeply, and almost surely will not fall.[3]

- There is a symmetrical instance to the previous one. Patients who have built up their system of connections, through personal ties and gratitude payments, fear that this may be destroyed by reforms. They should be reassured that although this may happen for a while, it will certainly be simpler and more pleasant to build up such relationships under the new forms of ownership and organizational structure.

- The recommended changes will go against the interests of the "free-riders" under the system of financing out of public funds. It has been emphasized that there needs to be a more equitable distribution of the load of public taxation, by broadening the tax base. This will be detrimental to those who have tried to escape from such taxation. They do not need compensating; the reform has to be carried out despite their opposition.

There have been some enquiries into the distribution of public opinion on the main choices affecting the reforms proposed here.[4]

Table 9.1 shows an international comparison of one of the main groups of problems that the book has discussed in

---

[3] There is a danger of the opposite process occurring. There are certain medical pressure groups that support the reform for purely financial reasons, while trying to divert the changes in directions favorable to them but undesirable from the broader social point of view. For instance, they are pushing for the introduction of unregulated fee-for-service payment, which would lead to cost inflation. This occurred initially with the Czech reform (Vepřek, Papes and Vepřek 1995). Polish professionals also lobbied for such a payment system but they did not gain support (Lawson and Nemec 1998; Bossert and Wlodarczyk 2000: 19).

[4] Several notable studies have appeared on the political economy of Eastern European health-care reform. Special mention can be made of the Nelson (2001) study, which compares the reform of the welfare sector in Hungary and Poland, and of the study by Bossert and Wlodarczyk (2000) on the Polish reform. Several lessons from these have been used in chapter 9 of this book. The title chosen by Bossert and Wlodarczyk, "Unpredictable Politics," accords with the conclusions that this book reaches on the political prospects for the reform.

Table 9.1 *Attitudes regarding the trade-off between welfare spending and lower taxes, Hungary, Czech Republic, and Poland, percentage of all responses*

Responses	Hungary	Czech Republic	Poland
Taxes should be raised in order to generate resources for extra welfare spending	8	14	2
No changes are necessary; the level of taxes and welfare spending should remain as they are	32	47	36
Taxes should be cut, even if that means a reduction in welfare spending	43	19	60
Don't know	17	20	2

Notes:
Respondents were asked the following question: "The volume of budgetary expenditure by the state depends on its revenues from taxation. If the government had to choose between cutting taxes or raising welfare spending, what do you think it should do?"

The survey was taken in September 1999 by the Central European Opinion Research Group, formed by TÁRKI of Hungary, CBOS of Poland, and IVVM of the Czech Republic.
Source: TÁRKI (1999).

detail: how much "public money" does society want to devote to purposes of solidarity? Those who phrased the questions did not concentrate their respondents' attention on the health sector. Nor did they define the concept of "welfare spending" precisely. Even so, the distribution of the responses is noteworthy. The responses from the Hungarians and the Poles have similar structures. Far more people would like to reduce taxes, even at the expense of welfare spending, than would like to retain the prevailing situation or see a change in the opposite direction. The Poles go further in this respect than the Hungarians. A far smaller proportion of the Czech respondents would like to see a tax reduction at the cost of a reduction in welfare spending.

Table 9.2 *Distribution of opinions about competition among health insurers and the level of social-insurance contributions, Hungary, 1999*

Responses	Percentage of all responses
I support both raising contributions and introducing competition.	20.1
I support competition as long as there is no contribution increase.	37.3
I don't support competition.	31.5
Don't know.	6.9
No response	4.2
Total	100.0

Note:
N=1,478.
Source: TÁRKI (1999).

The structure of opinion in all three countries suggests that an increase in the redistributive load would receive relatively little support among the public. Many of the public would like to gain control of more of their income than they have had so far. This (if indirectly) supports the forecast made at the end of chapter 8: increased macro-expenditure on health care will have to be achieved mainly by raising the proportion of household spending devoted to health care, rather than through channels of increased taxation and public spending.

It was mentioned earlier that TÁRKI, a Hungarian research institute, tried to explore public opinion on some of the dilemmas concerning the reform. One group of questions enquired into whether respondents would support the decentralization of insurance and the introduction of competition among insurers. The distribution of the responses is shown in tables 9.2–9.4. Less than a third of respondents

Table 9.3 *Age distribution of those preferring competition among health insurers, Hungary, as proportion of those saying "yes" or "no," percent, 1999*

	Age groups					
	18–29	30–39	40–49	50–59	60–69	70–
Supporters	55.3	54.2	54.2	41.8	38.2	37.4
Opponents	44.7	45.8	45.8	58.2	61.8	62.6

Note:
Number of cases excluding "Don't know" and "No response": 1,322.
Source: TÁRKI (1999).

Table 9.4 *Proportion of competition supporters, Hungary, by educational attainment, as proportion of those saying "yes" or "no," percent, 1999*

	8-grade elementary school or less	Technical high school	High school	Higher education	Together
Supporters	40.9	45.6	58.9	58.0	48.8
Opponents	59.1	54.4	41.1	42.0	51.2

Note:
Number of cases excluding "Don't know" and "No response": 1,322.
Source: TÁRKI (1999).

clearly reject the idea of decentralization and competition. The rest support it, unconditionally or conditionally, except for 11 percent, who take no position. The frequency of support increases with educational attainment and decreases with age, but it is less sensitive to income level. Sympathy for a "market-oriented" reform is neither more nor less frequent among those with high incomes than it is among those who are less prosperous.[5]

Another group of questions addressed attitudes towards supplementary insurance. To give just a single finding, 44 percent of the public are interested in this and do not reject the idea of taking out such a policy, although the inclination to do so depends strongly on how high the premium would be.

This revealed attitude cannot be taken as a piece of real market research because the respondents were not offered a specific insurance policy. The finding simply indicates what proportions of outright rejection and open interest there are.

A survey taken in Croatia (Chen and Mastilica 1998) indicates that there is quite a high degree of aversion to reform that has given greater scope to private ownership and the market. The structure of the responses appears in table 9.5, according to income categories. This differs from the Hungarian findings, with the responses strongly dependent on income level, perhaps because the questions were put in more general terms than they were in the more specific Hungarian survey. There was less for the poorer strata to fear in the reform measures outlined in the Hungarian questionnaire.

Finally, a Bulgarian opinion poll (Delcheva, Balabanova and McKee 1997) set out to explore the public willingness to move away from socialist-type health financing. The responses are shown in figure 9.1, broken down by age groups. Sympathy with the idea is commonest among the youngest age group and falls as a function of age. The Bulgarian distribution resembles the Croatian one in its pattern of preferences, and also in its sensitivity to income.

There are two lessons common to the public-opinion polls

---

[5] The proportion of unconditional or conditional supporters of decentralization among the three income categories are these: lower group 73.5 percent, middle group 68.7 percent, and upper group 73.7 percent (TÁRKI 1999: 70).

Table 9.5 *Knowledge of and attitude towards health reform, Croatia, by income groups, 1994, percent*

	Income group			
	Low	Middle	High	Combined
Do not understand reform at all	48	34	30	36
Reform will not succeed at all or will not achieve significant results	51	52	33	46
Reform worsens the respondent's position as a patient	52	46	20	40
Co-payment for visit to GP is high or very high	44	30	22	31
Co-payment for visit to specialist is high or very high	52	38	32	39
Co-payment for hospital care is high or very high	62	48	36	48
Co-payments for prescribed drugs are high or very high	48	44	33	42

Note:
The sample (*n* = 562) was divided into three income groups, each representing about a third of the whole sample. The monthly income of the low-income group was 740 kunas (about $140) or lower, that of the middle-income group was 740–1,480 kunas, and that of the high-income group was 1,480 kunas or more.
Source: Chen and Mastilica (1998: 1158).

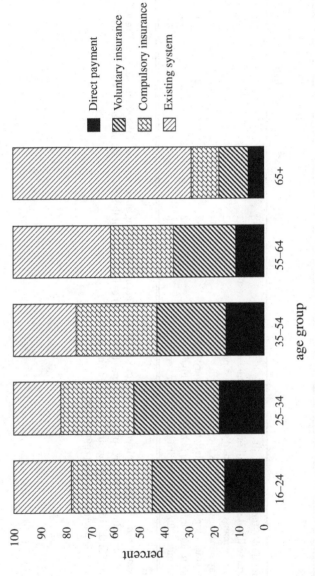

Figure 9.1 Preference for system of health-care financing, by age, Bulgaria, 1995

Source: Delcheva, Balabanova and McKee (1997: 96).

cited. The first is the need to strive in Eastern Europe to make known to the public easily distinguishable alternatives that are as specific as possible. Respondents should not be learning from the interviewer commissioned by academic researchers what possibilities lie ahead. The advocates and opponents of the alternative courses should be debating publicly with each other and explaining their points of view. Then the public should be asked for its opinion.

Broad, thorough debates have preceded reforms in several developed countries. Although the polemics hold up the passage of the measures, they ensure that people are not caught unawares. So far, there has not been much debate, at least not of *informed* participants regarding *specific* health-sector reform measures, in Eastern Europe. Politicians and the media often confine themselves to unacceptable generalities, which blur the alternatives. This means that when legislation is presented to Parliament, much of the public does not know what it contains. Pressure groups try to influence the decision in the background. Principle 6, the principle of transparency, should be applied more consistently in this respect as well.

The second lesson to be learned is not to expect a consensus to emerge. It is clear from a survey of the potential opponents, from considering the effects of the reform, and from analyzing the opinion polls, that public opinion is divided on all the difficult questions. There is no overwhelming majority for any of the strongly antagonistic positions that make up the dilemmas of choice. Even if there is a majority for one view, the opponents of it are relatively numerous.

This brings up one of the cardinal problems of democracy. To what extent should the current majority in the legislature avail itself of the opportunity to assert its own point of view, without making any concessions? This question becomes especially sensitive when people's health is concerned.

Taking the same approach as elsewhere in the book, the answer is to focus on the procedural aspect. This brings the discussion back to the point made in chapter 2, about the ethical principles 1 and 2, which was touched on again later in connection with the decentralization of insurance. In the authors' view, the majority in the legislature should not seek to impose its preferred alternative at all costs on those who disagree with it. Those who want to insist on public insurance and give private insurers a wide berth should have a way of doing so. On the other hand, people should not be prevented from taking out a policy with a private insurer. Those who have faith only in public hospitals should find public hospitals to meet their requirements. However, people should be free to go to private providers if they prefer. As for employers interested in playing a role in organizing medical insurance for their employees, they should be able, but not obliged, to do so.

Obviously, this open choice cannot be provided in everything. If contributions are compulsory, those who withdraw themselves arbitrarily must be penalized. If the single-payer monopoly of insurance is lifted, no one can offer to retain it. Everyone will lose the advantages to be gained from a monopoly, and of course gain those associated with competition, which many people do not appreciate.

The proposal for legislation on reforms, now qualified more accurately, goes as follows. The political sphere, wherever possible, should leave citizens with the choice between alternatives. The state should make decisions that restrict or pre-empt the choice of individuals only where the nature of the problem makes that inevitable. Will the parliamentary majority be capable of such self-restraint, of limiting its powers voluntarily? Time will tell. Either way, the result will be a good indicator of what importance legislators attach to principle 1, the principle of individual sovereignty.

Evolutionary and "constructivist" development

There were exciting debates at the beginning of the post-socialist transition about what features the process would possess. Distinctions were drawn between "shock therapy" and "gradualism", "evolutionary" and "constructivist" development.[6] More is now known about these questions, because experience with the development of the business sphere has given us hindsight. Several lessons can be drawn that are applicable to future reform of the welfare sector.

It would be mistaken to set up spontaneous, evolutionary transformation and state establishment of institutions based on a "design" as mutually exclusive, alternative types of development. Both occur, and each has its place, complementing the other.

A recommendation made earlier in the book is not to prescribe an exact form or compulsory schedule for privatizing state health-care institutions. The state should begin its measures by lifting bans and creating the legal opportunities for initiative and enterprise. Make way for the many innovations, including various provision and insurance organizations, and diverse contracts between state and nonstate forms. It will then turn out which of them are viable under the conditions of Eastern European countries. Concurrently the legal infrastructure, the supervisory authorities, and so on have to be developed as well.

There is a different situation with the things that have a governmental character according to classical criteria, such as the system of public finance. It would be foolish to expect a contributions system or a system of taxation to develop by evolution, of its own accord. Of course detailed blueprints are needed here, and legislation needs to be drafted after international experience has been thoroughly studied and appropriate analyses have been made.

The recommendations made in this book follow logically from principle 7: time must be left for the new institutions of the welfare sector to evolve and citizens to adapt. This

---

[6] The expression "constructivist" derives from Hayek (1935), who used it for previously planned formations forced upon society by state coercion.

Rather than picking any titles from the library of literature on the "gradualism versus shock therapy" debate, let us cite only two retrospective analyses: Roland (2000) and Kornai (2000).

prompted, for instance, the recommended cautious sequencing of the reform of basic-care financing. Partial decentralization must not begin before the necessary network of institutions and private medical insurance have gained a critical weight and the general public has become familiar with them. The same strand runs through the recommendations on gratuities. The way to eliminate these is not by force, through strict prohibitions. The chance has to be provided for the kind of legal, transparent payment relations to develop between doctors and patients that both sides prefer to the murky, opaque financial relationship it replaces.

Avoiding impatient actions is compatible with calling urgently for the legislative measures required for the reforms. The measures should not be hastily cobbled together, but they should not be protracted either, by an endless series of committee meetings and consultative talks, because the time has come to prepare the new laws.

There have been several references in this book to the way the debate on health-care reform raises again many questions that arose about socialism, especially during the debates about "market socialism." There are indeed similarities, but also a fundamental difference between the two debates. At that time it was a question of the economy and society *as a whole*, including the political structure that determined the method by which the economy was governed. The complex and extensive polemic arrived at the following dilemma: can economic activity be coordinated basically by the market while the communist party retains its monopoly of power and dictatorship over it, and while state ownership remains predominant? Those who were consistent advocates of individual freedoms and the market economy gave a negative answer to this question and rejected market socialism. Now, at the beginning of the twenty-first century, the impending reform of the health sector in Eastern Europe involves a well defined *part* of the economy. The political environment has also changed, so that the debates are held and the reform legislation is prepared under conditions of institutionalized, more or less consolidated democracy. The majority of the economy has also changed radically, since it works under a market economy based on private ownership. Surrounded by that democratic, market-based economic environment, it seems far more acceptable that there should be a circumscribed role for public ownership and administrative intervention in the health sector, with a permanent symbiosis between various ownership forms and coordination mechanisms.[7]

At the beginning of the post-socialist transformation, many of the sincerest advocates of reform felt they had to take measures that would close the way to a reversal of events as soon as possible. Perhaps the most important of these measures was codification of the new, democratic constitution, which certainly raised barriers to a return to dictatorship, even if it did not preclude it. At *that* time it was understandable and in many important matters legitimate to strive for irreversibility. It would be wrong to do that *now*, in a period of consolidated, continuing development, since the initial, stormy period of post-socialist development has ended before the health sector has been subjected to a similar process of reform. On the contrary, a trial-and-error approach is called for. No researcher or politician can be too self-confident. As emphasized earlier, there is no model country whose experience can be used to test the correctness of every

---

[7] The first author of this book feels the need to add a personal note at this point, as an active participant in the earlier debates on reforming the socialist system as a whole. He expressed repeated, emphatic doubts about the reforms and suggested in his work the idea that the dysfunctional features of the economy could not be overcome without changing the *foundations of the system*. That period more or less "conditioned" him to have an aversion to "mixed" solutions and antipathy towards cautious reforms.

He had to overcome this "conditioned reflex" and re-educate his thinking before he could bring himself to accept a mixed solution and a cautious strategy for introducing the health-care reform such as the one advanced in his Hungarian-language book (Kornai 1998b) and in this book.

proposal. There is no value-free blueprint ethically acceptable to all. The conflicts of interest mean that a comprehensive consensus cannot be expected. It is more important still
that regulations should not "cement down" any structure
that would block the way for other, alternative solutions. Let
it remain possible to experiment. Preference has to be given
to versatile solutions that can be altered with little loss and
leave open several alternative paths.

An attempt has been made here to create a strong link
between principles and practical proposals, and especially
between ethical convictions and proposals about legal and
economic institutions. In this respect, it differs strongly from
various other documents produced by researchers, government officials, or politicians that take the ostensibly pragmatic approach of beginning and ending with practical
detail.

Arriving at the end of this book, the authors cannot deny
that they remain uncertain about many questions. While they
adhere to their system of values, they realize that they cannot
derive every practical regulation from it *unequivocally*. That
is yet another reason for putting forward these proposals with
due humility. The authors have not shrunk from making a
proposal for reform, but they do not want to "sell" it at any
price. What if we are mistaken? Recognition of our own limitations and the risks of comprehensive reform impels us to
underline the importance of experimentation and the need
for careful oversight by duly authorized democratic institutions.

Without waiting for the work that immediately precedes
the legislative process, the intellectual preparations for
health sector reform in Eastern Europe have already begun,
among experts and among the broader public. This book is
intended as a contribution to that thinking process.

References

Adler, Nancy E., Boyce, Thomas, Chesney, Margaret A., Folkman, Susan and Syme, Leonard S. 1993, Socioeconomic inequalities in health, *Journal of the American Medical Association* 269: 3140–5

Akerlof, George A. 1970, The market for "lemons," *Quarterly Journal of Economics* 84: 81–108

Altman, Stuart H., Reinhardt, Uwe E. and Shields, Alexandra E. 1998, Healthcare for the poor and uninsured: an uncertain future, in Altman, Stuart H., Reinhardt, Uwe E. and Shields, Alexandra E. (eds.), *The Future U.S. Healthcare System: Who Will Care for the Poor and Uninsured?*, Chicago: Health Administration Press, pp. 1–22

Andorka, Rudolf, Kondratas, Anna and Tóth, István György 1994, *Hungary's Welfare State in Transition: Structure, Initial Reforms and Recommendations*, Policy Study no. 3 of the Joint Hungarian–International Blue Ribbon Commission, Indianapolis, Indiana: The Hudson Institute and Budapest: Institute of Economics

Arrow, Kenneth J. 1963, Uncertainty and the welfare economics of medical care, *American Economic Review* 63: 941–73

Arthur, Brian W. 1989, Competing technologies and lock-in by historical events: the dynamics of allocation under increasing returns, *Economics Journal* 99: 116–31

Atkinson, Anthony B. and Micklewright, John 1992, *Economic Transformation in Eastern Europe and the Distribution of Income*, Cambridge University Press

Banka Slovenje 1999, *Monthly Bulletin,* April, Ljubljana

Bardhan, Pranab K. and Roemer, John E. (eds.) 1993, *Market Socialism: The Current Debate*, Oxford University Press

Bator, Francis 1958, The autonomy of market failure, *Quarterly Journal of Economics* 72: 351–79

Baumol, William 1963, Health care, education and the cost disease: a looming crisis for public choice, *Public Choice* 77: 17–28

1988, Containing medical costs: why price controls won't work, *The Public Interest* Fall 1988: 37–53

Beattie, Roger and McGillivray, William 1995, A risky strategy: reflections on the World Bank Report "Averting the old age crisis," *ISSA Review* 48: 3–4

Benedict, Ágnes 2000, A cseh egészségügyi reformról (On the reform of the health sector in the Czech Republic), *Egészségügyi Gazdasági Szemle* 38: 83–98

Berlin, Isaiah 1969, *Four Essays on Liberty*, Oxford University Press.

Berman, Howard J., Kukla, Seven and Weeks, Lewis 1994, *The Financial Management of Hospitals*, 8th edn., Ann Arbor, Michigan: Health Administration Press

Bertko, John and Hunt, Sandra 1998, Case study: the health insurance plan of California, *Inquiry* 35: 148–53

Besley, Timothy and Gouveia, Miguel 1994, Alternative systems of health care provision, in Menil, George de and Portes, Richard (eds.), *Economic Policy: A European Forum*, Cambridge University Press, pp. 200–57

Bodenheimer, Thomas 1997, The Oregon health plan: lessons for the nation, *The New England Journal of Medicine* 337: 651–5

Bognár, Géza, Gál, Róbert Iván and Kornai, János 2000, *Hálapénz a magyar egészségügyben* (Gratuity money in the Hungarian health sector), *Közgazdasági Szemle* 47: 293–320

Bossert, Thomas and Wlodarczyk, Cesary 2000, *Unpredictable Politics: Policy Process of Health Reform in Poland*, Discussion Paper, no. 74, Boston: Harvard School of Public Health

Buchanan, James M. 1986, *Liberty, Market and the State: Political Economy in the 1980s*, Brighton: Wheatsheaf

Buchanan, James M. and Tullock, Gordon 1962, *The Calculus of Consent: Logical Foundations of Constitutional Democracy*, Ann Arbor: University of Michigan Press

Bureau of Labor Statistics of the United States 1999, *Current*

Population Survey: Employment and Earnings 1999, Washington, DC, pp. 213–18

Bútora, Martin and Skladony, Thomas W. (eds.) 1998, *Slovakia 1996–1997: A Global Report on the State of Society*, Bratislava: Institute for Public Affairs

Calnan, Michael, Halik, Janoz and Sabbat, Jolanta 1998, Citizen participation and patient choice in health reform, in Saltman, Figueras and Sekallarides (eds.), *Critical Challenges for Health Care Reform in Europe*, Buckingham, Philadelphia: Open University Press, pp. 325–38

Cassel, Dieter 1992, Eine Kassenwahlfreiheit ist herzustellen, *Wirtschaftdienst* 72: 287–91

Central Bureau of Statistics 1999, *Statistical Yearbook of the Republic of Croatia 1998*, Zagreb

Central Statistical Office 1998, *Statistical Yearbook of the Republic of Poland 1998*, Warsaw

Chawla, Mukesh, Berman, Peter and Kawiorska, Dorota 1998, *Financing Health Services in Poland: New Evidence on Private Expenditures*, Harvard and Jagellonian Consortium for Health, mimeo

Chawla, Mukesh, Tomasik, Tomasz, Kulis, Marzena, Windak, Adam and Rogers, Deirdre A. 1999, *Enrollment Procedures and Self-selection by Patients: Evidence from a Family Practice in Krakow, Poland*, Discussion Paper, no. 66, Boston: Harvard School of Public Health

Chen, Meei-shia and Mastilica, Miroslav 1998, Health care reform in Croatia: for better or worse? *American Journal of Public Health* 88: 1156–60

Chinitz, David and Israeli, Avi 1997, Health reform and rationing in Israel, *Health Affairs* 16: 205–10

Claxton, Gary, Feder, Judith, Shactman, David and Altman, Stuart 1997, Public policy issues in nonprofit conversions: an overview, *Health Affairs* 16: 9–28

Coulam, Robert F. and Gaumer, Gary L. 1991, Medicare's prospective payment system: a critical appraisal, *Health Care Financing Review* 13: 45–78

Csaba, Iván 1997, Fiskális illúziók és redisztribúciós csalás (Fiscal illusions and redistributive deception), *Századvég* 4: 109–18

Csontos, László, Kornai, János and Tóth, István György 1998, Tax awareness and reform of the welfare state: Hungarian survey results, *Economics of Transition* 6: 287–313

Culpitt, Ian 1992, *Welfare and Citizenship: Beyond the Crisis of the Welfare State*, London and Newbury Park, CA: Sage

Culyer, Anthony J. and Newhouse, Joseph P. (eds.) 2000, *Handbook of Health Economics vols. 1A and 1B*, Amsterdam: Elsevier Science BV (North-Holland)

Cutler, David M. and Reber, Sarah J. 1998, Paying for health insurance: the trade-off between competition and adverse selection, *Quarterly Journal of Economics* 113: 433–66

Cutler, David M. and Zeckhauser, Richard 2000, The anatomy of health insurance, chapter 11 in Culyer and Newhouse (eds.), vol. 1A: 563–643

Czech Statistical Office 1999, *Structure of Earnings Survey 1998*, Prague

Daniels, Norman 1985, *Just Health Care*, Cambridge University Press

   1998, Rationing health care – a philosopher's perspective on outcomes and process, *Economics and Philosophy* 14: 27–50

Davis, Lance E. and North, Douglass C. 1971, *Institutional Change and American Economic Growth*, Cambridge University Press

Delcheva, Evgenia, Balabanova, Dina and McKee, Martin 1997, Under-the-counter payments for health care in Bulgaria, *Health Policy* 42: 89–100

Diamond, Peter A. 1996, Government provision and regulation of economic support in old age, in *Annual World Bank Conference on Development Economics 1995*, Washington, DC: The World Bank, pp. 83–103

Donelan, Karen, Blendon, Robert J., Schoen, Cathy, Davis, Karen and Binns, Katherine 1999, The cost of health system change: public discontent in five nations, *Health Affairs* 18: 206–16

Dunn, Daniel L. 1998, Applications of health risk adjustment: what can be learned from experience to date?, *Inquiry* 35: 132–47

Eastaugh, Steven R. 1992, *Health Care Finance: Economic Incentives and Productivity Enhancement*, New York: Auburn House

Economist Intelligence Unit 1998, *EIU Country Report 3rd Quarter: Hungary*, London

Ellis, Randall P. and McGuire, Thomas G. 1993, Supply-side and demand-side cost sharing in health care, *Journal of Economic Perspectives* 7: 135–51

Enthoven, Alain 1978, Consumer choice health plan: a national health insurance proposal based on regulated competition in the private sector, *New England Journal of Medicine* March 23, pp. 650–8 and March 30, pp. 709–20

Epstein, Richard Allen 1997, *Mortal Peril: Our Inalienable Right to Health Care*, Reading, MA: Addison–Wesley

Féderer, Ágnes and Nemes, János 1999, Pontvadászat suvasztással: Mi minden látható a magyar egészségügy mély gödrében? (Hunting for points: what can be seen in the deep pit of Hungarian health care?), *Népszabadság*, February 13, p. 22

Feldstein, Martin S. 1973, The welfare loss of excess health insurance, *Journal of Political Economy* 81: 251–80

Feldstein, Paul J. 1994, *Health Policy Issues: An Economic Perspective on Health Reform*, Ann Arbor: Health Administration Press

Finland Ministry of Social Affairs and Health and WHO Regional Office for Europe 1996, *Health Care System in Transition (HiT) Profile for Finland*, updated April <http://www.vn.fi/stm/english/socinsur/socinsur_fset.htm>

Fuchs, Victor R. 1996, Economics, values, and health care reform, *American Economic Review* 86: 1–24

1998, *Who Shall Live? Health, Economics, and Social Choice*, Singapore: World Scientific Publishing Company

Gabel, Jon 1997, Ten ways HMOs have changed during the 1990s, *Health Affairs* 16: 134–45

Gawande, Atul A., Blendon, Robert J., Brodie, Mollyann, Benson, John M., Levitt, Larry and Hugick, Larry 1998, Does dissatisfaction with health plans stem from having no choices?, *Health Affairs* 17: 184–94

Gerdtham, Ulf-G. and Jönsson, Bengt 2000, International comparisons of health expenditure: theory, data and econometric analysis, chapter 1 in Culyer and Newhouse (eds.), vol. 1A: 11–53

Glied, Sherry 2000, Managed care, chapter 13 in Culyer and Newhouse (eds.), vol. 1A: 707–53

Goldstein, Ellen, Chellaraj, Gnanaraj, Adeyi, Olusoji and Preker, Alexander S. 1996, *Trends in Health Status, Services and Finance*, World Bank Technical Paper, no. 348

Greiner, Wolfgang and Schulenburg, J.-Matthias Graf v.d. 1997, The health system of Germany, in Raffel, Marshall (ed.), *Health Care and Reform in Industrialized Countries*, University Park: Pennsylvania State University Press, pp. 77–104

Gyenes, Monika and Kastaly, Ferenc 1998, Kérdőíves felmérések eredményei, elemzései (Results and analysis of questionnaire surveys), in Gyenes, Monika (ed.), *A fogászati privatizáció kézikönyve* (Handbook of Privatizing Dentistry), Budapest: Péztár 2000 Kft

Hakansson, Stefan and Nordling, Sara 1997, The health system of Sweden, in Raffel, Marshall (ed.), *Health Care and Reform in Industrialized Countries*, University Park: Pennsylvania State University Press, pp. 191–225

Hall, Jane 1999, Incremental change in the Australian health care system, *Health Affairs* 18: 95–110

Ham, Chris J. 1997, Priority setting in health care: learning from international experience, *Health Policy* 42: 49–66

Hausner, Jerzy 2001, Security through diversity: conditions for successful reform of the pension system in Poland, in Kornai, János, Haggard, Stephan and Kaufman, Robert R. (eds.), *Reforming the State: Fiscal and Welfare Reform in Post-Socialist Countries*, Cambridge University Press, pp. 210–34

Hayek, Friedrich A. (ed.), 1935, *Collectivist Economic Planning*, London: George Routledge & Sons

Haynes, Don and Florestano, Patricia S. 1994, Public acceptibility of taxing alternatives: evidence from Maryland, *Public Administration Quarterly*, 15: 447–67

Health Insurance Institute of Albania 1998, *Statistical Indicators for 1997*, Tirana

Health Insurance Institute of Slovenia 1999, *Annual Report of the Health Insurance Institute of Slovenia for 1998*, Ljubljana

Henke, Klaus-Dirk 1988, Auf dem weg zu mehr Rationalität im Gesundheitswesen, *Wirtschaftsdienst* 76: 64–8

Hofmann, Rainer, Hollandar, Pavel, Merli, Franz and Wiederin, Ewald (eds.) 1998, *Armut und Verfassung. Sozialstaatlichkeit im Europäischen Vergleich*, Wien: Österreische Statts-druckerei AG

Honigsbaum, Frank, Calltorp, Johann, Ham, Chris and Holmstrom, Stefan 1995, *Priority Setting Processes for Healthcare in*

Oregon, USA; New Zealand; The Netherlands; Sweden; and the United Kingdom, Oxford: Radcliffe Medical Press

Hsiao, William C. 1999, *Primer on Health Care Policy for Macroeconomists*, prepared for the International Monetary Fund

Hsiao, William C., Braun, Peter, Dunn, Daniel L., Becker, Edmund R., DeNicola, Margaret and Ketcham, Thomas R. 1988, Results and policy implications of the resource-based relative-value study, *New England Journal of Medicine* 319: 881–8

Iglehart, John K. 1992, The American health care system: managed care, *New England Journal of Medicine* 327: 742–7

1999, The American health care system (1): expenditures, *The New England Journal of Medicine* 340: 70–6

Ikegami, Naoki and Campbell, John Creighton 1999, Health care reform in Japan: the virtues of muddling through, *Health Affairs* 18: 56–75

ILO 1996, *Statistics on occupational wages and hours of work and on food prices: October Inquiry Results 1994 and 1995*, Geneva

1998, *Statistics on occupational wages and hours of work and on food prices: October Inquiry Results 1996 and 1997*, Geneva

1999a, *Statistics on Occupational Wages and Hours of Work and on Food Prices: October Inquiry Results 1997 and 1998*, Geneva

1999b, *Yearbook of Labour Statistics 1998*, Geneva

Institute of Health Information and Statistics of the Czech Republic 1998, *Czech Health Statistics Yearbook 1997*, Prague

Jakobs, Klaus 1991, Eine GKV-Organisationsreform ist dringlicher denn je, *Wirtschaftdienst* 71: 250–7

James, Estelle 1996, *Protecting the Old and Promoting Growth. A Defence of "Averting the Old Age Crisis,"* Policy Research Working Paper, no. 1570, Washington, DC: The World Bank

Jensen, Gail A., Morrisey, Michael A., Gaffney, Shannon and Liston, Derek K. 1997, The new dominance of managed care: insurance trends in the 1990s, *Health Affairs* 16: 125–36

Kanavos, Panos and McKee, Martin 1998, Macroeconomic constraints and health challenges facing European health systems, in Saltman, Figueras and Sekallarides (eds.), *Critical*

Challenges for Health Care Reform in Europe, Buckingham, Philadelphia: Open University Press, pp. 23–52

Knutson, David 1998, Case study: The Minneapolis Buyers Health Care Action Group, *Inquiry* 35: 171–7

Kocinska, Anna 2000, Racing toward real reform, *Warsaw Business Journal* February 7, p. 1

Kokko, Simo, Hava, Petr, Ortun, Vincent and Leppo, Kimmo 1998, The role of the state in health care reform, in Saltman, Figueras and Sekallarides (eds.), *Critical Challenges for Health Care Reform in Europe*, Buckingham, Philadelphia: Open University Press, pp. 289–307

Kornai, János 1972, *Rush versus Harmonic Growth*, Amsterdam: North-Holland

1980, *Economics of Shortage*, Amsterdam: North-Holland

1986, The softness of the budget constraint, *Kyklos* 39: 3–30

1992a, The post-socialist transition and the state: reflections in the light of Hungarian fiscal problems, *American Economic Review*, Papers and Proceedings 82: 1–21

1992b, *The Socialist System. The Political Economy of Communism*, Princeton University Press and Oxford University Press

1998a, Legal obligation, non-complience and soft budget constraint, in Newman, Peter (ed.), *New Palgrave Dictionary of Economics and the Law*, New York: Macmillan, pp. 533–9

1998b, *Az egészségügy reformjáról* (On the reform of the health care system), Budapest, Közgazdasági és Jogi Könyvkiadó

2000, *Ten Years After "The Road to a Free Economy": The Author's Self-Evaluation*, Washington, DC: The World Bank, mimeo

Kornai, János and McHale, John 1999, *Income, Technology or Demographics? An Accounting for Trends in International Health Spending*, manuscript

2000, Is post-communist health spending unusual? A comparison with established market economies, *Economics of Transition*, 8: 369–99

Koronkiewicz, Andrzej and Karski, Jerzy B. 1997, *Reviewing the New Polish Health Care Insurance System*, Warsaw: National Centre for Health System Management, mimeo

Krasnik, Allan and Vallgarda, Signid 1997, The health system of

Denmark, in Raffel, Marshall (ed.), *Health Care and Reform in Industrialized Countries*, University Park: Pennsylvania State University Press, pp. 29–48

Krugman, Paul 1994, *Peddling Prosperity. Economic Sense and Nonsense in the Age of Diminished Expectations*, New York and London: W.W. Norton

KSH 1999, *Statistical Yearbook of Hungary 1998*, Budapest: Központi Statisztikai Hivatal

Kuttner, Robert 1999, The American health care system (2): health insurance coverage, *The New England Journal of Medicine* 340: 163–8

Lawson, C. Michael and Nemec, Jiri 1998, Central European health reform: the case of Slovakia, 1990–1997, *Journal of European Social Policy* 8: 237–52

Lindbeck, Assar 1996, *Incentives in the Welfare State: Lessons for the Would-be Welfare States*, Seminar Paper, no. 604, Stockholm: Institute for International Economic Studies, Stockholm University, January

1997, The Swedish experiment, *Journal of Economic Literature* 35: 1273–1319

Lindbeck, Assar and Weibull, Jörgen W. 1987, *Strategic Interaction with Altruism: The Economics of Fait Accompli*, Seminar Paper, no. 376, Stockholm: Institute for International Economic Studies, Stockholm University

Lindbeck, Assar, Molander, Per, Persson, Torsten, Petersson, Olof, Sandmo, Agnar, Swedenborg, Birgitta and Thygessen, Niels 1994, *Turning Sweden Around*, Cambridge, MA and London: MIT Press

Liu, Yuanli and Jakab, Melitta 1999, *Reforming the Health Care System in a Transitional Economy: Experiences from Hungary, Czech Republic, Poland*, Harvard School of Public Health Program in Health Care Financing, mimeo

Losonczi, Ágnes 1986, *A kiszolgáltatottság anatómiája az egészségügyben* (The anatomy of defenselessness in the health sector), Budapest: Magvető Kiadó

1997, *Utak és korlátok az egészségügyben* (Paths and constraints in the health sector), Budapest, manuscript

Maarse, J. A. M. Hans 1997, The health system of the Netherlands, in Raffel, Marshall (ed.), *Health Care and Reform in*

Industrialized Countries, University Park: Pennsylvania State University Press, pp. 135–62

Marree, Jorgen and Groenewegen, Peter 1997, *Back to Bismarck: Eastern European Health Care Systems in Transition*, Aldershot: Avebury, Ashgate

Maskin, Eric S. 1996, Theories of the soft budget-constraint, *Japan and the World Economy* 8: 125–33

Massaro, Thomas A., Nemec, Jiri and Kalman, Ivan 1994, Health system reform in the Czech Republic: policy lessons from the initial experience of the General Health Insurance Company, *Journal of the American Medical Association* 271: 1870–4.

Mechanic, David 1997, Muddling through elegantly: finding the proper balance in rationing, *Health Affairs* 16: 83–92

Medicover 2000, *Medicover Health Care Provider*, <http://www.medicover.pl/indexen.htm>

Melnick, Glenn, Keeler, Emmett and Zwanziger, Jack 1999, Market power and hospital pricing: are nonprofits different? *Health Affairs* 18: 167–73

Mihályi, Péter 2000, Magyar egészségügy: Diagnózis és terápia (The Hungarian health-care sector: diagnosis and therapy), Budapest: Springer Orvosi Kiadó Kft

Milanovic, Branko 1996, *Income, Inequality, and Poverty during the Transition*, Washington, DC: The World Bank, mimeo

Murrell, Peter 1995, The transition according to Cambridge, Mass., *Journal of Economic Literature* 33: 164–78

Musgrave, Richard A. and Musgrave, Peggy B. 1980, *Public Finance in Theory and Practice*, New York: McGraw-Hill

Nagy, András 1997, *A jóléti rendszer Franciaországban* (The welfare system in France), manuscript

Nagy, György 2000, Magánklinikák gazdálkodása: Gyógyító tőke (Management of private outpatient clinics: capital that heals), *Heti Világgazdaság*, 2000/16

National Bank of Hungary 1999, *Annual Report 1998*, Budapest

National Center for Health Statistics 1999, *Health, United States, 1999, with Health and Aging Chartbook*, Hyattsville, Maryland

National Statistical Institute 1999a, *Statistical Yearbook of Bulgaria 1998*, Sofia

1999b, *Statistical Reference Book of the Republic of Bulgaria 1999*, Sofia

Naylor, C. David 1999, Health care in Canada: incrementalism under fiscal duress, *Health Affairs* 18: 9–26

Needleman, Jack, Chollet, Deborah J. and Lamphere, JoAnn 1997, Hospital conversion trends, *Health Affairs* 16: 187–95

Nelson, Joan M. 1992, Poverty, equity, and the politics of adjustment, in Haggard, Stephen and Kaufman, Robert R. (eds.), *The Politics of Economic Adjustment*, Princeton University Press, pp. 221–69

2001, The politics of pensions and health care: reforms in Hungary and Poland, in Kornai, János, Haggard, Stephan and Kaufman, Robert R. (eds.), *Reforming the State: Fiscal and Welfare Reform in Post-Socialist Countries*, Cambridge University Press, pp. 235–60

NERA 1996, *The Health Care System in the Czech Republic*, London: PPBH.

1998a, *The Health Care System in Hungary*, London: PPBH

1998b, *The Health Care System in Poland*, London: PPBH

1999, *The Health Care System in Romania*, London: PPBH

Netherlands Ministry of Health, Welfare, and Sport 1998, *Health Insurance in the Netherlands*, *available at* <http://www.minvws.nl/index. asp/Language=International>

Newhouse, Joseph P. 1992, Medical care costs: how much welfare loss?, *Journal of Economic Perspectives* 6: 3–21

1996 Reimbursing health plans and health providers: efficiency in production versus selection, *Journal of Economic Literature* 34: 1236–63

Newhouse, Joseph P. and the Insurance Experiment Group 1993, *Free for All? Lessons from the RAND Health Insurance Experiment*, Cambridge, MA: Harvard University Press

Niskanen, William A. 1971, *Bureaucracy and Representative Government*, Chicago: Aldine-Atherton

Nissenson, Allen R. and Rettig, Richard A. 1999, Medicare's end-stage renal disease program: current status and future prospects, *Health Affairs* 18: 161–79

North, Douglass C. 1990 *Institutions, Institutional Change and Economic Performance*, Cambridge University Press

Nozick, Robert 1974, *Anarchy, State and Utopia,* New York: Basic Books

Oberender, Peter 1992, Anforderungen eine Neuordnung des Gesundheitswesens, *Wirtschaftdienst* 72: 283–7

OECD 1992, *The Reform of Health Care: A Comparative Analysis of Seven OECD Countries,* Paris

   1993, *OECD Health Systems. Vol. 1: Facts and Trends 1960–1991,* Health Policy Studies no. 3, Paris

   1994a, *The Reform of Health Care Systems. A Review of Seventeen OECD Countries,* Paris

   1994b, *OECD Economic Survey: France 1993–1994,* Paris

   1998a, *Czech Health Care System. Delivery and Financing,* Prague: Czech Association for Health Services Research

   1998b, *OECD Health Data 98: A Comparative Analysis of Twenty Nine Countries,* Paris

   1999a, *Economic Survey, 1999: Hungary,* Paris

   1999b, *OECD Health Data 99: A Comparative Analysis of Twenty Nine Countries,* Paris

   2000, *OECD Economic Survey: Poland,* Paris

Office for National Statistics 1999, *New Earnings Survey 1999,* London

Office for Oregon Health Plan Policy and Research Homepage 2000, *Prioritized List of Health Services,* April 1, 2000. <http://www.ohppr.state.or.us/>

OMMK 1999, *Munkaügyi Adattár 1999/1,* Budapest

Oregon Health Services Commission 1999, *Prioritization of Health Services: A Report to the Governor and the 70th Oregon Legislative Assembly,* Office for Oregon Health Plan Policy and Research, Department of Administrative Services

Orosz, Éva, Ellena, Guy and Jakab, Melitta 1998, Reforming the health care system: the unfinished agenda, in Bokros, Lajos and Dethier, Jean-Jacques (eds.), *Public Finance Reform during the Transition: The Experience of Hungary,* Washington, DC: The World Bank, pp. 221–54

Pauly, Mark V. 1986, Taxation, health insurance, and market failure in the medical economy, *Journal of Economic Literature* 25: 629–75

   1992, The normative and positive economics of minimum health benefits, in Zweifel, Peter and Frech III, H. E. (eds.), *Health*

Economics Worldwide, Norwell, MA and Dordrecht: Kluwer Academic Publishers, pp. 63–78

Pfaff, Anita B., Busch, Susanne and Rindsfüsser, Christian 1994, *Kostendampfung in der Gesetzlichen Krankenversicherung*, Frankfurt and New York: Campus

PHARE 1998, *Recent Reforms in Organization, Financing and Delivery of Health Care in Central and Eastern Europe in Light of Accession to the European Union*, PHARE Conference, Brussels, May 24–26

Physician Payment Review Commission 1996, *1996 Annual Report to Congress*, Washington, DC

Poznanski, Kazimierz Z. 1995, *The Evolutionary Transition to Capitalism*, Oxford: Boulder

Rawls, John 1971, *A Theory of Justice*, Cambridge, MA: Harvard University Press

Reinhardt, Uwe E. 1998, Employer-based health insurance: RIP, in Altman, Reinhardt and Shields (eds.), *The Future U.S. Healthcare System: Who Will Care for the Poor and Uninsured?*, Chicago: Health Administration Press, pp. 325–52

Roland, Gerard 2000, *Transition and Economics*, Cambridge, Mass: MIT Press

Romanian National Commission for Statistics 1999, *Romanian Statistical Yearbook 1998*, Bucharest

Rose, Richard and Haerpfer, Christian 1993, *Adapting to Transformation in Eastern Europe: New Democracies Barometer – II*, Studies in Public Policy, no. 212, Glasgow: Centre for the Study of Public Policy, University of Strathclyde

Rose-Ackerman, Susan 1996, Altruism, nonprofits, and economic theory, *Journal of Economic Perspectives* 34: 701–28

Rothschild, Michael and Stiglitz, Joseph 1976, Equilibrium in competitive insurance markets: an essay on the economics of imperfect information, *Quarterly Journal of Economics* 90: 629–49

Rowland, Diane, Feder, Judith and Keenan, Patricia Seliger 1998, Uninsured in America: causes and consequences, in Altman, Reinhard and Shields (eds.), *The Future U.S. Healthcare System: Who Will Care for the Poor and Uninsured?*, Chicago: Health Administration Press, pp. 25–44

Saltman, Richard B. and Figueras, Josep (eds.) 1997, *European Health Care Reform: Analysis of Current Strategies*, Copenhagen: WHO Regional Office for Europe

Saltman, Richard B., Figueras, Josep and Sekallarides, Constantino (eds.) 1998, *Critical Challenges for Health Care Reform in Europe*, Buckingham, Philadelphia: Open University Press

Schieber, George and Maeda, Akiko 1999, Health care financing and delivery in developing countries, *Health Affairs* 18: 193–205

Scitovszky, Tibor 1997, *Egy büszke magyar emlékiratai* (Memoirs of a proud Hungarian), Budapest: Közgazdasági Szemle Alapítvány

Scott, Claudia D. 1997, Reform of the health system of New Zealand, in Raffel, Marshall (ed.), *Health Care and Reform in Industrialized Countries*, University Park: Pennsylvania State University Press, pp. 163–90

Sen, Amartya 1973, *On Economic Inequality*, Oxford: Clarendon Press and New York: Norton

  1990, Individual freedom as a social commitment, Acceptance speech at the award ceremony for the second Senator Giovanni Agnelli International Prize in 1990, published by the Agnelli Foundation, and also in *The New York Review of Books*, June 14, pp. 49–54

  1992, *Inequality Reexamined*, New York: Russell Sage Foundation and Cambridge, MA: Harvard University Press

  1996, Social commitment and democracy: the demands of equality and financial conservatism, in Barker, P. (ed.), *Living as Equals*, Oxford University Press, pp. 9–38

Shalala, Donna E. and Reinhardt, Uwe E. 1999, Viewing the U.S. health care system from within: candid talk from HHS, *Health Affairs* 8: 47–55

Sipos, Sándor 1994, Income transfers: family support and poverty relief, in Barr, Nicholas (ed.), *Labor Markets and Social Policy in Central and Eastern Europe. The Transition and Beyond*, published for the World Bank, Oxford University Press, pp. 226–59

Skocpol, Theda 1996. *Boomerang. Clinton's Health Security Effort and the Turn against Government in U.S. Politics*, New York and London: W.W. Norton

Sloan, Frank A. 2000, Not-for-profit ownership and hospital behavior, chapter 21 in Culyer and Newhouse (eds.),vol. 1, pp. 1141–74

Smith, Adam [1776] (1937), *The Wealth of Nations*, New York: Modern Library

Stark, David 1992, From system identity to organizational diversity: analyzing social change in Eastern Europe, *Contemporary Sociology* 21: 299–304

Statistical Office of the Republic of Slovenia 1998, *Statistical Yearbook of the Republic of Slovenia 1998*, Ljubljana

1999, *Rapid Reports: Labour Market*, no. 81, Ljubljana

Statistical Office of the Slovak Republic and VEDA 1999a, *Statistical Yearbook of the Slovak Republic 1998*, Bratislava

1999b, *Structures of Wages of Employees in the Republic of Slovakia 1998*, Bratislava

1999c, *Slovak Republic in Figures*, Bratislava

Stiglitz, Joseph E. 1986, *Economics of the Public Sector*, New York and London: W.W. Norton

TÁRKI 1999, Adótudatosság, fiskális illúziók és az egészségbiztosítás reformjával kapcsolatos vélemények. Kutatási beszámoló "Az állam és polgárai II" című kutatás adatfelvétele alapján (Tax awareness, fiscal illusions, and opinions on the reform of health insurance. Report on "The state and its citizens" research project), eds., Janky, Béla and Tóth, István György, mimeo

Tengs, Tammy O. 1996, An evaluation of Oregon's medicaid rationing algorithms, *Health Economics* 5: 171–81

Tobin, James 1970, On limiting the domain of inequality, *Journal of Law and Economics* 13: 263–77

Toth, Martin 1997, *Health reform in Slovenia*, manuscript

Tullock, Gordon 1965, *The Politics of Bureaucracy*, Washington, DC: Public Affairs Press

Tymowska, Katarzyna 1997, *The Private Sector in Polish Health Care: Possible Scenarios*, Economic Discussion Papers, no. 35, Warsaw: Faculty of Economic Sciences, University of Warsaw.

US Bureau of the Census 1996, *Statistical Abstract of the United States: 1996*, Washington, DC

van de Ven, Wynand P.M.M. and Ellis, Randall P. 2000, Risk adjustment in competitive health plan markets, chapter 14 in Culyer and Newhouse (eds.), vol. 1A: 755–845 van de Ven, Wynand P.M.M., van Vliet, Rene C.J.A., van Barneveld, Erik M. and Lamers, Leida M. 1994, Risk-adjusted capitation: recent experiences in the Netherlands, *Health Affairs* 13: 120–36

Vepřek, Jaromír, Papes, Zdanek and Vepřek, Pavel 1995, Czech health care in transformation, *Eastern European Economics* 43: 45–79

Viscusi, W. Kip 1992, *Fatal Tradeoffs: Public and Private Responsibilities for Risk*, Oxford University Press

Vyborna, Olga 1995, The reform of the Czech health-care system, *Eastern European Economics* 43: 80–95

Weiler, Paul C., Hiatt, Howard H., Newhouse, Joseph P., Johnson, William G., Brennan, Troyen A. and Leape, Lucian L. 1993, *A Measure of Malpractice: Medical Injury, Malpractice Litigation, and Patient Compensation*, Cambridge, MA: Harvard University Press

WHO 1996a, *Health Care Systems in Transition: Czech Republic*, Copenhagen: WHO Regional Office for Europe

   1996b, *Health Care Systems in Transition: Slovakia*, Copenhagen: WHO Regional Office for Europe

   1998, *Health for All Database*, Copenhagen: WHO Regional Office for Europe

   1999a, *Health Care Systems in Transition: Bulgaria*, Copenhagen: WHO Regional Office for Europe

   1999b, *Health Care Systems in Transition: Croatia*, Copenhagen: WHO Regional Office for Europe

   1999c, *Health Care Systems in Transition: Poland*, Copenhagen: WHO Regional Office for Europe

   1999d, *Health for All Database*, Copenhagen: WHO Regional Office for Europe

Wilson, Vicki M., Smith, Cynthia A., Hamilton, Jenny M., Madden, Carolyn W., Skillman, Susan M., Mackay, Bret, Matthisen, James S. and Frazzini, David A. 1998, Case study: The Washington State Health Care Authority, *Inquiry* 35: 178–92.

Windak, Adam, Chawla, Mukesh, Berman, Peter and Kulis, Marzena 1997, Contracting family practice in Krakow. Early experience. Data for Decision Making Project. Boston: Harvard School of Public Health, mimeo

World Bank 1993, *World Development Report 1993: Investing in Health*, Oxford University Press

　　1994, *Averting the Old Age Crisis: The World Bank Policy Research Report*, Oxford University Press, published for The World Bank

　　1997a, *Financing Health Care: Issues and Options for China*, China 2020 Series, Washington, DC: The World Bank

　　1997b, *Public Finance Reform in an Economy in Transition: The Hungarian Experience. The Hungarian Health Care System in Transition: An Unfinished Agenda*, Budapest, manuscript

Yip, Winnie C. and Hsiao, William C. 1999, *Economic Transition and Social Safety Net: The Case of Chinese Urban Health Care*, Harvard School of Public Health Program in Health Care Financing, manuscript

Zeckhauser, Richard J. 1970, Medical insurance: a case study of the tradeoff between risk spreading and appropriate incentives, *Journal of Economic Theory* 2: 10–26

Zweifel, Peter and Manning, Willard G. 2000, Moral hazard and consumer incentives in health care, chapter 8 in Culyer and Newhouse (eds.), vol. 1A: 409–59

Index